THE GOOD
PSYCHOPATH'S
GUIDE TO
SUCCESS

DR KEVIN DUTTON & ANDY McNAB DCM MM

THE GOOD PSYCHOPATH'S GUIDE TO SUCCESS

CARTOONS BY ROB MURRAY

BANTAM PRESS

LONDON · TORONTO · SYDNEY · AUCKLAND · JOHANNESBURG

TRANSWORLD PUBLISHERS
61–63 Uxbridge Road, London W5 5SA
A Random House Group Company
www.transworldbooks.co.uk

First published in Great Britain
in 2014 by Bantam Press
an imprint of Transworld Publishers

A CIP catalogue record for this book
is available from the British Library.

ISBN 9780593073995

The 'Reading the Mind in the Eyes Test' on page 243 was originally published in the *Journal
of Child Psychology and Psychiatry*, 42:241–252 (S. Baron-Cohen, S. Wheelwright and J.
Hill, 2001). The statistics on depression and anxiety on pages 302–3 are taken from the
following websites: http://talkbusinessmagazine.co.uk/depression-costs-uk-businesses-26-
billion-year/ and http://www.adaa.org/about-adaa/press-room/facts-statistics.

Every effort has been made to obtain the necessary permissions with reference to copyright
material, both illustrative and quoted. We apologize for any omissions in this respect and will
be pleased to make the appropriate acknowledgements in any future edition.

This book is not a substitute for a clinical intervention programme, nor does it replace the
specialist advice offered by qualified psychiatric, psychological and counselling professionals.
If you are in need of professional assistance or support regarding your mental health
condition, it is strongly recommended that you contact your local doctor or mental health
care worker for dedicated clinical assessment and advice over an appropriate treatment plan.

Addresses for Random House Group Ltd companies outside the UK
can be found at: www.randomhouse.co.uk
The Random House Group Ltd Reg. No. 954009

The Random House Group Limited supports the Forest Stewardship Council® (FSC®),
the leading international forest-certification organisation. Our books carrying the
FSC label are printed on FSC®-certified paper. FSC is the only forest-certification
scheme supported by the leading environmental organisations, including Greenpeace. Our
paper procurement policy can be found at www.randomhouse.co.uk/environment

Cartoons © Rob Murray
Design and illustrations by Julia Lloyd
Typeset in 11 on 14pt Electra LT Std
Printed and bound in Great Britain by
Clays Ltd, Bungay, Suffolk

10 9 8 7 6 5 4 3 2 1

 CONTENTS

Thus, when a superior intellect and a psychopathic temperament coalesce...in the same individual, we have the best possible conditions for the kind of effective genius that gets into the biographical dictionaries.

Such men do not remain mere critics and understanders with their intellect. Their ideas possess them, they inflict them, for better or worse, upon their companions or their age.

William James, 'Father of American psychology'
(1842–1910)

We are the Pilgrims, master; we shall go
Always a little further; it may be
Beyond that last blue mountain barred with snow
Across that angry or that glimmering sea.

From *The Golden Road to Samarkand* by James Elroy Flecker
(1884–1915). This verse is inscribed on the clock tower
of the Special Air Service base in Hereford.

 PROLOGUE

WANT TO COME UP TO MY PLACE AND SEE MY LAB . . . ?

The University of London's Birkbeck College is a sprawling complex with some 20,000-odd students rushing about with backpacks full of books. I was meeting Professor Kevin Dutton here because his colleague Professor Naz Derakhshan was Director of the Affective and Cognitive Control Laboratory in the Department of Psychology and she had some of the country's most up-to-date equipment for the type of experiment Kev had in mind for me.

After paying an outrageous university parking fee, I took a walk through the grounds and met Kev. He still had long, centre-parted hair and Buddy Holly-style thick rims, and looked more like the bass guitarist in a 1980s rock band than a professor.

But for once he had the university geek look.

He was dressed in a woollen, blue-checked Rupert the Bear three-piece suit, and a pink shirt buttoned up, but with no tie. He resembled one of those mad professors who forgot to dress properly or put his shoes on before leaving the house because his brain couldn't stop thinking professor stuff from the moment he woke up after dreaming professor stuff all night. All the normal life stuff – he just couldn't fit it into his day.

He greeted me with a very Cockney, 'All right, mate, how's it going?'

'Better than it is for you by the looks of things,' I replied. 'Where did you get that suit – Disneyland?'

Kev took me into one of the buildings and we squeaked along white-walled corridors with shiny lino flooring. 'Andy, thanks for doing this, mate. The more volunteers we have, the better the science gets, know what I mean?'

We pushed our way through a thick, wooden swing door and into a white, sterile laboratory. Six or seven young men and women hovered around, being busy in white sterile coats to match the room. It might have been a laboratory with waist-high tables, but the Bunsen burners had been put away. Instead, three of the tables were laden with monitors, hard drives and printouts. A mass of wiring spewed from the back of all that hardware and came together on the floor. From there, it was duct-taped all the way along the shiny lino to a rubber skullcap and a tube of KY jelly, sitting next to what looked like a dentist's chair with a 50-inch flat screen attached to the wall in front of it. Kev nodded proudly.

'Welcome to my world: brain science central, and I'm your chief tormentor.'

He pointed over to the chair that faced the wall and the screen. More wiring led from the chair and joined up to the stuff duct-taped to the floor.

Rupert the Bear was very pleased with his hardware. 'That seat, Andy, that's your world. That's where you will sit once we get the KY on and some of that headgear, and then we'll see what goes on in that nut of yours while you're under the cosh a bit. I'm going to show you some pretty nasty things on the screen and give you an ear bashing at the same time and then measure how you react to it. Easy enough, yeah? You just sit there and the girls will sort you out. Just imagine you're in a hair salon.'

I took the hint, and settled into the high-backed chair as a couple of the white-coated girls KY'd my hair. While I had the salon treatment other white coats unbuttoned my shirt and stuck heart-monitor sensors to my chest. Then came the Matrix skullcap with twenty or more electrodes on the inside, their wires trailing out of the back and down towards the floor like the world's longest hair. This was the EEG (electroencephalogram) recording equipment, Kev explained, the device that measured the electrical activity in my brain. The two girls squashed it down around my head so all the electrodes made contact with the KY jelly. Another white-coat wrapped Velcro around my fingers, with wires that went into a yellow box on the table. These were GSR (galvanic skin response) measures, Kev said, which assessed stress levels as a function of electrodermal activity. By the time all these students had finished, I looked like I was trapped inside a giant telecom junction box.

'I feel like Hannibal Lecter in here,' I laughed.

Kev laughed back, a lot more than he should have as he let go of the headset's cans and they slapped against my ears. He leant forwards and shouted as if the headset had blocked out the world completely.

'Mate, you're gonna be seeing the sort of handiwork he would have been proud of in a minute. I'm getting into professor mode now so I'm binning the jokes. Nothing personal, know what I mean?'

Directly in front of me, about two feet off the wall, was the flat screen. Kev flipped the switch and it crackled into life. The sort of music you'd hear in the elevator at a health spa wafted through the headset. Silky, twilight ripples on a lake filled the screen in front of my eyes. It was like watching an advert for incontinence pads.

'OK.' Kev's voice, in white-coat mode, was now coming through the headset. 'Andy, right now, on the screen in front of you, you can see a tranquil, restful scene, which is presently being accompanied by this lovely, relaxing music. All good, isn't it? Now what I'm doing at the moment is just establishing the baseline physiological readings from which we can measure subsequent arousal levels. So just lean back and relax, mate.'

I nodded the best I could with all the Matrix gear on.

'Make the most of it, because in a moment or two, some time in the next sixty seconds, the images are going to change. They're all going to be of a very different nature to what's on the screen right now. They're going to be violent, nauseating, graphic, disturbing. You name it, you're going to get it!

'As you view these images, we'll be monitoring changes in your heart rate, skin conductance and EEG activity. We're going to be comparing it with your resting levels. Piece of piss, mate. Any questions?'

'Bit late now, isn't it?'

Kev wasn't up for waffle, now that he was in mega professor mode. 'OK. Stand by.'

I sat and watched, and the screen suddenly changed. What I got next were graphic, florid images of decapitation, torture, execution, and limbs being cut off. At one stage, because they were so vivid, I actually started to smell blood: the sickly sweet smell that you never, ever forget. The spa music had also gone. The new images were now accompanied by blaring sirens and hissing white noise like the soundtrack to a bad science fiction film.

I sat and took it in. I wasn't sure how long it lasted, but soon the lake reappeared and the spa music was back in my ears. 'Job done,' I thought as I waited for someone to come and untangle me from Rapunzel's hair.

But no, the visuals and sounds started bursting out at me once more until the spa music came back along with the lake and – this time – even a low-flying swan!

'Shit!' I thought. 'This fucking incontinence ad is doing my head in!'

They all carried on taking readings for another minute or so, and then two female white-coats came and started to unplug me. It all came off easily, apart from the skullcap, and a couple of chest sensors that managed to create two hairless patches. The KY had created a perfect seal and the cap wanted to stay where it was. Eventually they eased it off with a slurpy pop and I caught my reflection in the flat screen. Hannibal Lecter had turned into Jedward.

By the time I got off the seat and went over to the table to join Kev, the printers were humming and he was busy studying paper readouts along with the monitors.

He couldn't keep his eyes off the data as I came over and joined him. 'Normally, I ask volunteers if they feel OK and offer them a coffee. But, mate, looking at these readings, I think it's me that needs one.'

'I'll still have one, anyway,' I said. 'Milk, no sugar.'

He didn't look up. There were scrolls of paper spewing out of monitors like tickertape, squiggly lines everywhere. 'Sorry, mate, only espresso. We need the caffeine for all this brain work we do here, know what I mean?'

'That'll do.'

One of the young guys nodded and disappeared with everyone's coffee order. I was offered a lab stool to sit on and Kev brought one over for himself and we sat together in front of the machinery. As he pointed, murmurs rattled about from behind me as they took a look at the data.

'Mate, your pulse rate was significantly higher than your normal resting levels after I told you to stand by. That's normal. It's in anticipation of what's to come. See that trace? That's your levels going up there.'

I nodded and agreed, but to me they were just squiggly lines going upwards.

He pointed again. 'But with the change of scene, an override switch somewhere in that brain of yours, I don't know – flipped. Your psychological readings slipped into reverse. Your pulse rate slowed. Your GSR dropped. Your EEG went down. In fact, by the end of the video show, all three of your psychological output measures were pooling below their baselines. You see that? Look, just a bunch of straight lines.'

He turned to me with a huge smile. Someone was having a good day at the office.

'Mate, I've seen nothing like it. It's almost as if your brain was saying: "Bring it on!" And then when the shit hit the fan it responded on autopilot, like a drone in human form. You might joke about feeling like Hannibal Lecter but I reckon the two of you have got more in common than you think!'

Kev kept looking at me and, now we were closer, his eyes were twice as big as they would have been without the thick-rims. His smile was slightly worrying. Like the kind all doctors have when they've found an exotic boil or awful disease on some poor unwitting victim. He was waiting for me to say something. But I wasn't speaking, I was just listening. Half of what he said went over my head anyway.

'Mate, no offence, but if someone showed me these readings and said they came from a human being – one that was *alive* – I'm not sure I'd believe them. You were so in the zone you were . . . in *another* zone. Yeeeaah!'

He clapped his hands together in a world of his own.

'So what does that mean,' I asked, 'apart from me not getting too sparked up about watching a video?'

His hand went on my shoulder. 'Mate, you seen *Blade Runner*?'

'Yeah.'

'You remember the test? The Voight-Kampff test, the polygraph-like machine used by Harrison Ford to test suspects to see whether they were replicants?'

I nodded. 'Good film.'

'Well this is the *real* Voight-Kampff test! And you know what it tells me?'

'Go on, you're going to anyway.'

Kev took a breath before making his announcement.

'It tells me that you might very well be a psychopath.'

He stuck his fingers in his hair and crossed his jam-jar eyes to accentuate the point and then saw the reaction on my face.

'Don't worry, it's not like you're going to go mad with an axe or anything. One of the things about psychopaths is that the light switches of their brains aren't wired up in quite the same way as the rest of the planet. One area that's particularly affected is the amygdala. It's a little peanut-sized structure – some say an almond, some say a peanut: who knows? Who cares? – located right in the centre of the circuit board.'

He knuckle-dustered the top of his head.

'Now, this amygdala is the brain's emotional control tower. It polices all our emotional air space and is responsible for the way we feel about things. But in psychopaths – people like you, mate – a section of this air space, the part that corresponds to fear, is empty. There's nothing there. Zilch.'

He held out his hands at the monitors and the printouts. 'That, mate, is you. But don't worry, you're not the Hollywood kind. There's good, and there's bad. Know what I mean?'

'No.'

He threw back the rest of his brew and wiped his lips. 'Alfred Hitchcock got us all thinking that every psychopath and his dog spend their days hanging around showers, and as for Hannibal Lecter . . . There are many reasons why those guys go the way of the West – it's their childhood, it's their genes, and of course the way that their heads are wired up.

'But, in the right context, certain psychopathic characteristics can actually be very constructive. Look at the lads in law. How do you think these great defence lawyers can annihilate an alleged rape victim under cross-questioning, sometimes causing the witness to break down to the extent she's affected for the rest of her life – yet still the guy goes home, cuddles his kids, and goes out for dinner with his wife?

'Or take banking and politics. The financial centres of the world and our leaders are filled with psychopaths – totally focused, totally ruthless. Sure, some of these fuckers have got us in the state that we're in now. But ironically, it takes the same kind of ruthless sentimentality to get us back out of it!'

He laughed to himself.

'I once tested a neurosurgeon who rated really high on the psychopathic spectrum. He described the mindset he entered before taking on a really difficult operation. He said it was like an intoxi- cation that sharpened, rather than dulled, his senses. In fact, in any kind of crisis, the most effective individuals are those who stay calm, who are able to respond to the demands of that moment, while at the same time remaining detached. I would say that's you, Andy.'

He didn't give me time to answer, even if I'd wanted to. He gave me a schoolboy nudge, shoulder to shoulder. I used to do that to mates in the classroom when the teacher was waffling on about something that we didn't understand.

But this one knew exactly what he was doing.

'Mate, I'd say you know something about that. I'd say you're more than familiar with that bring-it-on mentality that most of us find at the bottom of a bottle. It's almost . . . spiritual, transcendental, isn't it?'

He looked at me and nodded.

'Am I right?'

I wasn't letting him into my head. He'd gone in far enough already.

'Except you're *not* pissed, are you, Andy? You're not tired or uncoordinated or out of control. In fact, you feel exactly the opposite. You feel sharp, polished, super-aware, don't you, Andy?'

He paused and I let him take a sip of coffee as he waited for me to chip in. But all he got from me was a smile: in true mad professor style, the cup he was trying to drink out of was empty. He peered inside the blue china, confused as to where the coffee might have gone.

'OK, I get it. You're just going to listen. But let me tell you a bit more about yourself when whatever chips happen to go down, er, hit your fan.'

Mixed metaphors, disappearing coffee: he's losing it, I think.

'You feel as if your conscience is on ice, don't you? All your anxieties drowned, like you've had half a dozen shots of neuro-chemical vodka. You just cruise through life, don't you? All those psychological road signs that most people learn in their theory test of life don't mean anything to you, do they?'

He knew there wasn't going to be any reaction from me.

'Come on, you know I'm right. Why fight it? Everything that others see as a nightmare you see as a game, don't you? Maybe you see life like some psychopaths do – as if you're an alien sent to earth to study humans but never understand what the fuck they get up to. And, even worse, why. You just can't understand why others are always flapping about shit, can you?'

I shrugged. 'So which one are you: gamer or alien?'

He chuckled to himself as his eyes strayed back to the monitors.

'Mate, think about it. You came here not even asking if there was any risk. Not even asking what would happen if something went wrong. Not asking anything. Do you think that's normal? I've known people break down in that chair, throw the towel in, try to remove the electrodes themselves.'

He nodded over to the skullcap oozing KY on to a tray.

'I mean, you didn't even ask what that fucking thing was for.'

Kev leant over to me, our shoulders touching once more, and

half whispered as if we had a conspiracy going on between us.

Maybe we did?

'You know, there are some who say that psychopaths are evo-lution's next step. Mate, you could be the next trick that natural selection has up its sleeve. You could be one of the chosen ones. Know what I mean?'

I laughed. I couldn't help it. Me being part of some Darwinian fish-to-lizard story seemed like a joke. Kev also saw the funny side but still kept the conspiracy going. He was now so close he was almost chewing my ear off.

'Look, Andy' – he started to calm down – 'why not let me carry out more tests, both on the cognitive software and on the genetic hardware? They've got some great people here who are totally on top of their game.'

One of the machines went *ping* and Kev disconnected from me as he leant forward to pick up a read-out. The trace flat-lined along the bottom, as if I was dead. He tapped the paper with a pen.

'We could find out a hell of a lot more about your wiring. There are so many other tests we could do. Think of it as me giving you a psychological MOT – you know, opening up the bonnet and seeing what you've really got under there.'

I flattened my hair as I thought about what Kev had said. It made sense, even if I didn't want to admit it. I had always been up for stuff, not giving a single thought to the possibility of fucking up. It didn't matter if I was going to be number one through the door on a hostage rescue; or going undercover in Derry with a south London accent; or, these days, talking to the board members of a company that's going tits up because they don't know their arses from their elbows.

Fuck it, I'd get away with it. I always had, even as a kid. I never thought of anything as dangerous. I thought of it as fun – like going through the levels on a video game.

But when the action started, be it a fire fight, physical fight or just being chased, I was always 100 per cent aware of what was happening, always focused on what I needed to do. I certainly didn't think about failure. Sometimes I was even excited.

That feeling of 'fuck it' that Kev talked about, I definitely had it most days.

In a fight, physical or verbal, it felt like I was detached. It was almost like I was watching myself in slow motion and thinking clearly about what needed to be done and how I was going to do it. There was no fear, no emotional connection to what was happening.

Kev was right. I'd always thought I had a touch of the alien about me.

Why did people worry about things they had no control over?

Why did everyone think about tomorrow while ignoring today and fucking it up?

Why couldn't they break down what was happening around them and just deal with it instead of flapping about it?

After my time in Kev's world, everything started slotting into place. I'd always felt different, even from other kids on my estate.

But I'd never been able to put my finger on why . . .

 CHAPTER ONE

SORRY, I DON'T THINK WE'VE MET...

Hello! I'm Andy McNab.

You may have heard of me from one or two of my previous books. If you have, all well and good. But if you haven't, the introductions might as well start here.

I was in the British army for eighteen years. Eight as an infantryman and ten in the Special Air Service. I'm probably best known for my first book, *Bravo Two Zero*. It's the story of an eight-man Special Forces mission behind enemy lines in Iraq during the first Gulf war. I was decorated for bravery along with three other soldiers from the BTZ patrol. In fact, our BTZ mission became the most highly decorated action since the Boer war battle of Rorke's Drift in 1879.

Since then I have gone on to write more non-fiction, thrillers, film scripts, and to produce films. I am considered to be one of the top thirty writers of all time. The thing about success is that you need to control it. If you can do that and then use it correctly it'll breed even more success. That's why I'm also involved in business both in the UK and the US – particularly with start-up ventures.

But it's no big deal.

One challenge is pretty much like another to me. I've gone from enemy lines to movie lines and from battle plans to business plans without even thinking about it. Maybe that's why it's been so easy – because I *don't* think about it. Either way, I've never had a problem with problems.

I think they're scared of *me*.

The reason I'm telling you this is because I do know *one* reason why I'm successful – the main reason, in fact.

It's because I'm a psychopath.

But don't panic, I'm a *good* psychopath.

It comes as a bit of a surprise when you first hear it, doesn't it? It did to me. I had no idea until a few years ago when I met Kev – and discovered his liking for exotic suits and even more exotic perfumes. You've just met him too – and though he may not look like it (and certainly doesn't sound like it) he is a Professor of Psychology at the University of Oxford. The man knows his psychopaths – and he's impressive.

But enough of me (for now!). YOU want to know what this book will do for YOU. How will it change YOUR life?

Well, it works like this. In the pages that follow, we will reveal SEVEN SIMPLE PRINCIPLES that will make you more successful. And then we'll help you apply them.

We're not interested in what kind of success it is you're after. It could be big:

- Maybe you want a raise?
- Or a promotion?
- Or to clinch the deal that will *get* you that raise and promotion?

Or maybe it's the small things in life that you've never been able to nail:

- Putting off making that awkward and embarrassing phone call.
- Telling the neighbours that you LOVE their chihuahuas… but don't like them dumping on your lawn.
- Dealing with that friend or relation who still owes you money. You haven't forgotten but they are hoping you have.

Whatever it is, this book is designed to meet the EVERYDAY needs of EVERYDAY people in EVERYDAY life:

- in the workplace
- outside the workplace
- with colleagues
- with friends
- with family

It can:

- make you money
- save you money
- get you out of trouble
- get you into trouble!
- get you preferential treatment

Whatever kind of success it is that you're after, we are going to show you how to get it. But we're going to do more than that. We're also going to offer you a PHILOSOPHY FOR LIFE.

A philosophy for a SUCCESSFUL life.

A philosophy that WORKS.

Trust me – this book is a one-off.

Nothing else even comes close.

And as if that isn't enough, we also do . . . SCIENCE! To be honest, that's more Kev's department than mine. But I chip in when I can. He'll be examining how people like me tick – and how you can, too. I do the sleek stuff. Kev does the geek stuff. Basically, I'll be firing the gun and he'll be telling you why it goes bang.

So, I guess we'd better hear from him. The Geek . . .

Thanks, Andy. You're too kind, mate.

It's May 2010 and I'm at the launch party for my first book *Flipnosis*.

Picture the scene.

Twelve new magnums of vintage champagne have just appeared from nowhere, the world's supply of vol-au-vents is doing the rounds, and Blondie's 'Hanging on the Telephone' is blasting out of the iStation behind the bar.

Everyone is nicely plugged in and the place is in full swing.

Suddenly, from across the room, I hear someone call my name.

'Hey, Kev! Come over here a minute and sign these for us, will yer?'

I look round. Over in the corner, by the publisher's stand, a familiar face waves a handful of books, and a pen, in my direction. I edge through the crowd and we shake hands.

'Hello, mate. How are you?'

'Yeah, not bad. Just got in from Hawaii.'

The first thing I notice is the tan. More radioactive than Fukushima.

Then there's the shoes. So shiny they'd probably be banned in California in case they started a bushfire.

The suit is Armani. Charcoal, single-breasted.

I take the pen and pull up a nearby chair. If I didn't know better, I'd say this guy had class.

I open a book at the title page and pause.

'Who's it for?' I inquire, routinely.

'No one,' he says. 'Just sign it.'

'You sure?' I lament, therapeutically. 'What, Billy No-Mates, is it?'

He smiles and opens a Coke.

'I've got plenty of mates on eBay,' he says. 'And these little fuckers go for three times the price if they're signed!'

Who else could it be but the legend that is Andy McNab?

Hello, folks, I'm Kevin Dutton – Andy's immeasurably more fragrant, inordinately less tanned, and inestimably more domesticated other half.

If *Flipnosis* passed you by (which isn't beyond the bounds of possibility), you might have heard of me from the follow-up: *The Wisdom of Psychopaths – Lessons in Life from Saints, Spies and Serial Killers.*

In it, I argue that psychopaths possess wisdom. And to back up my claim I cite evidence from saints, spies and serial killers.

It took me ages to think of the title.

It's dayglo pink – exactly the same shade as Andy does his nails on a night out.

And oddly enough, he's in it.

I first met Andy when I interviewed him for a radio show I was doing for the BBC World Service. It was some time later that he showed up in my lab. I still get flashbacks today. When I checked out his brain scans in response to disturbing images – images that have most people's grey matter firing faster than Alan Sugar after a night on the piss – I did a double-take.

Far from it being the brain's answer to Guy Fawkes' night that I was expecting, the graphs were as flat as a pancake. He made Hannibal Lecter look like Dale Winton.

It's a good job he joined the SAS. He'd have scared the shit out of them in Broadmoor.

Andy has always been a bit of an outdoors person and he's got his mother to thank for that. He started off life in a Harrods bag on the steps of Guy's Hospital.

When he first told me my initial thought was: well, that's something we've got in common. After screwing up a gilt-edged education and a scholarship to Cambridge when I was at school I ended up working in the Harrods warehouse up the Great West Road in West London. I stacked shelves, took stuff off them and put it into lorries, then stacked them up again.

After two years of that it dawned on me that maybe university wasn't such a bad idea after all, so I started again at an adult education college down the road.

Most of the courses on offer were A levels – and I'd already made a balls-up of those – so I decided to branch out a bit. As luck would have it, Birkbeck College was running a two-year diploma course in psychology at the time so I signed up.

I never looked back.

Ten years later, I was teaching in Cambridge where all those years ago I should've been a student.

All things considered I reckon they got off lightly.

People often ask me: why psychology? And, apart from the teenage aversion to Λ levels, I often wonder myself.

I suppose, from an early age, it was in the blood. My old man was a market trader in London. I used to help him when I should have been at school – just one of the reasons why Cambridge happened later rather than sooner.

'You'll learn more on the stall than you ever will in a classroom,' he used to say.

And in my case he was probably right.

One summer, when I was around six or seven, I was about to break up for the school holidays. There's a star chart in the classroom and I'm second in the pecking order.

By two stars.

Mum cuts me a deal.

'I'll buy you a Monopoly set,' she says, 'if you top that chart by the end of term.'

Given the timeframe – a little under a week – I'm not getting my hopes up.

And so it proves.

When the bell sounds to signal the end of the year, the standings haven't changed. I'm two stars short of passing 'Go' and permanently stuck on Water Works. I'm not a happy camper.

Outside the gates Mum and Dad are waiting to pick me up. Dad takes my satchel and shoves it in the boot of the car.

'Kev,' he says, 'I've never seen your classroom. Any chance you could give me a quick tour?'

I sigh wearily.

'OK,' I say and lead him down a rabbit warren of empty, echoey corridors deep into the bowels of the school. The place is deserted. All the other kids left ages ago and the teachers are long gone. Only the caretaker remains, pottering about in the playground.

When we get there, Dad walks over to the star chart and inspects it.

Two short.

'Kev,' he says, 'go and get your mother from the car, will you?'

'Let's just leave it, Dad,' I say.

'Go and get your mother,' he repeats.

A couple of minutes later, when I return to the classroom with Mum, Dad's got a grin on his face the size of the South Circular.

'Just look at that, Clare!' he says, pointing at the chart. 'I knew he'd do it! I'm proud of you, boy!'

Mum shuffles forward and peers at it.

I peer at it.

We all peer at it.

I can't quite believe what I'm looking at.

Somewhere in the space of the last few minutes I appear to have accumulated three more stars.

All of a sudden I'm the cleverest boy in the class!

'Well,' Mum says, as we traipse back to the car, 'you really *did* pull your finger out this week, didn't you?'

I feel a dig in the back from Dad.

'I bet you can't wait to get your hands on that Monopoly set, can you, son?' he says.

A couple of days later – true to her word – Mum buys me one.

It's fabulous.

All colourful and shiny and new.

Later, when I'm ripping it out of the plastic in my bedroom, there's a knock on the door.

It's Dad.

'Here,' he says, throwing something on to the table, 'stick this lot in a drawer for next year. You never know, they may come in handy.'

He pulls the door to and I get up and take a look. It's a set of cheap, sticky-back stars from the newsagent down the road.

Three are missing.

Stuffed down the back is something small and bendy . . .

. . . a 'Get Out Of Jail Free' card.

My old man probably wasn't the only reason I took up psychology after concluding my packing and stacking tripos at Harrods. There must've been others, I'm sure. But his sheepskin-coated spectre can certainly be glimpsed in the books I've written since.

Flipnosis: The Art of Split Second Persuasion tells the story of how I hung out with some of the world's top con artists, both here and in the US, to see who knew more about getting people to do things: me or them?

The idea was to bring together the very best insights that the science of influence could offer with the top tips, the insider knowledge, that the great persuaders – past and present, good and evil – had amassed.

Having worked for much of my academic life as a social psychologist, I was fascinated by the science of persuasion. That science had thrown up some clear rules of engagement over the years, cogent guidelines as to what works and what doesn't – and my primary aim was to emancipate these tactics and principles, incarcerated, as many lamentably were, in obscure periodicals and quarterlies, and present them, unfettered, to a wider, less specialized audience.

I wanted to sequence the genome of persuasion. Uncover its DNA.

And then go one step further.

I was also intrigued by a highly mysterious subgroup of persuader, 'natural born persuaders' as I called them: influence black belts – like my old man – who wouldn't know one end of a psychology textbook from another, but who seemingly possess a God-given ability to derive the functions of persuasion from first principles and to bend lesser mortals to their will.

Many of these influence virtuosos – which count among their number some of the world's most venomous psychopaths – are the elite of the persuasion world: evil geniuses of social influence who learn their trade on their toes.

Could their deadly skills somehow be distilled into a few key principles of persuasion, I wondered?

Did the techniques they had honed in the bars, salesrooms and boardrooms stack up with what the academic study of persuasion had discovered over decades of painstaking research?

To find out, I spent a couple of years crisscrossing the globe interviewing this ruthless elite while, at the same time, running studies in my own lab and trawling the literature for scientific booty.

Once all the pieces of the influence jigsaw were in place I took a careful look at both sets of evidence – the scientific and the not-so-scientific – and slotted them together to form a number of common themes.

What I was left with was an elixir of success: an irreducible model of influence comprising five core principles of persuasion that are a sure-fire winner in any situation.

Which don't just turn the tables, but kick 'em over!

But more on that later.

The Wisdom of Psychopaths – Lessons in Life from Saints, Spies and Serial Killers, the follow-up to *Flipnosis*, took things one step further.

If (as I had found) psychopaths were brilliant at getting what they want, then how, I mused, precisely, did they do it?

What dark psychological thunderstorms lurked behind the madness in their method?

To find out, I interviewed psychopaths from every walk of life you can think of:

- **from ice-cool hedge-fund managers to nerveless neurosurgeons**
- **from silver-tongued barristers to ruthless CEOs**
- **from brutal, cold-eyed killers to Special Forces soldiers**

The result was a vast, labyrinthine subway map of the psycho-pathic mind. A sprawling, interconnected snakes and ladders board of the psychopathic personality – with as many ladders as snakes!

But quite a few readers wanted something more.

The Wisdom of Psychopaths, they pointed out, is a *popular science* book.

Not a *self-help* book.

And while it comprised a decent enough brochure for the Psychopathy Tourist Board, what it did NOT comprise was a list of bite-sized, step-by-step instructions on how we can all 'psychopath up'. On how we can each make friends with our own 'inner psychopath' and use psychopathic principles to become more successful during the course of our everyday lives.

It was never meant to, of course.

But suddenly there was an appetite for *exactly* that kind of book – a need for the 'bottom line'.

In particular, there seemed to be an overwhelming demand for a basic, no-nonsense guide summarizing the key things I'd learned during the writing of *The Wisdom of Psychopaths*. People wanted straightforward, in-your-face advice about what to do in familiar, day-to-day situations.

- How can I use psychopathic principles to get served first in a busy bar?
- How would a course in 'method psychopathy' help me to get an upgrade?
- How do I make friends with my inner psychopath to get that job...to get that *guy*?

This book – *The Good Psychopath's Guide to Success* – is here to fill that gap.

It integrates:

- niche, lightning-hot science from cutting-edge psychology labs around the world...*with*
- fun and revealing personality tests...*with*
- cloak-and-dagger Special Forces tips from one of the British Army's most famous and highly decorated soldiers...

to present:

- handy
- bullshit-free
- easy-to-follow

success recipes for practically any situation you can think of.

And some you can't!

You will learn, among other things:

- **Why 8 p.m. is the best time to sell insurance.**
- **Why taking a cold shower might help you get a raise.**
- **How much of a GOOD PSYCHOPATH you are.**

As Andy mentioned earlier, you won't just learn how to fire the gun, but also why it went bang.

That's something he's been trying to figure out for years.

Time we put him out of his misery.

 CHAPTER TWO

THE GOOD, THE BAD AND THE CUDDLY

Blood. Sometimes it sets
my teeth on edge,
other times it helps me
control the chaos.

Dexter Morgan, *Dark Passenger*

On 16 October 2012, at the Rubin Museum of Art in New York City, I sat onstage next to one of the most prolific serial killers in history.

Well, television history, that is.

'Dexter', aka Michael C. Hall, was in town to discuss my recently published book, *The Wisdom of Psychopaths*, and it was a packed house.

As the evening unfolded, the conversation ranged from the techniques Michael used to slip into Dexter's mindset before going in front of the cameras – how he 'serial-killered up' – to the psychological similarities between actor and character in real life.

I'm not sure the audience knew what to make of us, looking back on it. But they seemed to be enjoying themselves – amused, intrigued and scared half to death in equal measure.

And that was *before* the clingfilm!

Finally, as the show drew to a close, I posed Michael a question.

'If you could steal one of Dexter's personality characteristics,' I asked him, 'and pop it inside your own head, which would it be? Which of Dexter's qualities, if any, do you think you would benefit most from in everyday life?'

Michael thought about it for a moment and then a sly, Dexter-ish grin oozed across his face.

'Calmness under pressure. Stress management,' he drawled. 'The more the heat goes up, the cooler Dexter gets.'

THE PSYCHOPATH MIXING DESK

It's probably fair to say that the two questions I've been asked more than any other since *The Wisdom of Psychopaths* came out are these:

- Do psychopathic personality traits really help us get ahead in life?
- If so, what can we do about it? How can the everyday person in the street make themselves just that little bit more psychopathic?

And, of course, it's true, isn't it?

Whenever most of us hear the word 'psychopath' it's images of Ted Bundy and Hannibal Lecter that flash across our minds. Not scalpel-wielding surgical geniuses, silver-tongued secret agents or super-cool Special Forces soldiers.

The reality, however, is rather different.

In stark contrast to the headline-grabbing soundbites thrown out by the media pundits and the film industry moguls, when psychologists like myself use the word 'psychopath', we're actually referring to a specific subgroup of individuals with a distinct subset of personality characteristics.

These characteristics include:

- **Ruthlessness**
- **Fearlessness**
- **Impulsivity**

- **Self-confidence**
- **Focus**
- **Coolness under pressure**

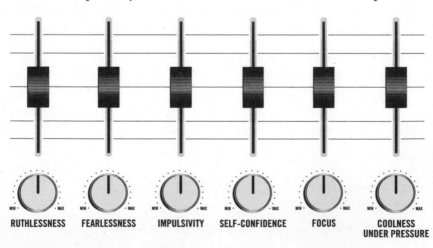

- Mental toughness
- Charm
- Charisma

- Reduced empathy
- Lack of conscience

Now, if we imagine each of these characteristics as being the dials on a personality 'mixing desk' which may be twiddled up and down in various combinations, we arrive at two conclusions:

1. There is no one-size-fits-all, objectively 'correct' setting at which these mixing-desk dials may be tuned. Instead, the most effective alignment will invariably depend on TIMING, and on the particular set of CIRCUMSTANCES you may happen to find yourself in.
2. By the same logic, there will be various jobs and professions which, by their very nature, demand that some of these mixing-desk dials are cranked up a little bit higher than normal – that demand a degree of what we might call 'PRECISION-ENGINEERED PSYCHOPATHY'.

In other words, none of the knobs and sliders on the mixing desk are 'bad'.

Far from it.

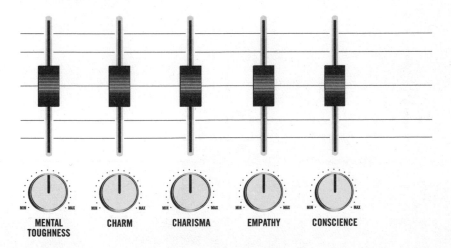

All of them have their place on it because:

- dialled up at the right LEVEL
- mixed and sequenced in the right COMBINATION, *and*
- deployed in the right CONTEXT

. . . each of them adds to the quality of the overall soundtrack.

KILLER TALENTS

Let's consider, for example, three well-known areas of employment: medicine, business and law.

In order to succeed in *any* profession you need two things:

- **TALENT – the requisite skill set necessary to do the job.**
- **AN OPTIMAL PERSONALITY FIT – the unique constellation of personality traits that will enable you to operationalize your professional skill set to maximum effect.**

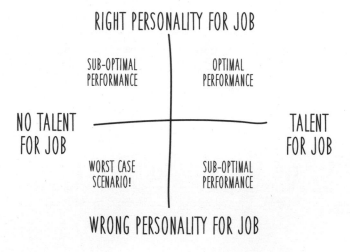

In MEDICINE, this synergy between talent and personality could easily mean the difference between life and death.

Imagine you've got the skill set to be a great surgeon – the manual dexterity, the technical ability and the specialist know-how – but you lack the capacity to DISSOCIATE YOURSELF EMO-TIONALLY from the person you're operating on.

You're not going to 'cut it'.

One top NEUROSURGEON I spoke to put it like this:

> I would be being less than honest if I said that I didn't get a kick out of the challenge. Surgery is a blood sport, and playing safe all the time just isn't in my nature . . . But one cannot allow oneself to become paralysed by fear if something goes wrong. There's no place for panic in the heat of battle. One must strive for one hundred per cent concentration, no matter what the eventuality. One must be remorseless, and have the utmost confidence in oneself to do one's job.
>
> The brain represents the high seas of modern-day med-icine, and twenty-first-century brain surgeons its pirates and buccaneers.

In the CORPORATE WORLD we may not be talking about life and death. But to some in that sphere, the difference between profit and loss is even more important.

Imagine you've got the strategic and financial smarts to be a top CEO – the motivational mojo, the visionary thinking, and an intuitive feel for the market – but lack the RUTHLESSNESS to fire people who aren't pulling their weight.

Or the COOLNESS UNDER PRESSURE to ride out a storm.

Or the basic business BALLS to take a calculated risk when appropriate.

No matter how smart you are, you're going to go under.

Here's what one of the world's leading HEDGE FUND MAN-AGERS told me:

It occurred to me that the times when I have produced my best returns are the times when the markets are chaotic and when panic is rife. Take 2008, when the market was down 20 to 30 per cent. I was up 20 per cent. When others are panicked and chaos is all around, that is when I am at my most calm. I find that environment relaxing.

It's odd, but absolutely true. When markets are calm and steady, my returns are not materially different to the average. I have no advantage in that environment. Panic creates calm for me in markets.

Lastly, imagine you've got the talent to be a great LAWYER – the ability to get your head around the twists and turns of a complicated case; the effortless eloquence and blistering turn of phrase of a consummate storyteller; a photographic memory – except for the fact that you lack that touch of NARCISSISM, that belligerent SELF-CONFIDENCE to be the centre of attention in the middle of a packed courtroom.

Again, it's not going to work, is it?

Listen to this, from an eminent QC I interviewed:

Information travels round the brain like electricity around a circuit. It takes the path of least resistance. The best barristers are the ones who can arrange the facts of a case, the pieces of the evidence jigsaw, to create the clearest, most coherent picture in the minds of the jury members.

In other words, those who are able to make their version of events easier for the jury to believe than the version presented by their opposite numbers.

And the barristers who can do that are the actors, the performers, the guys who, in the glare of the spotlight, are able to rise above the torpor of the courtroom and assume the mantle of Olympian wordsmiths…guys who don't just *tell* the story but who *are* the story.

In reality, of course, if you don't possess any of these Optimal Personality traits for the specific professions we've been talking about – emotional detachment and coolness under pressure for surgery; fearlessness and ruthlessness for business; self-confidence for law – then you're unlikely to get anywhere near the operating theatre or the boardroom or the courtroom in the first place. You'll be weeded out long before scalpels or mergers or silk become an issue.

And yet all of these traits comprise the central flagship features of the psychopathic personality…

…and are the dimensions of selfhood that unite serial killers and paedophiles with generals and captains of industry.

TO KILL OR NOT TO KILL?

Such an observation – stark, disturbing and unpalatable as it is in equal measure – brings us to a very important question.

Well, a couple of questions, in fact.

Questions that cut right to the heart of the core themes and values of this book and which I think we should get out of the way right now before we go any further:

- **What is the difference between a GOOD psychopath and a BAD psychopath?**
- **Is it possible to be BOTH?**

The answer to the first question is actually pretty simple.

Basically, there are three main differences between the GOOD and the BAD psychopath – differences that revolve around a number of the key components that make up our social environment:

- **other people**
- **social context (the interpersonal dynamic that exists between people in different social situations),** *and*
- **society at large**

Or, more specifically I should say, how we interact with these components.

These differences are summarized in the box below.

And to see how the pieces of the jigsaw all fit together we're going to get a little tutorial…

- on the judicious application of GOOD Psychopath principles…
- under the mind-warping pressure of some of the most extreme psychological G-forces out there in the moral universe…
- from the UK's most famous trained killer!

INTERACTION WITH	GOOD PSYCHOPATH	BAD PSYCHOPATH
Other people	Doesn't cause undue or unnecessary harm or distress to others.	Has no compunction about inflicting indiscriminate pain on others.
Social context	Is psychologically flexible: i.e. is able to regulate his/her actions according to the specific demands of particular situations.	The default settings for the various mixing-desk dials are at dangerously high levels – and are either stuck fast or very difficult to turn.
Society at large	Utilizes psychopathic personality traits to the benefit of society.	Has no concern over the consequences of his/her actions for anyone but self.
BOTTOM LINE	Psychopathy is a TALENT	Psychopathy is a CURSE

DIFFERENCES BETWEEN A GOOD PSYCHOPATH AND A BAD PSYCHOPATH

In *Bravo Two Zero*, Andy tells a story which captures the disparity between the GOOD psychopath and the BAD psychopath perfectly.

Holed up in the Iraqi desert behind enemy lines, his patrol was discovered by a shepherd boy tending his goats.

This posed a bit of a problem.

There were Iraqi anti-aircraft-gun positions just a couple of hundred metres from the hide. If they let the boy go, it would only be a matter of time before the gunners confirmed his story.

And then the shit would hit the fan.

But if, on the other hand, they chose to kill him and wound up being compromised anyway – well, you can imagine how *that* little scenario would've panned out. Whatever local reception committee pitched up to do the handshakes would hardly have looked favourably upon the taking of the shepherd boy's life.

Concealing the body wasn't exactly neighbourly either.

They had a decision to make. And fast. Or rather, Andy did, as patrol commander.

Should they spare the kid's life and thereby endanger their own? Or should they kill him and maintain their cover?

As it turned out, they decided to let him go.

And got caught.

'We are the SAS, not the SS,' as Andy put it at the time.

But from a purely practical perspective – putting the morality argument aside for a second – it was undoubtedly the right course of action.

And also, ironically, a rather psychopathic one.

It was the considered course of action of a clear-thinking, forward-planning GOOD psychopath. Not the murderous, kneejerk impulse of a BAD one.

To see where Andy is coming from, let's go back to our mixing-desk analogy for a moment and ask ourselves: what would the dial settings for NOT killing the shepherd boy look like in this instance? Well, according to Andy, they would look something like this . . .

And here, in his own words, are the reasons why:

In a situation like that you have to think of the whole picture. Not just what's in front of you. And you have to think fast! It's like chess. You have to be a few moves ahead. Dropping the kid just like that would simply have been flapping. And the Regiment is no place for flappers because that's counter-productive.

Even though your brain is racing at a million miles an hour, you have to stay focused on the Mission, what you really want out of the situation – in our case, finding the fibre optic cable that was buried somewhere close by and destroying it.

If we'd managed to drag the boy into our hide and killed him, we would've needed to take him with us and that would've slowed us down big style. We'd be carrying dead weight.

We would have done that if a dog had compromised us. We'd kill it, bag it up along with any blood-stained sand and take it with us, leaving no trace that we had been there.

If we were caught with a dead dog, so what? But caught with a dead child? That's a lot of explaining to do – if it had even got that far. Stalking round someone's backyard slotting kids is a no-no in anyone's book.

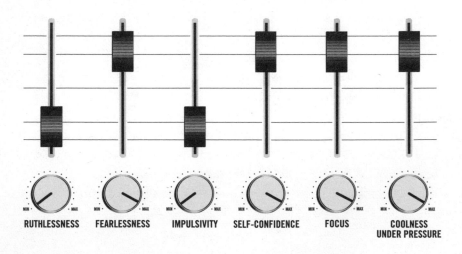

RUTHLESSNESS   FEARLESSNESS   IMPULSIVITY   SELF-CONFIDENCE   FOCUS   COOLNESS UNDER PRESSURE

So you have to weigh everything up – literally, in this case, bite the bullet – and believe that, whatever happens, you're going to be able to handle it.

In other words, you turn the following dials UP:
- **Fearlessness**
- **Self-confidence**
- **Focus**
- **Coolness under pressure**
- **Mental toughness**
- **Empathy**

You turn the following dials DOWN:
- **Ruthlessness**
- **Impulsivity**

And you leave the following channels out of it:
- **Charm**
- **Charisma**
- **Conscience**

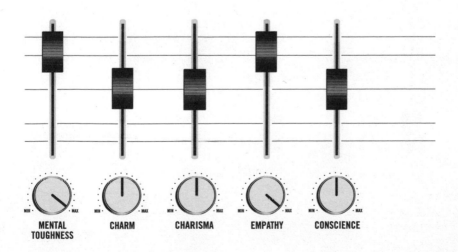

Or to put it another way, you:

- Avoid the deployment of indiscriminate suffering
- Regulate your behaviour in accordance with the demands of the situation
- Consider the wider consequences of your actions

Which begs, of course, the big unanswered question: what if killing the shepherd boy had actually conferred an *advantage* on the troop?

What if, just for the sake of argument, Andy had 'known' that, after killing the boy, they would make it – mission accomplished – to the Syrian border, unscathed?

Would that have changed the dial settings?

He gives me a wry smile when I put it to him.

'As a professional soldier you never take anything for granted,' he hedges. 'Human combat isn't a science. Certainty doesn't exist on a battlefield. And neither does hindsight. Which is a shame because life would be a hell of a lot easier if it did. Combat situations are too unstable, too fast-moving, too fluid to give you anything more than a few seconds to get your brain in gear and act on what it's telling you.

'Take any longer and you might not have a brain to *get* in gear. In the field, everything you do is a judgement call. It has to be.

'But – and it's a huge "but" – if I'd had that knowledge at the time, if I'd known that by killing him I could've carried out the mission, the very reason we were there, and got us all out of Iraq alive, then yes, that might well have changed the way things turned out for that boy.'

'Ruthlessness dial turned up a couple of notches?' I suggest.

'I had a responsibility not only to keep myself alive but the rest of the patrol,' Andy explains matter-of-factly.

The temperature plummets behind the peppermint-blue stare. Then he shrugs.

'So, yeah. As many notches as needed.'

THE CREAM AND THE SCUM

Andy's tacit admission that knife-edge situations can often code for uncompromisingly extreme solutions, that the hand of fate can twiddle the dials on the mixing desk up to levels that would ordinarily be considered highly dangerous in everyday life, raises a worrying and difficult issue:

The dividing line between being a GOOD psychopath and a BAD psychopath can at times be a vanishingly thin one.

This brings us to the second of our two questions: is it possible to be both simultaneously?

The answer, without a shadow of a doubt, is:

MAYBE!

But to understand *why*, we need to delve deeper into precisely what it means to be a GOOD psychopath.

There are a couple of labels currently doing the rounds that are often considered synonymous with each other.

These two labels are:

FUNCTIONAL PSYCHOPATH & SUCCESSFUL PSYCHOPATH

But far from being synonymous they are actually completely different. Or rather, *can* be – depending on what else you've got lurking at the back of your brain's personality locker.

Let's unpack these labels a little bit and get a better handle on what they really mean. I don't think it's going to come as a surprise to too many people that it's possible to lie, cheat, brag and manipulate your way up the ladder if you don't have the natural talent that your job requires.

They say two things rise to the top – the cream and the scum.

And they're right.

'Did anyone mention banking?' quips Andy.

But what I think is much more interesting, and might well come as a surprise to a lot of people, is that, if you *do* have the necessary skill set to do your job, certain psychopathic characteristics can actually make you *better* at it – as we saw a little earlier in medicine, law and business.

There are two different arguments here:

1. Psychopathic traits can get you up the ladder – in other words, can make you SUCCESSFUL
2. Psychopathic traits can help you capitalize on your natural abilities – in other words, can make you FUNCTIONAL

The two don't always go together.

Open a newspaper or turn on the telly and you'll soon see what I mean. In practically any line of work you can think of, a cunning, determined psychopath can bully, blackmail, backstab and schmooze their way to the top of their chosen profession using precisely such qualities to camouflage their lack of job smarts.

Such an individual might well wield significant power – and by that reckoning be considered SUCCESSFUL.

But FUNCTIONAL?

Nowhere near it.

They're about as functional as Tourette's in an auction house.

Wall Street presented Gordon Gekko (whom we'll be seeing more of) as the archetypal 1980s capitalist psychopath, and as he once put it:

'You had what it took to GET INTO my office; the real question is whether you got what it takes to STAY.'

KILLING IN THE MARKET?

'So being a GOOD psychopath, then, isn't nearly the same thing as being a SUCCESSFUL psychopath,' says Andy, as we pace around a London square during an endless TV shoot, nicking the production team's cheese and pickle sandwiches. 'Is that what you're saying?'

'Exactly,' I say. 'On a superficial level, it's an easy mistake to make. But no, not by a long way.'

Sure, many GOOD psychopaths *will* be SUCCESSFUL. But so will many BAD psychopaths. That's something we need to remember.

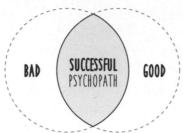

YOU DON'T NEED TO BE A GOOD PSYCHOPATH TO BE A SUCCESSFUL PSYCHOPATH

But something else we need to remember is this: things aren't that simple! The relationship between GOOD psychopaths, BAD psychopaths, FUNCTIONALITY and SUCCESS further depends on another couple of other factors at least:

- Level of INTELLIGENCE
- Predisposition to VIOLENCE

And that's when things start to get *really* interesting!

To see what I mean, take a look at the following simple grid. Let's start top right and work our way clockwise:

PSYCHOPATHIC	HIGH INTELLIGENCE	LOW INTELLIGENCE
Violent	4. FUNCTIONAL SUCCESSFUL (e.g. Special Forces, criminal mastermind)	1. DYSFUNCTIONAL UNSUCCESSFUL (e.g. low-level thug; enforcer)
Non-violent	3. FUNCTIONAL SUCCESSFUL (e.g. lawyer; surgeon; CEO)	2. DYSFUNCTIONAL UNSUCCESSFUL (e.g. petty criminal)

TIME AND PLACE: WHEN PSYCHOPATHIC TRAITS DO AND DON'T PAY

1. Let's say that you are:
   - a psychopath.
   - You get a poor start in life.
   - You are low in intelligence.
   - You are violent.

Your prospects, to be perfectly honest, aren't exactly great. You're going to end up as a low-level thug or an enforcer for a criminal gang – or something along those lines.

Either way, you're going to end up in prison pretty quickly.

2. Remove violence from the equation and your prospects are little better. You're going to be a:
   - crook
   - small-time con-artist
   - drug-dealer
   - pimp

or, more likely than not, all four in combination. And again, you're going to wind up in prison pretty sharpish.

3. But now let's say that you are:
   - a psychopath.
   - You are not naturally violent.
   - You get a *good* start in life.
   - You are *intelligent.*

Now, it's a different story altogether.

Now, as the famous Reuters headline once put it, you'll more likely make a killing in the *market* than anywhere else.

4. Finally, if you're:
   - a psychopath,
   - intelligent, *and*
   - violent . . .

. . . well, any number of exotic occupations might await you.

Anything from being the next Andy McNab to the head of a criminal syndicate.

JAMES BOND VERSUS GORDON GEKKO

'To help you get your head around it a bit better,' I say to Andy, 'think of it in terms of famous film characters.'

I grab a serviette and sketch out the diagram below:

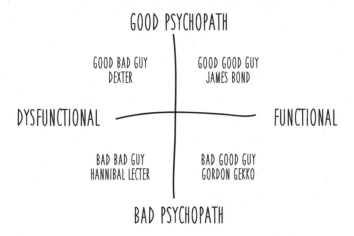

GOOD PSYCHOPATH

GOOD BAD GUY
DEXTER

GOOD GOOD GUY
JAMES BOND

DYSFUNCTIONAL ——————— FUNCTIONAL

BAD BAD GUY
HANNIBAL LECTER

BAD GOOD GUY
GORDON GEKKO

BAD PSYCHOPATH

TWO GOOD TWO BAD: FOUR DIFFERENT TYPES OF PSYCHOPATH

Top right, you've got what I call the GOOD GOOD guys. These are the FUNCTIONAL psychopaths who are acting in the interests of society – and for whom James Bond is the pin-up boy of choice.

Andy raises his eyebrows.

'Well, think about it,' I say.

He's skied off the edge of a mountain; used crocodiles as stepping stones; bungee-jumped in the dead of night off the world's highest dam, and killed a man in his bath by throwing him an electric fire to play with.

Bond is a secret service vampire. He throws no reflection in the looking-glass of guilt and casts no shadow in the glare of mortal danger. He is an icon of icy ingenuity and lord of the beatifically brutal whose Union Jack brain possesses some of the most functionally psychopathic neurochemistry in cinematic history.

'And all for Queen and country!' laughs Andy.

Bottom right, in contrast, are the BAD GOOD guys. These are the FUNCTIONAL psychopaths who, like 1980s financial genius Gordon Gekko, are 'in it' for themselves.

They *could* be in it for the rest of us, *could* act for the common good if they put their minds to it—

'But they choose not to,' interjects Andy. 'Right?'

'Right.'

Gekko is a remorseless corporate raider who, as soon as he gets his hands on an enterprise, sells off its most lucrative assets and tosses the rest – including the workforce – on to the scrapheap. He's the Lionel Messi of the business world, running rings around corporate stakeholders like the diminutive Argentine football maestro runs rings around opposing defenders.

He's got the charisma:

Greed, for lack of a better word, is good. Greed is right. Greed works. Greed clarifies, cuts through, and captures, the essence of the evolutionary spirit . . .

He's got the drive:

Lunch is for wimps.

And when it comes to making money, he's as ruthless as a junkyard pit bull:

You get it right. Or you get eliminated.

But does Gekko give a shit about anyone else apart from himself? You've got to be joking!

HANNIBAL LECTER VERSUS DEXTER MORGAN

Continuing on in a clockwise direction – across the Tropic of Dysfunction – and we plunge from a glittering suite at the top of a New York skyscraper to a glass-fronted cell in the basement of a supermax prison.

Here, we meet Hannibal Lecter – the epitome of sibilant menace and the archetypal poster boy for the BAD BAD guys.

Eloquently evil, dispassionately depraved, and more predatory than a skint loan shark on the last Friday of the month, Lecter is as chilled as he is chilling.

His highest recorded pulse rate is 85: a measurement, we are told, recorded shortly after he dismembered a nurse . . . and while he was tucking into her tongue.

'Enough said!' agrees Andy.

But jump to the cell above Lecter, home of the GOOD BAD guys, and it's a different story. Here we run into my old buddy Dexter, the blood-spatter expert cum clingfilm-loving serial killer, in the middle, as he might put it, of 'taking out the trash'.

Dexter is the cuddliest serial killer in the business. On the one hand he satisfies our deep-seated delectation for death, while on the other hand offering us protection from it.

Yes, he is brutal, bestial and barbaric. But he's also decent, demure and discerning.

The enduring appeal of Dexter – seven years is a pretty good innings for any serial killer, even on *Showtime* – is that he offers us the best, and the worst, of both worlds.

'So, is Dexter your GOOD psychopath and BAD psychopath all rolled into one?' asks Andy, scrunching up the serviette, giving his mouth a good old going over with it, and tossing it into the bin.

I stare at him in mock disbelief.

'Well,' I say, 'maybe I should let YOU be the judge of that. One thing's for certain: his heart's in the right place!'

Andy shrugs. 'Yeah,' he says. 'Question is: does it go above 85?'

THE UPS AND DOWNS OF PSYCHOPATHY

Already during the course of this chapter we've covered a lot of ground. We have:

- looked at precisely what it means to be a psychopath.
- debunked several popular myths surrounding psychopaths.
- introduced the concept of the GOOD psychopath.
- outlined exactly what it takes to be a GOOD psychopath.
- compared the characteristics of a GOOD psychopath with those of a BAD psychopath.
- considered how the traits of a GOOD psychopath and a BAD psychopath might sometimes coexist within the same person.

This stereotype-busting joyride across the Psychopath Midwest – via a corporate suite at the top of a New York skyscraper and a dugout in the Iraqi desert – should hopefully have provided you with a basic level of psychopath map-reading skills that will help you keep your bearings on the road ahead.

But just as we're about to walk back on set for the next shoot, Andy poses a question that we need to take a look at – a question that cuts right to the heart of a lively scientific debate currently going on between psychopath experts around the world.

In his own words:

Is being a psychopath a bit like being from Mars – either you are or you aren't? Or is it like being tall – you can be very tall, quite tall, or not tall at all?

The answer to this question has changed a few times over the years. Up until not so long ago, consensus was built around the first option: it was generally thought that you either *were* a psychopath or you weren't. Which, with Hannibal Lecter and Patrick Bateman as the poster boys of choice, I guess seems fair enough.

Psychopathy, in other words, was seen as a bit like a light switch. It was either ON or OFF – and when it was ON the difference was pretty obvious!

But recently scientists have come to view the condition in a slightly different 'light'. Rather than psychopathy being ON or OFF, it's now more a case of whether it's UP or DOWN.

'Psychopathicity', in other words, is now hooked up to a dimmer switch.

And we all have our place on the dial.

(To find out what *your* setting is, why not take the simple test at the end of the chapter? Andy did, but I'm sworn to secrecy over his score – ahem, 30!)

PERSONALITY WITH A TAN

Light is actually a good analogy for psychopathy. Because just as it disperses into seven constituent colours when shone through a prism (hence the rainbow) so the psychopathic personality disperses into a number of different sub-traits when subjected to psychometric analysis[*] (hence our psychopath mixing desk).

---

[*]Psychometrics is a mathematical procedure that breaks down particular aptitudes or skill sets into smaller component parts by analysing statistical associations between the various elements that comprise those facilities. For instance, one's overall score on an IQ test may be broken down into sub-scores on questions measuring numerical, verbal, spatial and reasoning ability.

These traits (or, in mixing-desk parlance, channels) are, as we have seen, each hooked up to their own individual dimmer switches which can be dialled up HIGH or LOW – resulting, needless to say, in a high degree of play within the system.

Shunt all of them on MAX and you overload the circuit. You get thirty years inside.

But twiddle some up HIGH and some down LOW depending on the circumstances, become, as we saw in the desert a little earlier with Andy, a METHOD PSYCHOPATH – and you'll be ripping it up in a different way to the Lecters and Batemans and Dexters.

A new consensus is now beginning to build. The question of whether you're a psychopath or not is not cut and dried. It's not black and white.

There are, a bit like the fare zones on a tube map, inner and outer intensity bands of psychopathy – with only a tiny minority living in the city centre.

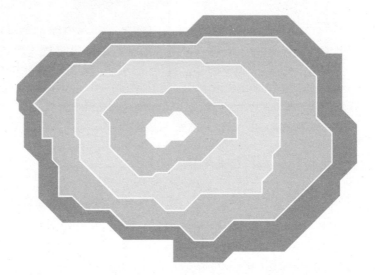

'Which isn't to say,' as Andy points out, 'that if you happen to live out in the sticks, heading into the centre of town every now and again is a bad idea. I mean, it's not, is it? Sometimes you have to. Sometimes the only place you can get what you want is Up West.'

I bow to his genius.

'You know,' I say, 'you were talking about coming from Mars just now. Well, imagine this. Imagine a Martian comes to Earth and the first thing they do is they get a job in a medical unit dedicated exclusively to the treatment of sun-related problems. You've got people in there with melanomas, sunburn, heatstroke, dehydration . . . you name it, they've got it. Immediately, the Martian would think: "The sun is bad. Let's ban the sun!" Right?'

'I suppose,' says Andy.

'But, of course, *we* know that the sun *isn't* bad. We know that the sun *can* be bad if we're exposed to it too fast or in large doses, but that, actually, at weaker dosages and with more controlled levels of exposure, the sun doesn't just make us look better and feel better – without it we wouldn't be here at all!'

'And your point is?' yawns Andy, casually snaffling a last-ditch chocolate éclair from the clutches of one of the runners and shoving it into his mouth.

'My point is,' I continue, 'it's exactly the same with psychopathy. Sure, if you lie out in it day after day you're going to get badly burned. And so are the people around you. You'll have what we might call a carcinoma of the personality. But with regulated exposure psychopathy can have intrinsic benefits. At high levels, yes – psychopathy is personality CANCER. But at low levels it's a different story. It's personality with a TAN.'

ARE YOU A PSYCHOPATH?
TO FIND OUT...

Indicate the extent with which you agree or disagree with each of the statements below. If you strongly agree give yourself 3 points, if you agree give yourself 2 points, disagree 1 point, and strongly disagree 0 points. Then add up your total and check it against the scale to provide a rough idea of where you are on the psychopathic spectrum.

	strongly agree 3	agree 2	disagree 1	strongly disagree 0
1. I rarely plan ahead. I'm a spur-of-the-moment kind of person.	○	○	○	○
2. Cheating on your partner is OK so long as you don't get caught.	○	○	○	○
3. If something better comes along it's OK to cancel a longstanding appointment.	○	○	○	○
4. Seeing an animal injured or in pain doesn't bother me in the slightest.	○	○	○	○
5. Driving fast cars, riding rollercoasters and skydiving appeal to me.	○	○	○	○
6. It doesn't matter to me if I have to step on other people to get what I want.	○	○	○	○
7. I'm very persuasive. I have a talent for getting other people to do what I want.	○	○	○	○
8. I'd be good in a dangerous job because I can make my mind up quickly.	○	○	○	○
9. I find it easy to keep it together when others are cracking under pressure.	○	○	○	○
10. If you're able to con someone, that's their problem. They deserve it.	○	○	○	○
11. Most of the time when things go wrong it's somebody else's fault, not mine.	○	○	○	○

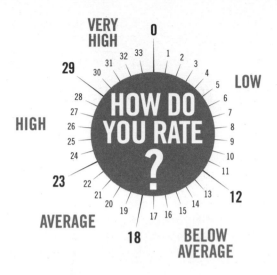

SO . . . WHAT DOES IT MEAN?

When most people think of psychopaths, Hannibal Lecter typically springs to mind. But, actually, being psychopathic doesn't necessarily mean you're a serial killer. Or even that you'll break the law.

In fact, within the framework of clinical psychology, a psychopath is someone with a distinct cluster of personality traits, including ruthlessness, fearlessness, self-confidence, charm, charisma, impulsivity, persuasiveness, mental toughness, and a lack of conscience and empathy.

Sure, these traits may well come in handy if you aspire to be an axe-murderer. But they can also come in handy in the courtroom, on the trading floor, on the battlefield or in the operating theatre. It just depends on what else you've got going on in your personality, and the start you get in life.

Another misconception about psychopaths concerns diagnosis. A lot of people think that you're either a psychopath or you're not, that it's all very black and white. But there is evidence to suggest that things aren't as clear-cut as they seem. And that psychopathy – like height and weight, for example – in fact lies on a SPECTRUM.

Sure, at the sharp end you may well find your serial killers and axe-murderers. But at the same time, all of us have our place at some point along the continuum. Some of us may score higher on some psychopathic traits than on others. In other words, some of us have our dials twiddled further to the right than others.

But unless you've got *all* of your dials twiddled to the right – or, for that matter, the left – you really don't have anything to worry about! In fact, even if you *do* have all of your dials cranked up high or low, you still don't have anything to worry about.

Unless, that is, they're all on max. And *stuck*.

In which case, well . . . you might!

Remember – no one setting is necessarily bad in isolation. Instead it depends on the situations you find yourself in.

So let's start by getting a GENERAL INDICATION of where your OVERALL psychopathy dial is set.

Then, in the pages that follow, we'll help you fine-tune your INDIVIDUAL mixing-desk dials to ensure you get the success you want out of life.

SCORE BREAKDOWNS

LOW You are warm and empathic with a heightened awareness of social responsibility and a strong sense of conscience. You like to carefully weigh up the pros and cons of a situation before you act and are generally averse to taking risks. You avoid hurting others and are easily hurt yourself. You are very much a 'people person' and dislike conflict. 'Do unto others . . .' are your watchwords.

AVERAGE Though your conscience is in the right place, you also have a pragmatic streak and generally aren't afraid to do your own dirty work. You're no shrinking violet – but no daredevil either. You generally have little trouble seeing things from another person's perspective but, at the same time, are no pushover. 'Everything in moderation – including moderation' might sum up your approach to life.

HIGH You can play hardball with the best of them. You know what you want and are not afraid to go for it – even if it means bending the rules occasionally and putting a few noses out of joint on the way. Nothing fazes you. You are decisive, self-confident and pretty much up for anything. You are a 'means-to-an-end' person. For you, it's not necessarily a matter of right or wrong but of what gets the job done. 'Bring it on!' is your mantra.

GOOD
CHOPATH
IFESTO

**Great men are forged in fire.
It is the privilege of lesser men
to light the flame.**

Doctor Who

BUS STOP BUST-UP

You are driving along in your two-seater car on a cold, stormy night. You pass by a bus stop and notice three people waiting for a ride home:

- **A very old lady who's clearly seriously ill and needs to get to a hospital.**
- **An old friend who once saved your life.**
- **The perfect partner you have spent many years dreaming about.**

Knowing that you only have room for one passenger in your car, who do you decide to give a lift to?

You could:

- **Pick up the old lady and help save her life.**
- **Select your old friend as he once saved yours,** *or*
- **Choose that perfect partner you may never see again unless you make an immediate move.**

Which is it to be?

Andy and I are sitting having a coffee in a glass-fronted restaurant with a view across London to die for. It's early December, late afternoon, and the twinkling lights of MI6, Canary Wharf and the Old Bailey are gold and glittery against a dark, pre-Christmas sky.

Bond, Gekko, Dexter and Lecter are all out there somewhere, I think to myself. Doing their thing. No doubt it'll only be a matter of time before we hear about their latest incarnations.

The shimmering skyline is a fitting backdrop to the dilemma Andy has just posed me.

'It's meant to be an initiative test,' he tells me in between loud slurps of his cappuccino, 'for people working in an investment bank.'

He picks up a spoon and starts skimming the froth off the top.

'Andy, mate,' I say. 'This place has got a Michelin star.'

'I know. This foam tastes great!'

I have been giving Andy's conundrum some serious thought. Or, rather, have been *trying* to give it some serious thought while he deconstructs his coffee. But as soon as I hear the words 'initiative test', that's it. I throw in the towel.

'Go on then,' I say. 'What's the answer?'

'Well,' he says, 'according to what I've heard, the answer they're looking for is this. You mow the old girl down to put her out of her misery, get your perfect partner's telephone number, then drive off for a few bevvies with your old mate. Apparently, this shows that you're ruthless, well organized and loyal to those who've been good to you in the past – the qualities, so they say, of a perfect investment banker.'

I stare at him blankly.

'Well organized?' I say. 'So hang on, let me get this right. Your perfect partner is supposed to give you her contact details, and your best mate is supposed to go out for a drink with you, after just seeing you plough into an old lady right in front of them?'

Andy takes another slurp.

'The wrong answer is to take the old lady to hospital and leave your perfect partner alone at the bus stop with your old friend,' he continues. 'This shows that you are easily distracted from the main task at hand, fail to grasp opportunities as they arise, and allow your competitors to get the jump on you.'

'You're taking the piss.' I laugh. 'So, OK, how about this then? You bung your mate your car keys to take the old dear to hospital, see your dream partner on to the bus to make sure she gets home all right – and while you're at it you get her mobile phone number. This shows that you have more than one brain cell, a bit of common sense, and the ability to avoid being banged up for life in a hospital for the criminally insane. Where does that fit into the equation?'

Andy shakes his head. 'Don't know,' he says. 'But it's what I'd do. Chances are the old dear's going to have an artificial hip and if you catch them wrong those things can be a real bugger for your paintwork.'

'Banks,' I mutter. 'No wonder it all went tits up.'

HOT SEAT

Andy's moral dilemma/initiative test is a brilliant example of how *not* to live your life. Of how *not* to go about pursuing your own self-interest.

There's nothing wrong with getting what you want. But running an old lady over in your car? That's not ruthless. It's malicious, boneheaded stupidity.

Stupidity like that is *not* what this book is about. Instead, this book is about getting what you want in a way that may, at times, be tough but which is always within the rules . . .

. . . though admittedly, there can sometimes be grey areas!

I once remember taking the F line into Manhattan on the New York subway. I was on my way to some store or other when it dawned on me that I didn't actually know which station to get off at.

The train was packed so I decided to ask the guy standing in front of me.

'Next one,' he said.

'Thanks,' I said, and stood up.

He sat down.

'Actually,' he said, 'it's 34th Street. That's another five stops, man. But you know what? My legs are killing me!'

Everyone else in the carriage started laughing so hard I had little choice but to 'suck it up', as they say in that part of the world. 34th St station couldn't have come round fast enough.

But is what this guy did acting within the rules? It's a difficult one to call. Yes, he pulled a fast one. There's no doubt about that. But, looking back on it, I have to ask myself this:

In hindsight, was the ignominy and inconvenience of standing up for a few extra minutes on the New York subway worth what I got in return – a story I've been telling ever since?

An unstoppable free kick of a scam that screamed straight into the top corner of my brain?

A quick and dirty master class in how to be a CHEEKY psychopath if not an entirely GOOD one?

I reckon so!

Some people have asked me whether I might have looked more favourably on what this guy did if it had been for the benefit of someone else as opposed to himself. If, for instance, after getting me to stand up, he then ushered an old lady into my seat.

Or the partner of his dreams.

Or his best mate.

I don't think so. If *that* had been his game it would've seemed, to me, a little too patronizing. A little too smug. A little too much like he was trying to teach me a lesson. And no one likes being taught that kind of lesson. Especially not by that kind of guy!

Besides, surely the right thing to do in that situation would be to punch the old lady to the floor, get the number of your perfect partner as you settle them into their seat, then jump off at the next stop to have a celebratory drink with your mate?

Or maybe I've been knocking about with too many investment bankers.

The first time I met Andy he told me something that has stuck in my mind ever since.

'You can get away with anything,' he said, 'so long as you can get away with it.'

He's right.

The trick is to get away with it.

NOT SHAKEN, NOT STIRRED –
THE GOOD PSYCHOPATH MIX

Sometimes Andy can be cleverer than he looks – not often, but sometimes – and over the years I've occasionally found myself reflecting on those words.

They're shallower than they sound!

Basically, I think, the bottom line is this:

Everything is impossible until someone comes along and does it. And then, all of a sudden, it becomes possible.

Possible and impossible, in other words, are not Harry Pottery super words with the power to define reality. In fact, it's the other way around. REALITY defines THEM. Whether something is possible or impossible very much depends on what WE are going to do about it. It's an incredibly empowering thought.

It is also, I think, a philosophy – a philosophy which pretty much encapsulates what being a GOOD PSYCHOPATH is all about.

In Chapter One Andy made a very important point. He said, if you recall, that what we're offering you here isn't just a Jamie-style recipe book for success: a handy hints manual to get you up the ladder.

It's a PHILOSOPHY OF LIFE.

Which it is.

But what kind of philosophy *is* it, exactly?

And where does it come from?

In the rest of this chapter we're going to answer these questions by sketching out for you the ethical, cultural and intellectual traditions that the Good Psychopath philosophy draws upon – the theoretical foundations of this lifestyle we're describing. The resulting ideological cocktail may surprise you: an unlikely blend of hedonism, existentialism and Judaeo-Christianity.

On the other hand, however, philosophical tasting notes may not be your thing. So if you're not really bothered about how the brew was mixed and are more concerned with what the concoction tastes like, then please feel free to skip the next few pages. The less you think, the quicker you get your drink!

NATURAL UNBORN KILLERS

We begin our degustation in the company of the ancient Greeks. Well, *an* ancient Greek to be precise: the philosopher Epicurus.

In the third century BC, Epicurus put forward a notion that most of us now take for granted. As we make our way through life, we have two primary motivations:

- The attainment of PLEASURE
- The avoidance of PAIN

These dual motivations are not exclusively human. In fact, so fundamental is Epicurus's idea that it applies at even the most rudimentary levels of life. Under powerful microscopes, for example, simple, single-celled microorganisms may be observed moving TOWARDS REWARD STIMULI (e.g. a food source) and AWAY FROM THREATENING STIMULI (e.g. a sharp probe).

'A bit like someone who's overweight ordering more cake instead of binning the carbs and going on a diet!' Andy chimes in, picking up a menu.

Epicurus called this preference for pleasure over pain *hedonism* (from the Greek word *hedonismus*, meaning delight) – and even the most masochistic of us are hedonists at heart. Not only that, but we start off rather early!

Here's an example.

Harvard University biologist David Haig has spent the last few years systematically debunking the notion that the relationship between a mother and her unborn child is anything like the rose-tinted idyll that one usually finds on the glossy covers of maternity magazines.

In fact, it is anything but.

Pre-eclampsia, a condition of dangerously high blood pressure in pregnant women, is brutally kick-started by nothing short of a foetal coup d'état. It begins with the placenta invading the maternal bloodstream and initiating what, in anyone's book, is a ruthless biological heist – an *in utero* sting operation to draw out vital nutrients.

And I'm not just talking about baby Gordon Gekkos here – I'm talking about all of us.

The curtain-raiser is well known to obstetricians. The foetus begins by injecting a crucial protein into the mother's circulation which forces her to drive more blood, and therefore more nourishment, into the relatively low-pressure placenta.

It's a scam, pure and simple, which poses a significant and immediate risk to the mother's life.

'The bastard!' says Andy. 'Shall we get some olives?'

'And it's by no means the only one,' I continue.

In another embryonic Ponzi scheme, foetal release of placental lactogen counteracts the effect of maternal insulin thereby increasing the mother's blood sugar level and providing an excess for the foetus's own benefit.

'A bowl of the citrus and chilli and a bowl of the sweet pepper and basil,' Andy says to the waiter.

Then he peers at me over the menu.

'So basically what you're saying then is this: forget the Gaddafis and the Husseins. When it comes to chemical warfare it's the unborn child that's top dog!'

'Well they definitely nick stuff that isn't theirs,' I say. 'And they don't give a damn about the consequences.'

Andy smiles.

'So in other words they're psychopaths!' he says.

BABY YOU'RE THE BEST

Epicurus's observation that we are all motivated by self-interest, by the attainment of pleasure and the avoidance of pain – accompanied, some two millennia later, by the supporting scientific evidence that we're all at it from the moment we can manage to scrape a couple of bog-standard nerve cells together – should, in theory, go some way towards making us feel good about ourselves.

Or better, at least.

Towards soothing our troubled consciences.

But it doesn't.

Besieged, as we grow up, by the pressure of social norms and the personal and professional consequences of stepping on others' toes, we carry the burden of getting what we want, of unpasteurized self-interest, very heavily.

We ruminate . . .

We cogitate . . .

We deliberate . . .

We hesitate . . .

. . . not just over decisions of life-changing importance but also over those of considerably lesser magnitude.

We sweat the small stuff, the big stuff, and all the differently sized stuff in between. In *Flipnosis*, I – like Andy – drew a number of striking parallels between newborn babies and psychopaths. It ruffled quite a few feathers at the time. Most notably among readers who didn't have kids!

Babies are charming, manipulative, heartless, and in it totally for themselves, I wrote. Like their equally ruthless counterparts. And also, like psychopaths, engage in uncomfortable periods of prolonged, unblinking eye contact – a reliable indicator of social disinhibition.

Psychopathy, I argued at the time, is our natural state. We are born that way. At the precise moment that we come into this world, natural selection has already kitted us out for the hazardous mission ahead – tooling us up with a deadly psychopathy starter pack chock to the brim with every trick in the black-belt con artist's book to get us what we want.

Which, of course, it does.

Little did I know that we opened that pack in the womb!

But as we get older things begin to change. Our ruthlessness mellows and our psychopathic fearlessness subsides.

It is – in varying degrees – loved, punished, educated and indoctrinated out of us so that, by the time we reach adulthood and begin to take control of our lives, by the time we've grown up and have the power to make our *own* decisions rather than have others make them for us, we are absolutely terrified of doing so.

We freeze in the glare of the consequences of our actions.

We stand dazzled and confused in the immobilizing headlights of choice.

We are paralysed by the freedom we fought so hard to win.

The olives arrive and Andy dives straight in.

'You know what we need don't you, mate?' he says.

'Go on,' I say.

'An updated version of that *in utero* psychopathy starter pack.'

THE DIZZINESS OF FREEDOM

This idea of existential angst that Andy and I are talking about is, needless to say, not new. It's as old as the philosophical hills.

But the first person to really put their finger on it, to properly sit down and quantify it was not, in fact, an ancient bearded colossus classically bedecked in a laurel wreath and toga, but the nineteenth-century Danish philosopher Søren Kierkegaard.

To illustrate his point, Kierkegaard came up with a brilliant analogy. Imagine that you're standing on the edge of a cliff, he wrote.

You will experience two kinds of fear.

The first kind is the fear of falling (which is fair enough).

The second kind is the fear of throwing yourself off – the terrifying realization that whether or not you plunge into the abyss below is COMPLETELY UP TO YOU.

You have total FREEDOM OF CHOICE.

In keeping with the vertiginous theme of his analogy, Kierkegaard coined a beautiful phrase to describe the ontology (a philosophical word combining reason and origin in one) of this fear.

'Anxiety,' he wrote, 'is the dizziness of freedom.'

Even Andy nods his head. 'But he couldn't have been talking just about standing on cliff tops,' he says. 'I mean, if that were true we wouldn't still be talking about him now.'

'You're right,' I reply. 'He wasn't. His insight goes much deeper than that.'

Kierkegaard proposed that we experience this kind of dizziness all the time – when we teeter on the edges of personal or moral or financial cliff tops (to name but a few) during the course of our everyday lives.

And, in the grand scheme of things, he didn't think it did us much harm.

Quite the reverse, in fact.

It kept our wackier impulses in check and society on the straight and narrow by ensuring that we didn't go and do anything too 'over the top'.

Sure, it may get us down from time to time. It may drive us into depression or spill over into the full-blown psychological vertigo of anxiety disorder.

But in general, Kierkegaard maintained, the benefits outweigh the costs. It heightens our self-awareness and gives us a greater sense of both personal and communal responsibility.

'Fair one,' says Andy. 'But the downside, I guess, is that some people develop an unhealthy fear of heights. And a lot more, even

if they aren't afraid of going up the mountain to begin with, are reluctant to jump even a small distance when they get to the summit.'

'Got it in one!' I say.

The problem, it seems, lies in striking the right balance.

In direct contrast to our *in utero* and newborn personas, we've scampered too far up the other end of the spectrum.

We've become too risk averse.

TALENT VERSUS SUCCESS

Banks didn't exist back in Jesus' time. Well, not the big multinationals that piss us about today anyway. If they *had* done, and the Roman Empire had experienced the same kind of credit crunch that we did a few years ago, then the following tale might well have panned out differently.

But as it stands there is no better example of the failings of risk aversion, of *too much* risk aversion, and of the moral responsibility that each of us has to roll the dice and get the very best out of ourselves, than that provided by the immeasurably surprising story that Andy brings up next.

It's one of the most elegantly discerning treatments of healthy and unhealthy mindsets, of positive and negative outlook, in the history of Western thought.

And an exquisite encapsulation – some two thousand years before he came up with it – of Kierkegaard's big idea.

Unfortunately, Andy's rendition isn't as good as some of the others out there on the market (a mouthful of olives doesn't help).

So here it is, the Parable of the Talents, in the narrator's original words.

Again, it will be like a man going on a journey, who called his servants and entrusted his property to them. To one he gave five talents of money, to another two talents, and to another one talent, each according to his ability. Then he went on his journey. The man who had received the five talents went at once and put his money to work and gained five more. So also, the one with the two talents gained two more. But the man who had received the one talent went off, dug a hole in the ground and hid his master's money.

After a long time, the master of those servants returned and settled accounts with them. The man who had received the five talents brought the other five. 'Master,' he said, 'you entrusted me with five talents. See, I have gained five more.'

His master replied, 'Well done, good and faithful servant! You have been faithful with a few things; I will put you in charge of many things. Come and share your master's happiness!'

The man with the two talents also came. 'Master,' he said, 'you entrusted me with two talents; see, I have gained two more.'

His master replied, 'Well done, good and faithful servant! You have been faithful with a few things; I will put you in charge of many things. Come and share your master's happiness!'

Then the man who had received the one talent came. 'Master,' he said, 'I knew that you are a hard man, harvesting where you have not sown and gathering where you have not scattered seed. So I was afraid and went out and hid your talent in the ground. See, here is what belongs to you.'

His master replied, 'You wicked, lazy servant! So you knew that I harvest where I have not sown and gather where I have not scattered seed? Well then, you should have put my money on deposit with the bankers, so that when I returned I would have received it back with interest.

'Take the talent from him and give it to the one who has the ten talents. For everyone who has will be given more, and he will have an abundance. Whoever does not have, even what he has will be taken from him. And throw that worthless servant outside, into the darkness, where there will be weeping and gnashing of teeth.' *(Matthew 25:14–30 NIV)*

This brutally simple story, as Andy rightly observes, holds a perfect psychological mirror to Kierkegaard's altitudinous analogy. But it also goes one further.

Because the main thing we notice, alongside the element of RISK, is that success is completely RELATIVE. It is *not* absolute.

'Whenever we look at the final standings, be it at the end of a race, competition, selection process or whatever,' Andy points out, 'it's important to remember that we all begin from different positions on the starting grid. In other words, whatever it is that we're setting out to achieve in life there are always going to be some lucky bastards who have it easy, who are blessed with natural ability (five talents). And there will always be those who aren't (one talent).

'I think that getting your head around this simple, basic truth is key to how you see success. And key to how you achieve it. That Danish bloke you were on about is right. It's true that a lot of people don't get what they want because they're scared of taking the plunge.

'But I reckon there's another reason why people fail at stuff – and it's got nothing to do with a lack of application or the way they go about it. It's purely and simply because they have unrealistic expectations of what is actually possible. They set themselves goals which, given where they are on the starting grid, are impossible to reach.

'Earlier, you were talking about success being a byproduct of two things: talent on the one hand and the right kind of personality to maximize that talent on the other. Well, that's just it, isn't it? One without the other just won't work.'

By way of example, Andy tells me about a common occurrence on SAS selection – the most fearsome military selection process in the world.

'Some of the guys who turn up on Day One look like Olympic athletes,' he says. 'They train for months to get themselves into peak condition only to discover, at some point down the line, that peak condition for *them* still falls short of the benchmark physical talent required to get into the Regiment.

'These guys are in bits when they're "binned" and returned to their units. They've worked so hard and yet they've still "failed".

'Except that they haven't failed at all. They've failed Selection, yes. But they haven't failed *themselves*. They've given the very last drop of what they've got to give. But it just wasn't good enough. It never *was* going to be good enough. There's no shame in that.

'On one SAS Selection a few years ago a couple of the candidates died. The Commanding Officer summoned the Training Officer who ran the course to his office and asked him how he was supposed to justify it. There were questions being raised in the Commons.

'"The way I see it," said the Training Officer, "it's Nature's way of telling them they've failed Selection!"

'His answer was immortalized as a print, set in a frame and hung in the Training Wing's accommodation block for all Selection candidates to read.'

But it works both ways.

The story might be called the Parable of the TALENTS. But notice how the narrator places equal emphasis on the PERSONAL-ITY side of the equation. On how those talents are managed.

If you happen to be one of the lucky ones, like Five-Talent Man for instance, it just isn't good enough to rest on your laurels and take it easy on yourself. If you happen to be naturally gifted, the return you get on those gifts should be consistent with the outlay.

In contrast there may be times in your life when, like One-Talent Man, you simply have to do the best you can with it. Which does not translate to burying it in the ground! A one-talent return on one talent is just as good as a five-talent return on five.

'Agreed,' says Andy. 'In fact, that's one of the guiding principles on which the SAS operates. Selection is open to everyone within the British Army, Navy and Air Force – from head chefs on submarines to airframe mechanics who keep the RAF Chinook helicopters flying to Regimental Sergeant Majors from a Para battalion.

'But it doesn't matter what you are, the Selection training staff will expect a level of knowledge and expertise from you consistent with where you came from. It's all about the ability to learn, not what you already know. That means there is no way you can judge your progress by comparing yourself with others. The only person you are competing against is YOU. Pass *him* – and you're in.

'They are perfectly happy to teach the navy chef the basics of stripping and assembling a weapon. But a Para regiment RSM? You've got to be joking!'

GIVING WHAT YOU'VE GOT

We order dinner and look out at the MI6 building. It hass started to rain and with the lights and the opaque windows, the place is enveloped in a greeny-gold haze. I ask Andy if he's ever been in there.

'What, Legoland?' he replies. 'Yeah, loads of times.'

As we begin to get more comfortable, Andy tells me a story about his own time on Selection, which is a perfect demonstration of the SAS's approach to talent.

Having completed the initial four-week endurance and navigation phase, those who remained on the course (and there weren't many) were flown off to Brunei to begin what is called 'continuation' (or jungle) training.

As the boys settle down to learn basic Morse Code beneath the sweltering emerald canopy of the rainforest, one of them, whose parent regiment is the Royal Corps of Signals, decides to loaf about drinking cups of tea.

As a signaller, he is already skilled in Morse Code and sees no reason to sit in on stuff he could quite easily do in his sleep.

As soon as they return to England, he's packing his bags and is gone.

'It was a fair one, for two reasons,' says Andy. 'First, if he's getting a brew on it shouldn't have been just for himself; he's part of a team. And second, as soon as he'd made it he should've then started pitching in – helping us get our heads around all those dots and dashes.

'It's not just Who Dares Wins. It's Who *Shares* Wins, too.'

In an ironic twist, once news of his fate got out, a mysterious note composed of strange hieroglyphics turned up on his bed.

'Morse Code?' I ask Andy.

'Yes,' he grins, shoving his bacon and sun-dried tomato bread roll into his mouth. 'For "Fuck off, teaboy!"'

There are two sides to success: SUBJECTIVE and OBJECTIVE.

When the two coincide it's brilliant. But when you get one without the other, the results, for the most part, are usually less than optimal.

Subjective without objective can code for disappointment.

Objective without subjective can lead to laziness and under-achievement.

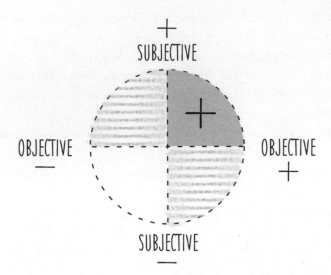

The bottom line, as we can see from the way the Parable of the Talents eventually pans out, is self-confidence.

Not *over*-confidence.

Self-confidence.

It is:

- **Believing in yourself.**
- **Throwing down the gauntlet.**
- **Facing down your demons.**

The Parable of the Talents is an audacious invitation – to return to Kierkegaard's 'cliffhanger' metaphor – to overcome the 'dizziness of freedom' and to throw in your lot with the person you dare to become.

It is a licence to go for your shots.

'Many years ago, when he was still with us, the American tennis player Vitas Gerulaitis dumps Jimmy Connors out of some tournament or other,' I tell Andy. 'Connors – who's gone into the match on a sixteen-game winning streak against Gerulaitis – is livid. At the post-match press conference tensions were widely expected to boil over. Until, that is, Gerulaitis takes the stand.

'"No one beats Vitas Gerulaitis seventeen straight!" he booms.'

The remark has everyone laughing.

Including Connors.

But, despite what had gone before, Gerulaitis had played brilliantly that day. And his quip was as much a mantra as it was an icebreaker.

He had stood on the edge of the precipice and had taken the plunge.

He'd suffered innumerable losses but had refused to cash himself in.

'He refused to bury his talent,' says Andy.

LEARNING TO FAIL

Vitas Gerulaitis had the guts to keep believing in the person he dared to become. He had the guts, as Epicurus might've put it, to persist in stumbling towards a dreamed-of oasis of pleasure even when the route took him time and time again through the parched and lonely killing fields of pain.

Which is easier said than done.

A classic experiment conducted back in the 1960s showed that dogs repeatedly given electric shocks with no way of escaping those shocks, subsequently chose to passively accept their fate EVEN WHEN AN ESCAPE ROUTE WAS MADE AVAILABLE TO THEM.

They lay down and whimpered instead of getting up and walking away.

This strange tendency that the brain sometimes has to be brainwashed into submission – called 'learned helplessness' by psychologists – can also be observed in humans.

It explains, among other things, why battered women often remain loyal to abusive husbands when the door to a new life is, quite literally, thrown wide open in front of them. And why, when they have the chance, long-term hostages and kidnap victims do not make a break for freedom, and instead, against all the laws of objective common sense, choose to remain incarcerated.

And going back to SAS selection, it also explains why candidates throw in the towel – even in the latter stages, when the physical stuff is over and there are only a few days left to run.

Here's Andy again:

'On the final week you're dumped in the middle of the Brecon Beacons with a hunter force after you. You're set up to be captured because they have to interrogate you, see how you stand up to it.

'It usually lasts seventy-two hours. They hood you, blindfold you, tie you up, yell at you, throw water over you, throw *everything* at you – white noise, stress positions, the lot – to see if they can break you.

'And a lot of people *do* break. Even blokes who have got that far and have got only a few hours left on the course will break.

'I've never understood it myself. Interrogation was easy for me. I remember thinking: "Just a few more hours of this and that's it. Pull on the beret, one of the boys."

'That was the goal I'd set myself. That's who I wanted to be. I wanted to look at myself in the mirror wearing the famous winged dagger and say: "Mate, you've come from the gutters of Peckham to take your place among some of the finest soldiers who ever walked the face of the earth. Good on you!" And no amount of beasting was going to take that away from me.

'But the problem for some blokes is that they start believing it's real. They start believing that it actually *means* something.

'When you're cold, wet, tired and hungry, blindfolded and handcuffed and being bombarded with bursts of white noise in some minging shithole in the middle of fuck-knows-where that stinks of bat, rat and cat piss, it's easy for your mind to start playing tricks on you.

'It's easy to start thinking that they've got it in for you. That they're trying to kill you. That they don't want you to pass. That it's never going to end and that there's no way out.

'But it's not like that at all. They just want to see if you're good enough. And if you start thinking like that – that it means something, that it's all about *you*, that there's never going to be an end to it – then, quite frankly, you're not good enough.

'Fuck it – when it came to noise and piss and stress positions, I knew nightclubs in Hereford that were worse!'

BREAKING THE MOULD

Andy's take on the final few hours of SAS selection, which, in a unique and unlikely narrative, unites Epicurus, Kierkegaard and Jesus under the one metaphysical roof, brings us to the halfway point in our historical and philosophical excavation of the core principles and values of the Good Psychopath psychology.

But before we progress from mantra to methodology we need to touch base with a second triumvirate of philosophical greats whose thinking comprises the high-wire, existentialist suspension bridge between the PRINCIPLES of being a Good Psychopath and their PRACTICE: Jean-Paul Sartre, Albert Camus and Friedrich Nietzsche.

The food arrives and we start tucking in. Fillet of John Dory for me: lightly grilled.

Burger for Andy: burnt.

'You know, you're probably not going to like this,' I say, as the ketchup does a flypast over the burger and touches down at an undisclosed location somewhere to the right of our shiny Conran table, 'but I'd put you down as a disciple of Sartre and Camus. During the final few days of SAS selection anyway.'

Andy's not listening – too busy sorting the sauce bottle malfunction.

Sartre, a Parisian who was at the height of his philosophical powers during the mid-twentieth century, is famous for his contention that, when it comes to us humans, 'Existence precedes essence.'

Or, to put it more simply, we are

born without purpose so we are free to become whoever we wish to become.

We are at liberty to shape our own destiny.

To clarify, Sartre uses the example of a paper knife. It is inconceivable, he suggests, that a paper knife could exist without the prior intention of the craftsman who made it. In other words, in order to fashion a paper knife, as opposed to, say, a carving knife or a Stanley knife, the craftsman would have to know exactly what it was going to be used for.

To cut paper. Not fabric or meat.

But humans, Sartre reasoned, are different to paper knives. A devout atheist, he maintained that there was no Master Plan behind the creation of the human form – no envisaged purpose – and that each and every one of us was teeming with unique potential.

'First of all man exists, turns up, appears on the scene, and only afterwards defines himself,' he proclaimed. 'As far as men go, it is not what they are that interests me, but what they can become.'

'A bit like ketchup then!' says Andy.

I ignore him, drizzling some white asparagus velouté over my grilled fish.

'Whatever,' I say. 'But get this: what Sartre was mulling over some half a century ago in the coffee houses of the Left Bank is exactly the same thing that *you* were mulling over as you lay hooded and gagged on the floor of some Brecon Beacons hay barn on your journey from Peckham to Hereford!'

The bottle farts and a big dollop of tomato ketchup lands slap bang in the middle of his burger.

'Perfect,' says Andy.

THE CLARK KENT WITHIN ALL OF US

With its emphasis on freedom and possibility, on breaking the mould of a preordained natural order, Sartre's philosophy is seen as profoundly liberating.

But he is quick to point out that we do have to accept *some* limits on the scope of our personal achievement.

Unless you are blessed with the VO2 max, lactate threshold, and ratio of slow to fast twitch muscle fibres of, say, a Mo Farah then you are never going to be . . . Mo Farah!

Likewise, as Andy told us earlier, unless you have the innate physiological capabilities required to pass SAS selection you're never going to pull on the famous sand-coloured beret, no matter how fit you are.

On the other hand, however, within the range of realistic options that we *do* have at our disposal, the choices we make are often distorted by powerful societal forces way beyond our control: by ancient psychological jet streams that have, over time, expediently sculpted the supple neural forests of our brains.

Over millions of years of complex biological development these withering evolutionary trade winds – fear of failure, social norms, self-consciousness and the like – have weathered our decision-making landscape into coppices of convention and conformity: a psychic malaise which the Parable of the Talents neatly captures.

Friedrich Nietzsche, a German philosopher of the late nineteenth century, wrote on a similar theme.

But for Nietzsche – like Sartre an atheist – the constraints on human potential were not customs and norms like tradition and expectation, but the prevailing Christian values of his day.

Nietzsche railed against the way that Christianity devalued life as just a warm-up act for the infinitely more rewarding 'life after death' – how it advocated turning our backs on what seemed important in the here and now in readiness for life on an eternal, ethereal, more exalted plane of existence. By doing this, Nietzsche argued, Christianity was essentially urging us to 'de-friend' life itself – a pompous and universally restrictive philosophy which threatened to undermine us as a species.

Instead he called for a 'revaluation of all values' – a comprehensive audit of all the things that we habitually think of as 'good'.

Were they genuinely good?

Or, when you cast a cold eye over them, were they extraneous codes of conduct that simply held us back?

Is staying in a boring job, or an abusive relationship or a toxic friendship merely out of a sense of duty, for instance, really the right thing to do? Are the so-called 'sins of the flesh' actually sins at all? Is 'turning the other cheek' a legitimate strategy by which to live one's life?

Science, I tell Andy, has in fact come up with an answer to this last question.

And it's NO!

Research has shown that responding to nice people by being nice and to not nice people by being not nice is by far the most effective way forward.

'So the meek don't inherit the earth after all,' he says. 'They get jack shit!'

I degust the last of my truffle ravioli.

'Man is a rope tied between the animal and the Superman,' Nietzsche asserted. 'A rope over an abyss . . . human life is a dangerous wayfaring, a dangerous looking back, a dangerous trembling and halting.'

Kierkegaard would have approved.

To be who we CAN be as opposed to who we SHOULD be, we have to brave the storm.

In our quest to be our very own Clark Kents we have to transcend the dizziness of freedom.

THE ILLUSION OF MEANING

I doubt if Albert Camus knew much about elite military selection procedures – although he did work for the French Resistance during the Second World War editing an underground newspaper. But were his indomitable revolutionary spirit to have attracted him into the military fraternity as opposed to the hotbed of anarchist and communist activism – in Algeria in the 1930s and then Paris in the 1940s and 1950s – I have a feeling he might have excelled.

Like Sartre and Nietzsche, Camus was struck by the profoundly empowering meaninglessness of existence.

'I looked up at the mass of signs and stars in the night sky,' intones Meursault, the central character in Camus's 1942 novel *L'Etranger*, 'and laid myself open for the first time to the benign indifference of the world.'

'I know where he's coming from,' says Andy. 'I did the same through the bars of an Iraqi prison cell. It feels great.'

For Meursault and Camus – and Andy – the celestial cupboard is bare.

But *unlike* Sartre and Nietzsche, the illusion of meaning was not, for Camus, a guilt-laced fuzzy-headedness that stemmed from the torpor of some moral or religious hangover.

It was a little bit more psychological.

It's long been accepted by psychologists and neuroscientists that each of us is fitted with a meaning detector in our brains. We are rational, thinking beings and we look for patterns in everything.

Sometimes, these patterns are there. They form part of the fabric of an objective, coherent reality. The symmetry of a snowflake, for example. Or the 'eyes' on the wing of a butterfly. But sometimes these patterns are *not* there and our brains fill in the gaps. They jump to conclusions to make themselves look useful – one of the taxes we pay on the bumper evolutionary windfall that we call consciousness. (See the Bullshit Grid overleaf for an idea of how this works.)

But Camus took things one step further – and extended the argument beyond the cognitive stratosphere of mental computation deep into the realms of philosophical outer space. For Camus, the truth was absurdly and brutally simple.

Nothing meant anything anywhere!

Well, anywhere, that is, except the space between our ears.

Sure, lots of things *seem* meaningful, conceded Camus – significanced-up by our pattern-seeking, sense-addicted consciousness. But the reality is very different. There is no rhyme or reason to anything in the universe.

Or, for that matter, the universe itself.

THE BULLSHIT GRID

	ONE	TWO	THREE
0	INTEGRATED	MANAGEMENT	OPTIONS
1	HEURISTIC	MONITORED	MOBILITY
2	SYSTEMATIZED	ORGANIZATIONAL	CAPABILITY
3	PARALLEL	RECIPROCAL	FLEXIBILITY
4	FUNCTIONAL	DIGITAL	PROGRAMMING
5	RESPONSIVE	LOGISTICAL	SCENARIOS
6	OPTIONAL	TRANSITIONAL	TIME-PHASE
7	SYNCHRONIZED	INCREMENTAL	PROJECTION
8	COMPATIBLE	3RD-GENERATION	HARDWARE
9	FUTURISTIC	POLICY	CONTINGENCY

THE POWER OF BOLLOCKS

Need to get the jump on someone fast? Then quickly consult this handy business bullshit grid. It works like this. Think of any three-digit number (eg. 2-6-6) and then select the corresponding buzzword word from Columns One, Two, and Three respectively (eg. the selection 2-6-6 produces: 'Systematized Transitional Time-phase') You will immediately come up with a meaningful corporate phrase that will massively impress your boss and completely bamboozle your work colleagues. It's as easy as 1, 2, 3 . . . or Heuristic Organizational Flexibility!

ROCK AND ROLL

Camus was killed in a car crash in 1960, aged 46. He'd torn up a train ticket to Paris to accept a lift with a friend. Not that he would have taken such a thing to heart. Life, in Camus' book, didn't have it in for you. It didn't give a damn.

It just wanted to see, as Andy put it earlier, whether you were good enough.

No need to take it personally.

The SAS have even devised a selection test based around

Camus' thoughts on meaninglessness. Or more accurately, I suppose, around his thoughts on *meaning*.

'During the first month of Selection, life consists of climbing up and down the Brecon Beacons and Black Mountains in Wales with a Bergen [rucksack] on your back,' Andy tells me. 'The Bergen weighs between 16 and 25 kilograms and the distance covered can be anything from 15 to 62 kilometres. But to make things more interesting you don't know the cut-off time, how fast you have to get from A to B. There are two reasons for that.

'First, it means that you're performing under uncertainty, which is much harder psychologically.

'Second, if any Olympic-class racing snake gets across those mountains in record time and is feeling a bit smug, the training team have the opportunity to set them another little test to see if they have as much mental stamina as they do physical stamina.'

The test involves carrying rocks in their Bergen up a hill . . .

then carrying them back down . . .

then carrying them back up . . .

then carrying them back down . . .

ad infinitum.

Until the instructor tells them to stop.

This was exactly the fate that befell the Greek king Sisyphus in Camus' essay *The Myth of Sisyphus*. Sisyphus fell out of favour with the gods and was duly transported to the Underworld. There, for all eternity, he was condemned to heave a huge rock up a mountain, only to watch it roll all the way back down again once he reached the top.

It's not a nice feeling.

'That was a bastard,' admits Andy, looking back. 'There's nothing like a task that's both pointless and physically draining to rip the shit out of you. Especially if you don't know when it's going to end. Quite a few of the lads jacked it in on that one. Talking of which: shall we get the bill?'

Meaning is like psychological oxygen. Without it we wither and die. But not all of us, it would seem.

For the men who pass SAS selection, the ability to:

- let things wash over them
- not take things personally
- not dwell on the past
- not overthink the present
- not worry unduly about the future

is second nature. As it has to be in their line of work.

Here's Andy again:

'I remember the RSM saying to a few of us not long after we'd first been badged: "The secret of success is this. Train like it means everything when it means nothing – so you can fight like it means nothing when it means everything." And he was right. That just about sums up Regiment mentality. Sums up any winning mentality, in fact.'

'Sounds like the geek's version of *Who Dares Wins*,' I tease.

He laughs. 'Exactly,' he says. 'And you should know!'

GOOD PSYCHOPATH TAKEAWAY

The philosophy tour is over – our sightseeing trip around a few of the more popular beauty spots concluded. We pulled out of the station with some words of advice from Andy – that *The Good Psychopath's Guide* should not be seen as *just* a handbook of success but as an all-encompassing PHILOSOPHY OF LIFE – and we embarked on a quest to find out what it was.

What were the roots – classical and modern, moral and psychological – of the Good Psychopath way of life?

What are the guiding principles underpinning its no-nonsense mindset?

Arriving back at the terminus it seems that we've come full circle. We set off on the trail of a philosophy of life and have ended our journey with a Special Forces maxim of success.

Somewhere along the way – via Epicurus, Jesus, Kierkegaard, Sartre, Nietzsche and Camus – the two got tangled up.

But what do we pack in the way of souvenirs?

What can we take from the ideological gift shop?

Well, the first thing of note, which we can take from Epicurus and Kierkegaard, is that, hiding behind success, embedded within the genome of achievement, there lurks a mutant paradox.

On the one hand, as Epicurus observed, we have an inbuilt desire for the positive over the negative. To favour pleasurable experiences over less pleasurable experiences.

On the other hand, however, in order to get what we want – to attain that pleasure and to avoid that pain – we have no option but to square up to pain head on. We have to move out of our comfort zones. We have to overcome the 'dizziness of freedom' of which Kierkegaard spoke so eloquently and take the plunge into the unknown.

We have to have the courage to take chances. To take a chance on *ourselves*. To make the most of our talents instead of burying them under a mountain of excuses.

'Going back to our mixing-desk analogy,' observes Andy, picking up the tab and shooting me a knowing look, 'you have to make sure that your FEARLESSNESS dial is twiddleable . . . ahem . . . and in the pages that follow we'll be giving it a bit of a workout.'

But there are other dials that might also need some twisting and turning. Sartre's obsession with becoming all we can be, with sawing through the shackles of convention and becoming the masters of our own destiny, demands that we play with our RUTHLESSNESS dials a little.

Likewise, Nietzsche's idea that some of the classical virtues that we traditionally think of as good are in fact psychological restraining agents that prevent us from reaching our full potential suggests that we adjust our CONSCIENCE and EMPATHY dials.

Not to the point where we start to harm those around us.

But certainly to the point where levels become low enough not to start harming *ourselves* – not to actively endanger our own self-interests and life-goals.

Last, the hand of Camus hovers ghostlike over our FOCUS dials.

So often in life our preoccupation with meaning . . .

- **What's in it for ME?**
- **What's in it for THEM?**
- **What do I stand to LOSE?**
- **What do I have to GAIN?**

. . . starts to get in the way of . . . well, life itself!

We get so caught up in the consequences of what we're doing that we start not to do it very well.

Things begin to MATTER.

Stuff begins to MEAN SOMETHING.

And before we know it we're not just making decisions. We're making decisions about making those bloody decisions!

'Anyone can walk along a three-foot-wide plank if it's three feet off the ground,' says Andy, handing me my coat. 'But three thousand feet off the ground? That's a different story.'

'But why? It's still a three-foot-wide plank, isn't it?'

The reason, of course, is that at three thousand feet we're no longer focusing just on the plank. In fact, we're probably not focusing on the plank at all! We're focusing on everything *but* the plank.

We're focusing on what's either side of it . . .

NOTHING!

EVERYTHING!

NOTHING *and* EVERYTHING!

And that's just it.

We're focusing on nothing and everything instead of just putting one foot in front of the other. Instead of w-a-l-k-i-n-g. Instead of just getting to the other end of the plank.

The result is that we freeze.

We hesitate.

We dither.

And when you're three thousand feet off the ground with no margin of error, such indecisiveness can be deadly.

Andy again:

'The reason planes don't fall out of the sky is simple. The

principles of aerodynamics aside, the bottom line is because they're going too fast.'

Absolutely right.

If, mid-flight, they suddenly developed consciousness and routinely started to think about it, every airline in the world would go bust.

It's the same with us and planks.

The same with us and LIFE.

Focus on what's in front of you, not what's on either side of you, and you'll stand a far better chance of making it across the abyss. The abyss, as Nietzsche put it, that separates the animal from the Superman.

Of course, it's easier said than done. But in the pages that follow we'll set you on your way.

We'll help you change out of your horn-rimmed, collar-and-tie, short-back-and-sides personality to reveal underneath the DECISIVE, FEARLESS and SUCCESSFUL persona of a Good Psychopath.

Our Good Psychopath Manifesto will transform you from someone who pussyfoots about on the left to a dynamic, go-getting achiever who maxes out on the right:

UNSUCCESSFUL PERSONALITY TRAITS		GOOD PSYCHOPATH PERSONALITY TRAITS
MAKES EXCUSES	>	DELIVERS
BLAMES OTHERS	>	TAKES RESPONSIBILITY
TRIES TO PLEASE	>	IS TRUE TO ONESELF
WIMPS OUT	>	DOES WHAT ONE HAS TO DO
TAKES IT LYING DOWN	>	TAKES IT ON THE CHIN
DWELLS ON THE PAST	>	MOVES ON SWIFTLY
PUTS IT OFF	>	GETS IT DONE
OVERTHINKS	>	CUTS THROUGH THE CRAP

UNSUCCESSFUL PERSONALITY TRAITS		GOOD PSYCHOPATH PERSONALITY TRAITS
TAKES IT PERSONALLY	>	TAKES CARE OF BUSINESS
WORRIES TOO MUCH ABOUT THE BIGGER PICTURE	>	FOCUSES ON THE JOB AT HAND

So what are the principles of the Good Psychopath Manifesto? And what can they do for YOU?

THE SEVEN DEADLY WINS

All is revealed in the seven-point action plan below – a psychological blueprint not just for success but for a richer, happier, more fulfilling life in general. These SEVEN DEADLY WINS of Good Psychopath living will help you achieve your goals not just at work but in all aspects of your life.

They will help you:

- **get that job**
- **get that deal**
- **get that guy or girl**
- **get that raise**
- **get that opportunity**

. . . that you've always been striving for but have never been able to nail.

They will also get you peace of mind. Because the more you begin to take control of your life, the more you will start to realize something amazing: so many of the things that you used to do BEFORE, you did for OTHER PEOPLE! You did them:

- **to impress your boss.**
- **to make your colleagues like you** (after you'd **impressed the boss!**).

- to keep the peace at home.
- because you owed it to a mate.
- to make the girl at the bus stop think you're cool.
  (Run over any old ladies recently?)

Jesus once said: 'Do unto others as you would have them do unto you.' A fine sentiment!

Disrespecting others is NOT in the GOOD Psychopath Manifesto. But it's equally important not to disrespect YOURSELF. So we would like to amend that venerable and honourable statement to the following:

'Do unto YOURself as others would do unto THEMselves.'

And here are the principles to put it into action.

The following seven chapters will focus on each one in turn.

Good luck in overcoming the dizziness of freedom!

Good luck in unmasking your own GOOD Psychopath Superman!

1 JUST DO IT

Psychopaths go for it. Research shows that procrastination uses up valuable mental resources. If they want something, psychopaths just go for it. They are very reward-driven and don't waste time thinking about things. They just do it!

2 NAIL IT

Psychopaths know how to win. This ability to 'switch on' when it really matters is a trait common to both psychopaths and top sportspeople. A study found that when psychopaths were rewarded for success, rather than being punished for making mistakes, they learnt a lot quicker. They play to win!

3 BE YOUR OWN PERSON

Psychopaths have immense self-belief. You can't please all of the people all of the time, so psychopaths don't see the sense in voting against themselves. Most of us are scared of putting our head above the parapet but psychopaths don't care what people think. They're not afraid to speak out.

4 BECOME A PERSUASION BLACK BELT

Psychopaths study people. They are genius-level psychological code-breakers because, like any predator, getting inside the mind of their prey gives them a distinct advantage. As one of the world's top con-artists once said: 'I can read your brain like a subway map. Shuffle it like a deck of cards.'

5 TAKE IT ON THE CHIN

Psychopaths move on. They focus on what they are good at and do it – avoiding emotional hangovers. They don't beat themselves up and they don't have regrets. Research shows that in mock business scenarios, psychopathic negotiators make more money than other negotiators because they're way less bothered by being screwed by unfair deals. As the Zen proverb goes, 'Let go – or be dragged.'

6 LIVE IN THE MOMENT

Psychopaths are focused when it matters. Believe it or not, the ability to 'live in the moment' is something that psychopaths and elite Buddhist monks have in common. It's also another trait they share with top sportspeople. Next time you're going for that interview, remember this quote from the athlete Michael Johnson: Pressure is nothing more than the shadow of great opportunity.

7 UNCOUPLE BEHAVIOUR FROM EMOTION

Psychopaths aren't ruled by emotions. In fact, they take a step back and surgically remove emotion from the situation. When stressing over a difficult task, ask yourself: what would I do if I didn't feel this way? What would I do if I didn't give a damn what other people thought? What would I do if it just didn't matter?

CHAPTER FOUR

JUST DO IT

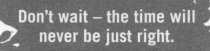

**Don't wait – the time will
never be just right.**

Napoleon Hill

PRESSING QUESTION

'Everyone has heard the story of the little boy who cried wolf. But very few have heard of the classic psychology experiment this famous folktale inspired. Want me to tell you about it?'

'Go on,' says Andy, chucking a knackered piece of carburettor into an already overflowing bin. 'I'm all ears.'

We're in his garage and he's dismantling his latest acquisition – a Moto Guzzi V7 Racer.

'OK,' I say. 'Listen up. Imagine that there are twenty telephone boxes all in a line. I show you into one of these telephone boxes and close the door. In front of you, where the telephone would usually be, is a big red button. Underneath the button are the following instructions:

> You must remain in this telephone box for ten minutes without pressing this button. There are nineteen other people in the same position as you in the other boxes.
>
> If, after the ten minutes is up, no one has pressed the button, everyone will receive £10,000.
>
> But if, before the ten minutes is up, someone *does* press the button, then the experiment will immediately terminate – with the person who pushed the button receiving £2,500 and everyone else getting nothing.
>
> The time will commence when the button lights up.
>
> Thank you for participating in this study.

'All of a sudden, while you are still trying to get your head around the ins and outs of the deal, the button lights up. What do you do?'

Andy looks up, his face spattered with gunk.

'I'd push the button,' he says.

'What?' I say, open-mouthed. 'No, you wouldn't!'

He rubs his nose with his oily, grease-black hands and screws his face up at me as if I'm demented. It's a comical scene. He looks like the naughty kid in the middle of a finger-painting class.

'Of course I would,' he repeats. 'I'd push the fucking button. Why wouldn't I?'

I'm stunned.

This fiendish experiment is known as the Wolf's Dilemma – for obvious reasons. It is a brilliant window on to the fraught, troubled, and often stormy relationship between the way we THINK and the way we FEEL.

Between LOGIC and EMOTION.

Between HEAD and HEART.

When most people are asked this question, they say that they'd do nothing. They'd 'play the game' and hold out for the full ten minutes. And why not? If everyone thinks the same and 'pulls together', then each player goes home ten grand richer.

But the question, of course, which obviously occurred to Andy, is: *Will* everyone think the same?

What if one of the other nineteen players decided that they wanted to save the researcher a couple of hundred thousand quid and pressed the button? Or what if one was paranoid that everyone else was going to gang up against them and decided to press it themselves to beat them at their own game? Or what if one simply pressed the button by accident?

When you go down this road – the road Andy immediately went down – the doubts start creeping in.

What are the chances that one of the other nineteen players will:

- **freak out,**
- **have issues, or**
- **just be plain selfish and press the button?**

The odds are fairly high.

Moreover, what are the chances that one of the other nineteen players won't have exactly the same thought themselves? And press the button!

In fact, seeing that it's already occurred to YOU, what are the chances that one of the other players isn't having exactly that thought right now? And is going to press the button right now?

When you weigh all of this up you come to a startling conclusion. The conclusion that Andy came to. Though your HEART might tell you to hold out for the full ten minutes, to pull together, to trust your fellow competitors and have a bit of faith in humanity, the cold, clinical, LOGICAL thing to do is to press the button as soon as it lights up.

The others may hate you. But so what? You're walking away with £2,500. And they're walking away with nothing. You'd have felt the same if you'd been in their position. But you're not. You're smart. You cut through the sentiment and worked out the correct strategy.

Or you would've done, at least, if you were a psychopath like Andy!

SEE YOU LATER

There are many ways to avoid success in life. But if you're really serious about it you might just want to try procrastination.

Procrastination can be defined as 'putting off activities that were planned or scheduled for activities that are of a lesser importance'. And with the advent of modern technology – Angry Birds, Xboxes, Facebook and Twitter – it's steadily on the increase.

In the late 1970s, roughly 5 per cent of the population thought of themselves as chronic procrastinators whereas today that figure hovers around 25 per cent.

GOOD PSYCHOPATHS, like Andy, are clearly not among them.

But here's the deal. Though it may offer temporary relief when you're doing it, every time you procrastinate you sabotage yourself.

You place obstacles in your own path. You actually make choices that IMPAIR, rather than ENHANCE, your performance.

Procrastination costs billions of pounds a year in lost profits; decreases personal effectiveness; destroys teamwork by shifting *your* responsibility on to others, who become resentful; has a negative effect on health (studies have shown that students who are chronic procrastinators have weaker immune systems and report more cold- and flu-like symptoms than those who aren't). And it cuts across all areas of your life. Below is a list of some of the most common things people procrastinate over. Do any of these sound like you? If they do, you may wish to take the questionnaire at the end of this chapter to see how bad you've got it.* (Andy scored zero.)

1. Going to the doctor.
2. Calling your family and friends.
3. Paying your bills.
4. Answering your emails.
5. Going on a diet.
6. Leaving on time.
7. Getting fit.
8. Telling the truth.
9. Apologizing.
10. Saying, 'I love you.'
11. Starting your own business.
12. Looking for a new job.
13. Doing the laundry.
14. Cleaning the dishes.
15. Asking a favour.
16. Giving up smoking.
17. Getting married.
18. Shopping for groceries.

---

*A little test will appear at the end of the next six chapters, each of which provides a general assessment of the particular personality characteristic under discussion. To find out how you measure up on each of the Seven Deadly Wins, just fill out the respective questionnaire and check your score against the scale provided.

19.   Taking the rubbish out.
20.   Ending a relationship.

Of course, at some time or another, we all procrastinate. We all have a tendency to take the easy way out and put the hard stuff off until later. And, moreover, it seems to be perfectly natural.

As he sets about scrubbing some sparkplugs with a manky old toothbrush, I tell Andy about a study that was conducted recently. Participants were presented with a list of twenty-four movies and were asked to make three choices:

- **Which one they wanted to watch RIGHT AWAY.**
- **Which one they wanted to watch in TWO DAYS, and**
- **Which one they wanted to watch TWO DAYS AFTER THAT.**

The movies were split into various types. Some were light-hearted like *Sleepless in Seattle* or *Mrs. Doubtfire*. Some were a bit more highbrow, such as *Schindler's List* or *The Piano*. In other words, participants were given a choice between movies that were fun and forgettable and movies that were meaningful and memorable. Movies that could be watched without effort, and those that required higher levels of viewer concentration and commitment.

'Which ones do you think they went for?'

This gets Andy's attention and he stops scrubbing for a moment.

'Unsurprisingly,' I say, 'most people went for *Schindler's List* as one of their three choices. I mean, it's widely regarded as one of the best films ever made. But here's the deal. Despite the fact that it's one of the best films ever made, it didn't make it on to most people's list for the first showing. Instead, people tended to pick lighthearted or action flicks for their first sitting, with only 44 per cent going for the loftier stuff first.'

'And why's that?' he asks.

'Simple. The heavier gear was thought to require more concentration and effort to watch, and so was put on the backburner for later. In fact, talking of later, people chose more serious movies 63 per cent of the time for their second movie and 71 per cent of the time for their third.

'And when the researchers did the experiment again with a slight modification – this time participants were told that they had to watch all three of their selections one after the other – *Schindler's List* was 13 times *less* likely to be chosen at all.'

'OK, OK,' says Andy. 'Don't get too excited – you'll knock yourself out. That's the problem with you geeks. Soon as numbers get involved you start hyperventilating.'

'Fair enough,' I say. 'But it's interesting, isn't it? Even when we're doing something we enjoy – such as watching movies – we often put off harder, more demanding activities – even though they might be great – for activities that will give us that instant fix.'

Of course, knowing procrastination when we see it is one thing. Understanding WHY we do it or what makes the habit BETTER or WORSE is another. Science, however, is beginning to come up with some answers. And it's time to check them out.

No, not later. NOW. You can't put this off any longer!

THREE TYPES OF PROCRASTINATOR

When you ask people the question WHY, exactly, they wouldn't press the button in the Wolf's Dilemma immediately, WHY they wouldn't jump at the chance to win £2,500, they typically come up with two different types of reason.

- **I'd need more time to weigh up the pros and cons.**
- **I'd be worried about how it might look to the other players.**

Both of which are fair enough. We love to veg out in our COMFORT ZONES. Our brains put their little fear kettles on, whip out their little fear chocolates, and whisper between our ears: 'Now's not the time. You can do this, no problem. But, just to be on the safe side, it's probably best to wait. Have a cup of No Rush coffee and a Perfect Moment soft centre and see how things pan out.'

Whatever the reason, the bottom line is simple. More likely than not, you're going to come away empty-handed.

In fact, these two reasons actually reflect three different types of procrastinator. And, needless to say, three different causes of procrastination:

- **RUMINATORS who cannot make a decision.**
  Motivation: Not making a decision absolves them of responsibility for the outcome of events.

- **AVOIDERS who are avoiding fear of failure (or, in some cases, fear of success).**
  Motivation: They are concerned with what others think of them and would rather have others think that they lack effort than ability.

- **PERFECTIONISTS who aren't happy with anything they do unless it's 100 per cent error-free.**
  Motivation: They would prefer to do nothing rather than face the prospect of having to measure up to their own exacting standards.

All three types of procrastinator tell whopping great big lies to themselves:

- **I'll feel more like doing this tomorrow. (They don't!)**
- **I work best under pressure. (They don't!)**
- **This isn't important. (It is!)**

But why?

If we know, deep down, what we're up to – and ninety-nine times out of a hundred we do – what's going on? More to the point: what can we DO about it?

THE GOVERNMENT OF BRAIN

In order to answer these questions, we first need to delve into a bit of neuro-anatomy. Don't worry, it's perfectly painless.

Let me introduce you to two basic brain structures:

- The amygdala
- The prefrontal cortex (PFC)

The amygdala forms part of what is known as the limbic system – a set of evolutionarily primitive brain structures involved in many of our emotions and motivations. In particular, those emotions – such as fear, anger and pleasure – that are chiefly related to survival.

If you think of your brain as your own personal 'government', then the amygdala may be seen as the Ministerial Office of the Department of Emotion. It is the part of the brain where the big and instant decisions are made, such as fight or flight. It is ancient, steeped in evolutionary tradition and wields a heck of a lot of power.

'Like a colonel then,' says Andy.

It has the authority to veto ordinary, everyday decision-making processes – to order a Code Red – if it thinks it is in our interests to do so.

Which often it is.

But like any powerful collective, the amygdala is open to corruption and sometimes takes bribes from less pressing and helpful motivations to exert influence over our behaviour.

'*Exactly* like a colonel then,' says Andy.

These are the times when we:

- RUN instead of FIGHT
- DREAM instead of DO
- TURN ON THE TELLY instead of FILING THAT REPORT

The prefrontal cortex, on the other hand, is the official headquarters of the Department of Rational Thought. This is the part of our brain that tells us that we should be working: that we should turn off the telly and start filing that report.

Compared with the amygdala and the limbic system, it is a relative new-build and is responsible for the heightened self-control that separates us from our ancient ancestors and the rest of the animal kingdom. It enables us to:

- plan,
- weigh up different courses of action, *and*
- refrain from responding to immediate impulses and doing things we'll probably later regret..

It is the cornerstone of wisdom and willpower.

Now, when we procrastinate, it often feels as if there's an argument going on inside our heads. An argument between our 'good', rational side and our 'bad', emotional side. And that's because there is!

More specifically, this argument is between our logical, conscientious, forward-thinking PFC, and our emotional, hedonistic, heat-of-the-moment amygdala.

'But why is it that nine times out of ten, the emotion side of the brain always seems to win?' asks Andy.

It's a good question. And one directly related to our innate reaction to disturbing or threatening stimuli – the fight or flight response mentioned earlier. Whenever we encounter something we find intimidating – let's say we open our bathroom door and find a pissed-off king cobra staring straight back up at us – the first thing we do is FREEZE.

Our pulse rate quickens. Our palms start to sweat. And we develop tunnel vision.

We forget all about anything else that we might have been thinking about at the time. The rational decision-making part of our brain, the PFC, shuts down, in other words – while the Department of Emotion (liaising, in this case, with a specially appointed COBRA committee) quickly works out an immediate plan of action:

SHUT THE DOOR!

But it's not just pissed-off king cobras that set up this temporary no-fly zone over our brain's decision-making infrastructure.

The same thing happens when we encounter *anything* that we find threatening: heights, enclosed spaces, the dream girl/guy from accounts, the dream job *in* accounts—

'The letter from the Inland Revenue *about* that job in accounts!' interjects Andy.

'I wouldn't know!' I shoot back.

We experience what amounts to a low-level dose of anxiety, our amygdalae take over from our PFCs, and we SHUT THE DOOR on whatever it is that is scaring us.

It'll be gone tomorrow, we tell ourselves.

We'll feel better tomorrow, we tell ourselves.

Let's do something else, we tell ourselves.

NO GAIN – LOTS OF PAIN

As mentioned previously, there are a number of reasons why procrastination is bad for us – not least of which is the fact that, as a long-term life-strategy, there is scientific evidence that it's flawed.

One study, for instance, which looked at college students, showed that on a 4.0 scale, chronic procrastinators achieved a final grade point average of 2.9 whereas those who procrastinated very little averaged 3.6.

But as Andy points out between sparkplugs, not only is procrastination flawed in the LONG RUN, it's also flawed in the short run.

'You actually end up experiencing more pain, not to mention more lost opportunities, *not* doing something than doing it,' he observes.

Which is true. Research has shown that:

- People who take ages getting into a cold swimming pool in fact experience more physiological discomfort than those who 'get it over with' and jump straight in.
- Imagining giving people bad news over the phone is more painful than doing so in real life.
- Deliberation uses up valuable mental resources. In one experiment, for example, women who were forced to make difficult choices between wedding presents to buy for their friends were later found to crack much sooner on a standard lab-based test of willpower (keeping their hands immersed in a bucket of ice-cold water) than women who weren't exposed to such difficult choices.

But there is one group of people who never put things off. Psychopaths!

Quite the opposite, in fact.

If psychopaths want something, they go for it immediately – just one of the positives of having an under-strength amygdala. Psychopaths just don't feel anxiety in the same way as the rest of us. Which means that not only do they not fear failure, but that the rational, logical cockpits of their brains are at less risk of being hijacked and commandeered by the black-and-white extremists of emotion.

Of course, this often leads psychopaths into trouble. With no Minister of Emotion to order a recce or a strategic withdrawal when necessary, they are often guilty of the *opposite* of procrastination.

Of fighting instead of running.

Of doing instead of dreaming.

But they, needless to say, are the BAD PSYCHOPATHS.

The GOOD PSYCHOPATHS, like Andy, are different.

Rather than being stuck and permanently set on max, the Fearlessness dial on the GOOD PSYCHOPATH'S mixing desk is flexible. And can be twiddled up and down depending on the context. And one of the contexts in which it's shunted up to high is when the chips are down and something needs to be done about it.

So next time you find yourself putting off filing that report or filling in that job application, or asking someone you fancy for the time when you should've been asking them out:

- Unchain your inner psychopath.
- Jumpstart your motivation.
- Toughen your resolve.
- THINK about the way you're thinking, *and*
- Ask yourself this . . .

SILENCE.

'Ask yourself what?' snaps the oil-infested grease-monkey from behind a barrel of God-knows-what.

'*You* tell *me!*' I say.

'OK then,' he says. 'SINCE WHEN DID I NEED TO *FEEL* LIKE DOING SOMETHING IN ORDER TO DO IT?'

I have to admit – the monkey's pretty good!

Then, when you've got the answer you're looking for – YOU DON'T NEED TO WAIT UNTIL YOU *FEEL* LIKE DOING IT! – turn to the exercises that follow in the next few pages and start putting them into practice. They'll help you roll your sleeves up and get down to the task at hand.

LEAP OF FAITH

Talking to Andy about procrastination is like talking to Charlie Manson about a pension plan. He just doesn't get it.

'Tomorrow doesn't exist in Regiment mentality,' he says, handing me a cup of tea that's one part Typhoo and nine parts Castrol GTX. 'Because it's got a funny old habit of not coming round. If you've got something to say, you say it. If you've got something to do, you do it.

'Everyone knows the phrase "Better late than never". Well, in the Regiment, "late" and "never" can sometimes mean the same. Brew OK?'

I nod through gritted teeth. If the gunk in my cup got washed up in the Channel, Greenpeace would send a flotilla.

And it's not just on the battlefield that Andy is talking about. The same kind of split-second decision-making that is called for in combat situations crops up time and again in SAS training. One occasion that stands out particularly vividly for Andy was his first ever HALO (High Altitude Low Opening) parachute jump, with full kit.

(Oddly enough, it might well have stuck in *my* mind too!) Here, in his own words, is how he remembers it:

I sat there in the C130 [Hercules transport aircraft] and checked the altimeter on my wrist: 20,000 feet – nearly four miles above the earth. Only another half mile higher to go before I jumped out the back of this thing – my first time at such height.

There were two four-man patrols and two bundles on this jump. As part of a patrol we had to free-fall together, carrying full equipment loads weighing in excess of 120 pounds. We also had to follow our bundle holding extra gear which was going to do its own free-fall with us, attached to its own parachute.

The oxygen console, which was keeping us alive, ran down the middle of the aircraft. There was a certain amount of gas in our own bottles but we would need that when jumping. So for now we were on the central console instead, linking us up to the aircraft's main supply.

We were in full kit. Our Bergens were strapped between our legs, ready to hook up behind our arse when we jumped, and our weapons were fastened to the left-hand side of the parachute, which was already attached to our backs. The helmets and their oxygen mask tubes running to the console looked like something out of *Star Wars*.

This was a big test for us as we were all on the Military

Free-fall Course and didn't want to fail this jump. The idea behind it was to get men and kit all landing in the right place at the right time so whatever mission they had to carry out, they had the gear and the manpower to do it.

So far, I wasn't feeling worried. All the things that we were about to do, like getting on to the oxygen, were drills that we had been taught and practised. Without oxygen we wouldn't be able to breathe – and by the time you hit 22,000 feet there isn't enough of the stuff around to keep you alive.

Everybody was mentally and physically dry-drilling: simulating pulling their handle that would deploy their main canopy and then looking above them to see a big bag of washing billowing out. Just in case the clothes line wasn't there, they were also going through Plan B: pulling the emergency cut-away of their main canopy and deploying the reserve.

I couldn't see the point of dry-drilling just minutes before jumping. Whenever we 'jumped kit' or jumped at night we would have an AOD [automatic opening device] attached to the parachute. This worked by barometric pressure. At 3,000 feet it automatically kicked in so if you got into a spin, had a mid-air collision, knocked yourself out or broke your pulling arm, it at least got the canopy out of its bag.

There were horrendous stories of people going into spins, especially with heavy kit. If the kit isn't packed right or balanced right then as soon as you jump and the wind hits it, it does its own thing. And then you're really in the shit – because it keeps doing its own thing, only faster and faster.

I could tell there were a couple of lads who were flapping. Either that or they wanted to show the instructors they knew the drills. They were giving it the old thumbs-up like something out of *Top Gun*. They might as well have thrown in a few salutes for good measure.

I was going to jump, there were no problems with that. But I just didn't want to cock it up. I didn't want to be the one who didn't land next to the bundle.

One of the things about barometric pressure is that the less there is of it, the more gases will expand. All of us were farting big time but thankfully due to the oxygen we couldn't smell anything!

I eventually joined in the dry drills and kept the instructors happy by showing them I was putting their teaching into practice. But to be honest, if I didn't know the drills by now, I never would.

It wasn't long before there was a loud electrical winding sound as the ramp at the rear of the C130 started to come down and daylight burst in making us squint. It was like God had started shouting at us. I wasn't really thinking all that much about anything now. I was just going through the rigging-up drills as I'd been taught. I had no control over anyone else and certainly not over the bundle. Nothing else mattered. All I was going to do was jump and try really fucking hard to land within spitting distance of the kit.

I checked the altimeter on my arm – 22,000 feet – as we got the command to rig our kit up. All the commands were printed on large flash cards because of the noise and the oxygen masks. I pushed the Bergen behind me and attached it by hooks to my rigs harness. We were now waiting for the command to go up towards the tailgate. When it came we unhooked the oxygen from the main console and attached it to our own bottles.

A couple of the lads gave some more *Top Gun* thumbs-ups. All I wanted to do now was just get out of the aircraft. The combined weight of the equipment and rig together was well over 200 pounds.

On the command, our patrol moved to the ramp like a line of ducks, waddling from foot to foot, weighed down by all the gear. I was on the left-hand side of the bundle, another lad was on the right and a third bloke was at the rear. It looked like a thick, two-metre-long bullet with a rig strapped on it.

We pushed it on its trolley wheels towards the tailgate

with the wind blowing against us as it lapped on to the ramp area. About six inches from the edge of the tailgate there were two chocks that stopped it toppling over into space. The aircraft started doing corrections, jockeying us around as we semi-stooped over the bundle, holding it in position.

I checked my altimeter: just under 25,000 feet.

I didn't even bother looking out at the blue sky and clouds which were now way below us. Why bother? It wasn't going to get me off the ramp any quicker or help me keep up with the bundle.

The fourth member of the patrol had his toes on the edge of the ramp. Everybody was bunched up over the bundle, really close to each other, because we all had to get out at the same time to keep with the thing.

We were waiting for the two-minute warning which would signal that we were on the run-in. Even through goggles it was clear to me that everybody was tensed up on the ramp.

I couldn't understand why.

Everyone wanted to do the jump. Everyone wanted to pass this part of the training. We'd all been trained up to the eyeballs. So what was the problem? It seemed to me that the time to worry was if you fucked up or had a malfunction in mid-air which you couldn't get out of.

All of a sudden the RAF loadmaster, who was also on the ramp holding the paracord that was keeping the chocks in position, held up two fingers and everybody started banging the next man doing the same.

'Two minutes!'

I'm not sure we heard each other through our oxygen masks and above the deafening roar of the wind and the aircraft engines. But that didn't matter. It was part of the drill to make sure that anyone flapping big style knew it was nearly time to jump.

All eyes were now fixed on the unlit red and green lights either side of the ramp. More banging and shouting.

'Red On!'

Then, as the green light came on and the loadmaster pulled the chocks away:

'Ready!'

We gripped the bundle as high as possible for a clean exit.

'Set!'

Now we rocked back ready to push it out.

'Go!'

We piled over the ramp, all four of us trying to keep hold of the bundle and drop with it for as long as we could before the jet stream ripped us away from it.

I still didn't bother looking at the ground. It was a full three minutes away yet and I wanted to use every second of that time to keep up with the bundle.

Basically, because of all the equipment you've got on, you can't move about the sky that well. It's as if your whole body is an arm shoved out a car window at 120mph. You fall – and fight as hard as you can to keep yourself stable, stay in a group and get down to the bundle that now seems miles below while all the time your Bergen is catching air and trying to shunt you into positions you don't want to be in.

I watched the bundle's AOD deploy its canopy below me and started to look about at the ground. There was total silence. It felt as if I was suspended in the sky. But before I knew it the earth was rushing up to meet me and I hit with both feet, landing about five metres from the bundle.

And that was it. Not much to think about apart from the fact that I'd passed the test.

Then it was straight on to a vehicle for the half-hour drive back to the airfield and the waiting C130 for another go.

ON THE GREEN LIGHT: GO

Practical Tips for Getting It Done, Getting It Over With, and Getting It Not Quite Right . . .

Andy once gave *me* a bit of advice about parachute jumping. I did one in Australia several years ago and texted him the night before.

'Keep your eyes open and your arse shut!' came the reply. 'And make sure you get it the right way round!'

Fortunately, I didn't have to make any decisions that day. The guy I was strapped to made them all for me. But if it *had* been down to me, who knows?

'I do,' says Andy. 'You geeks are so full of hot air you'd have probably gone *up*.'

'Which is why we can walk on water,' I retort.

But for those of you out there *not* as well endowed in the helium department as I am, and not as well endowed in the psychopath department as Andy, here are some tips that will help you take the plunge. That will lure you out on to the nerve-shattering tailgate of life – then off into the rush of terminal velocity decision-making!

'We used to have a saying in the Regiment,' Andy says, taking off his boiler suit and binning it for the day. 'Leave till tomorrow only the stuff that you're prepared never to do.'

A sentiment echoed by the racing driver James Hunt in the film *Rush*: 'The closer you are to death, the more alive you feel,' he observed. 'It's a wonderful way to live.'

1. Visualize what you want to do

If you procrastinate you will actively seek out distractions, particularly ones that don't take a lot of commitment on your part (this, incidentally, is why email was invented). Distraction serves as a method of emotional self-regulation. It's a diversionary tactic to keep your fear of failure under control.

To counteract this, start planning what you do – and then close your eyes and VISUALIZE yourself doing it. The more specific, detailed and graphic your visualization the better. Picture yourself carrying out the task, and executing it successfully – avoiding interruptions and focusing on the job at hand.

This is just one of the methods used by members of the SAS's Counter-Revolutionary Warfare (CRW) team when training for hostage rescue scenarios.

'Before storming the Killing House* we would go through in our heads the precise drill for engaging the enemy and getting the hostages to safety,' says Andy. 'Lobbing in a flash-bang, a stun grenade . . . quick scan of the room . . . short burst – tap-tap – of machine-gun fire if necessary . . . room clear, move on.'

And with good reason. Research shows that when we *imagine* doing something – say, playing tennis, for instance – the exact same areas light up in the sensorimotor region of our brain as if we were doing it for real.

Especially important when you practise with live ammunition!

2. Dissect and analyse the task

While you picture yourself performing the task, try to access precisely what it is about it that you don't like, exactly what it is that makes you reluctant to attempt it in the first place. Forewarned is forearmed.

And once you start putting your finger on what lies behind your avoidance behaviour – be it practical, workable problems or irrational, illogical fears – you can begin to work through it.

3. Focus on the future

Because of their dictatorial amygdalae, procrastinators tend to fold in the face of immediate challenges, opting for short-term pleasure over long-term gain instead. So next time you find yourself putting off something important, put off putting it off for a moment, stick

---

*A building on the SAS barracks in Hereford which serves as a mock-up for terrorist situations.

your feet up in a quiet corner, and ask yourself this:

Is how BAD I'm going to feel when I have to rush this task under pressure going to be anything like how GREAT I'll feel when I've got it under my belt in good time?

As Andy memorably put it when we first started writing this book together: 'This time next year we're going to be glad we started TODAY.'

4. Contract out your time to yourself – then ring-fence it

Work, to a procrastinator, is a bit like Pringles to the rest of us. They take ages to open the packet. Then once they pop, they just can't stop! Which is why, of course, they dread getting started in the first place.

To get around this energy-sapping vicious circle, here's what you do.

Set a predetermined period of time in advance – say, an hour – during which you make a contract with yourself to work on whatever it is you need to get done. And then RING-FENCE it. This means closing the door and putting up the 'Do Not Disturb' sign, turning off your phone, email, Facebook . . . anything that isn't DIRECTLY RELEVANT TO WHAT YOU ARE DOING RIGHT NOW. And then lifting the curfew once the 60 minutes is up. And make sure you lift it on time!

Not after 59 minutes.

Or 61 minutes.

But after one hour DEAD.

Transform your attentional spotlight from a strip light into a laser beam.

5. Downsize your time

When it comes to work, a procrastinator is like a prize fighter waiting to land the one big knockout punch – except it never materializes, and by the time the awful truth dawns, the fight is over, and they've lost on points to an opponent who has thrown more leather.

Procrastinators wait for large, unbroken, marble-smooth slabs of time upon which to get started instead of rolling their sleeves up and making do with more temporary, makeshift, rough-and-ready surfaces.

So now you know, don't hang around for the perfect opportunity to present itself any longer. Don't keep saving up for huge, uninterrupted wads of time. Instead, start getting rid of some of that loose, opportunistic change that's been rattling around for ages deep in the lining of your brain.

Andy once told me that he hammered out large chunks of his books not in some big comfy armchair at home or some sun-dappled villa on the Algarve, but on the West Coast Mainline and in the food courts of motorway service stations.

'I spend a lot of time on the move,' he said, 'and you just have to work when you can. But there's something – I don't know – a little bit sneaky about working on the train or in a cafe. It's like you're nicking time off yourself.'

The glamour!

AND FINALLY . . . A WORD ON PROCRASTINATION AND PERFECTIONISM.

GET IT DONE, NOT PERFECT

As mentioned earlier, procrastination and perfectionism often go hand in hand. Knowing the effort required to live up to their own unrelentingly high standards, a procrastinator is beaten before they even start – remember the concept of 'learned helplessness' in the previous chapter? – and so prefers not to try in the first place.

In fact, research suggests that procrastinators are frequently self-handicappers. Rather than risk the prospect of not being up to the challenge, their deep-seated lack of confidence combined with a Walter Mitty-like fantasy of unrivalled, heroic success fiendishly join forces to render legitimate success impossible.

To the procrastinator, being seen to lack ABILITY is the worst-case scenario. Better, instead, to be seen to lack OPPORTUNITY.

Even if they do eventually manage to get down to a task, the perfectionist-procrastinator endeavours to make things difficult for themselves. They spend so much time trying to get it 'right' that other, more important tasks suffer as a result. And a vicious cycle sets in.

They seem completely unmoved by the Law of Diminishing Returns – that, for any given task, the continuing application of effort steadily declines in effectiveness after a certain standard has been reached – and plough on regardless.

Ask yourself this!

If it takes 20 minutes to do something to 70 per cent (that's a return of 3.5 per cent per minute), is it really worth spending another 40 minutes (on a return of 0.75 per cent per minute) to get it 100 per cent?

LAW OF DIMINISHING RETURNS

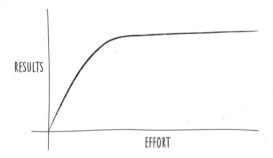

Unless the project is a matter of life and death, most people answer NO. In fact, when you put it like this, even perfectionist-procrastinators answer no.

But it's easier SAID than DONE.

THINKING it isn't the same as FEELING it – and when perfectionist-procrastinators are engaged on a task, the emotion area of their brains, their amygdalae, keep their noses to the grindstone until they're finally convinced they can't do it any better.

Ring any bells?

If it does, here's something you can do about it:

You can relax your FUNDAMENTALIST black-and-white standards and start thinking more MODERATELY in graduated shades of grey.

Let's imagine, for example, that you are a student, and a perfectionist when it comes to your academic work. You will probably be having the following internal dialogue with yourself on a daily, if not hourly, basis:

'Unless I get distinctions in my assignments then I am worthless.'

This dialogue is a THOUGHT BULLY that is pushing you around and getting you to run errands for it which you don't want to run.

So, what's the solution?

Well, it's the same as for any bully.

You STAND UP TO THEM!

Overcoming your perfectionism involves coming to terms with the fact that, although the standards INSIDE YOUR HEAD may appear in black and white, those OUTSIDE it, in EVERYDAY LIFE, in general do not.

They fall on a spectrum of grey.

So instead of studying for five hours a night, you may want to cut it down to two hours a night, and throw in some relaxation time instead.

e.g. not caring how you do on an assignment

NO STANDARDS

e.g. studying for two hours a night

REASONABLY HIGH STANDARDS

e.g. studying for five hours a night

REMORSELESSLY HIGH STANDARDS

In other words, for whatever kind of perfectionism you may be harbouring, you need to:

1.	Identify the BULLY – 'I need to get a distinction in all my assignments.'
2.	Engage in the appropriate SELF-TALK – 'I know that if I stand up to the bully and down tools after a couple of hours I will feel anxious in the short term but better in the long term.'
3.	Take the appropriate ACTION – down tools after a couple of hours, invite a friend round for dinner, and raise a glass to the benefits of not studying for five hours a night.
4.	Do this REPEATEDLY, braving the anxiety of your newfound freedom and resisting the temptation to go back to your old five-hour-a-night habit.

Until: PRACTICE MAKES NOT PERFECT!

But that's not all.

You can also . . . ask yourself this: WHAT'S THE WORST THAT CAN HAPPEN ANYWAY?

You see, most of the time our fears are completely unfounded. As mentioned earlier, we have a spectacular capacity for imagining things to be far worse than they really are. And guess what? This is just as true for failure as it is for anything else.

When cognitive behavioural therapists talk about procrastination, they often talk about the importance of 'putting down the whip'. Of:

- **Permitting ourselves the luxury of making mistakes.**
- **Not beating ourselves up when we make them, *and***
- **Not allowing the concept of PERFECTION to become tangled up in our concept of OURSELVES ('If I'm not PERFECT I'm NOBODY').**

Well, Andy and I go one better than that. We recommend that every now and again you don't just make the odd mistake here and there. That would be too easy. No, instead we recommend that you actually set out with failure as your goal.

Why?

Because once you start doing it, succeeding to fail becomes harder and harder to achieve.

I remember a BAD PSYCHOPATH I spoke to in a maximum security unit once telling me about a game he and his mates used to play when they were younger and out on the town. They used to have competitions to see who could get the most rejections from girls in bars. The incentive was pretty big. Whoever it was would have all their drinks taken care of the next time they went out.

Not bad!

But guess what started happening? The more they got used to rejection, the more they realized that – in the grand scheme of things – getting the elbow actually meant bugger all, the harder it became to pull off.

And the easier it got to go home with a girl on their arm!

QUESTIONNAIRE
HOW MUCH DO YOU PROCRASTINATE?

Assign a rating to each of the following statements, then add up your total and check it with the scores on the next page.

		always	typically	sometimes	rarely
		0	**1**	**2**	**3**
1.	I let other people down by not keeping my promises.	○	○	○	○
2.	I find it difficult to get started on new projects, or switch from one project to another.	○	○	○	○
3.	I worry about making mistakes before getting started on a task.	○	○	○	○
4.	I do easy tasks first and leave difficult tasks for later.	○	○	○	○
5.	I miss deadlines because I dedicate too much time to less important tasks.	○	○	○	○
6.	My workspace is cluttered and disorganized.	○	○	○	○
7.	I am late for appointments.	○	○	○	○
8.	I think dreaming is often better than doing.	○	○	○	○
9.	I avoid conflict or unpleasant situations by doing something else.	○	○	○	○
10.	I prefer it if people think I lack effort rather than ability.	○	○	○	○
11.	I find it difficult to say no to requests from others.	○	○	○	○

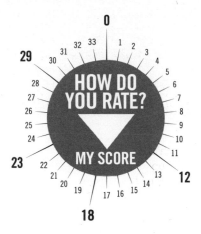

0–11 Procrastination is significantly reducing your quality of life. Get it sorted! Now!

12–17 You already have suspicions about yourself – but hey, you'll deal with those later.

18–22 Room for improvement – but you can probably cut it off.

23–28 You have the odd lapse every now and again but generally get things done.

29–33 You are disciplined and organized and usually do things when you need to.

✳ *Keep a note of your scores for each questionnaire because at the end of the book we'll be inviting you to take part in a unique nationwide survey which will enable you to find out where you sit on the overall GOOD PSYCHOPATH spectrum.*

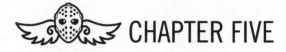

CHAPTER FIVE

NAIL IT

Whatever you are, be a good one.

Abraham Lincoln

FARE POINT

It's a hot summer's afternoon in the West End of London and Andy and I are sitting in the back of a black cab on our way to lunch. We've just finished filming for Channel 4's *Psychopath Night* and the session has proved interesting, to say the least. In the lab, I had subjected Andy to one of the gold standard tests for psychopathy and he had emerged with first-class honours.

The *emotion-modulated startle response* paradigm involves bombarding volunteers with random bursts of white noise, interspersed with nauseating images of road accidents, torture and death presented on a computer screen, and then measuring subsequent brain activity in the amygdala (which, if you recall from the previous chapter, is the Ministerial Office of the Department of Emotion).

Most people's amygdalae implement a state of emergency – the natural reaction to encountering threatening stimuli. But Andy's had pretty much flatlined. It had barely registered the graphic and disturbing onslaught that I'd spent the last half hour assailing him with. The atmosphere in the lab had been electric as, in a remote viewing room, everyone sat gawping in total disbelief while the motion-picture graph that was secretly mining the deep uncharted minerals of his brain inched ant-like and *horizontal* across the hypnotic green oscilloscope in real time.

By the time the experiment was over no one was in any doubt. We had the real thing on our hands here. No question about it. The results were impossible to fake. In fact, after we'd unhooked him from all the wires and sensors Andy was more concerned about what the electrode gel had done to his hair than he had been about the eyes and the testicles and the intestines he'd just been looking at.

As we round Trafalgar Square and watch all the tourists taking their holiday snaps by the fountain, I make up my mind.

If he orders liver and chianti for lunch, I'm off!

'So how's business?' Andy shouts to the cabbie through the grill. 'Plenty of people about.'

The driver shakes his head.

'No, mate,' he says. 'The sun brings them out all right. But no one wants to take a cab in this weather. All they want to do is sit about in parks and get pissed. I wanted to watch the football tonight but instead I'll probably be working now. I have to make £200 a day just to cover the cost of hiring this thing. Then there's the diesel on top of that. Give me the rain and the cold any day of the week. Once I've reached my quota I can knock off early.'

We pay the guy and go into the restaurant. In spite of the fact that there are a couple of Michelin stars knocking about, Andy has fish and chips and a Diet Coke so I decide to stick around.

I'm glad I do. Because over the cappuccinos he raises an interesting point.

'That taxi driver earlier,' he says. 'Now I might be missing a trick here but hasn't he got it the wrong way round?'

'How do you mean?' I ask.

'Well,' says Andy, 'if it was me I'd be working my bollocks off on the good days and knocking off early on the bad days instead. Think about it. If you're going to knock off early, why do it on a day when you're coining it right, left and centre? It's madness! On a day like that you should keep your foot on the gas and maximize your profits, surely?

'On the other hand, it actually makes sense to knock off early on a slow day because not only is your profit margin going to be jack shit anyway, you'll be conserving energy for your next shift – which could turn out to be a good 'un.' He looks at me quizzically. 'Or am I barking up the wrong tree entirely?'

I laugh.

'You're certainly barking, mate,' I say. 'But actually, you might well be on to something there.'

He orders a couple more coffees.

'Thanks,' he slurps. 'I may be a psycho – but I'm not stupid.'

TAKE IT OR LEAVE IT

Andy's observation over lunch that day stuck in my mind. And pretty soon it really started to bug me. I wasn't sure how many taxi drivers followed the same pattern as the guy who picked us up. But something told me it might be quite a few. So I did some digging around.

For the next couple of months, every time I got into a cab in London I asked the driver to tell me his routine. What did he do on a slow day and what did he do on a good day? I couldn't believe my ears. A heck of a lot of the drivers I talked to worked harder on slow days than on good days.

But why? It just didn't make any sense. Not since Andy had put on his Apprentice hat anyway. Then again, Andy was a psychopath. And despite the U-turns in the middle of Piccadilly Circus you don't find too many of *those* sitting behind the steering wheels of London taxis. If you did, their weekly takings would probably go through the roof.

To explain what I mean, I'm going to let you in on a little secret that psychologists have known about for quite some time now. It's a secret that, once YOU know it, will change the way you think about things for ever. It's all about how we quantify success.

Back in the 1970s a group of researchers conducted a brilliant experiment. They got a bunch of volunteers together and handed each of them twenty quid. The volunteers were then given a choice.

They could either walk – with the twenty quid tucked safely

away inside their back pockets. Or they could choose to gamble their unexpected windfall on a roulette table to see if they could make even more money out of the bungling boffins.

What do you think they did?

Before you answer, let me tell you about another group of volunteers that the researchers approached – only this time with a slightly different proposition.

Just like the first group, this lot were also given twenty quid as a sweetener. But with a twist. First they were handed *fifty* quid – but thirty of that fifty was then immediately taken back to leave them with a *net* gain of twenty.

If they wanted to reclaim the 'lost' thirty then they had to earn it. Yep, you guessed it – by gambling the twenty they *did* have on a roulette table.

Alternatively, of course, they were free to call it quits and walk away twenty quid up.

What do you think *they* did?

If you think that the volunteers in the first group were way more likely to say thank you very much and walk away than those in the second group then you'd be right.

Nearly all of them said: 'See you later!'

But for some strange reason the volunteers in the second group stuck around. Instead of realizing that they were twenty quid UP they couldn't help thinking that they were thirty quid DOWN. And they tried to win it back.

Exactly like the taxi drivers working harder on SLOW days to

AVERT A LOSS as opposed to putting in the hours on GOOD days to MAXIMIZE PROFIT, they were far more interested in STAYING OUT OF THE RED than they were in MAKING A KILLING.

And because of that they walked away with less.

THE BRIGHT SIDE OF THE DARK SIDE

The results of this experiment stunned the world of psychology. And, as you might imagine, that of economics. Many more followed but for all of them the take-home message was the same. We are way more inclined to turn off the NEGATIVE tap than we are to turn on the POSITIVE.

And it cuts across all aspects of our lives, not just the money side of things.

Why was it that you didn't approach that great-looking girl or guy in the bar the other night when you had the chance? Could it have been because the risk of getting the elbow in front of your mates outweighed the kudos of getting the dreamboat's number?

Why didn't you stick your hand up at the project launch yesterday morning when the head of marketing asked if there were any questions? Could it have been because the risk of looking stupid in front of the rest of the team mattered more to you in the short run than getting your head around those dodgy-looking sales charts?

Why didn't you go for that vacant seat on the tube on Tuesday evening when you were coming home from work? Could it have been because if that other guy eyeing it up opposite you had beaten you to it you'd have been standing there facing the music for the next couple of stops?

I bet I'm not far off.

So what happened instead?

You left the bar without pulling.

Again!

You had to ask a colleague about those projected figures and she got on her high horse because she had a million and one other things on her plate without having to give *you* a personal tutorial on sales drives!

The other guy *did* get the seat simply because he went for it and you didn't.

Even though YOU were nearer!

Of course, we all know people who are brave. Who go for it. Who would prefer to 'die trying' rather than sit about twiddling their thumbs wondering 'what if?' And most of the time they seem to come up smelling of roses. And while on the one hand we might think they're a little bit crazy, we also, deep down, wish we had a piece of their action.

Some of us – like Andy, though it pains me to say it – have always been more 'rational' than others.

But why? Is there something fundamentally different between these super-logical 'reason surgeons' and the rest of us? With the arrival of modern brain-imaging technology recent studies have begun to shed light (quite literally!) on the answer to this question.

And guess what?

The preliminary findings have a strangely familiar ring to them.

Those of us who make more money on mock gambling scenarios like the should-I-stay-or-should-I-go set-up of earlier – who walk instead of play – have a distinct biological signature in their brains. Their prefrontal cortices (the municipal offices of the Department of Logical Thought) are better staffed, and are much better equipped, than the PFCs of those who spin the wheel.

In other words, they are far less likely to be pushed around by their amygdalae – to cave in to pressure from the brain's Emotion Select Committee – than their more rationally challenged counterparts.

So does this mean that psychopaths, with their understaffed Emotion Departments, are more likely to 'go for the win' than the rest of us? Are psychopaths less bothered about bad things happening to them and more inclined to look on the bright side of life? Is *this* why Andy was suddenly able to put his finger on where every London taxi driver and his dog seemed to be going wrong?

Science suggests that it is.

When the performance of psychopaths and non-psychopaths was compared on a simple learning task, for instance – a task that required volunteers to pick up a simple rule as quickly as possible – a whopping great difference emerged. When mistakes were PUNISHED by a painful ELECTRIC SHOCK, the psychopaths were slower on the uptake than the non-psychopaths. But when the incentive to do well was modified – when success was REWARDED by FINANCIAL GAIN, as well as by avoidance of shock – fortunes changed dramatically. This time it was the psychopaths who learned the rule quicker.

The bottom line is a psychological game-changer.

We might, as we learned from Epicurus in Chapter Three, have a natural inclination to pursue pleasure at the expense of pain. To win and not to lose. But on closer inspection it's not a level playing field.

When the chips are down and our necks are on the line something rather curious happens. Avoiding pain becomes way more important to us than pursuing pleasure. We work a damn sight harder to AVOID DEFEAT than we do to GAIN VICTORY.

Unless, that is, you're a psychopath.

If a psychopath can 'make' out of a situation, if there's any kind of reward on offer, they go for it. To hell with the 'should haves' and 'what ifs'. Just bring it on!

WHO DARES WINS

These days, Andy and I can't get into a taxi without at some point uttering the immortal words: 'How's business?' That first time was a sobering insight for both of us into how a hidden flaw in basic human reasoning could have such a bearing on one's fortunes in everyday life. And how simply being aware of it can make all the difference.

Intrigued, I asked Andy what difference it had made in his *own* life. How had his psychopathic focus on reward benefited *him*?

His answer was fascinating.

Here, in part, is what he had to say:

In 1984, I passed the toughest military selection process in the world and became a member of the Special Air Service. Immediately, I felt at home.

The Regiment, as it's known, was different to the regular, or what we called the Green Army, in a lot of ways. You didn't have to wear a uniform. You didn't have to cut your hair. You didn't have to salute. And you didn't have to get up at the crack of dawn every morning and go on parade.

If that sounds easy, it isn't.

In contrast to the regular army, the emphasis in the Regiment is on *self*-discipline. On *personal* responsibility. They assume you *want* to be there. And if you aren't where you need to *be* with all the kit you need to *have* then you obviously don't.

In those days the SAS was not as well known as it is today. But it was better known than it had been in May 1980 when B Squadron, one of the four Sabre Squadrons that make up the Regiment, ended the Iranian Embassy hostage siege in full view of the world's media.

Before the world got to hear of the SAS, it already had a mythical status within the British Army. Squaddies talked about 'The Regiment' in hushed tones, as if they weren't normal soldiers at all but somehow had superhuman powers the rest of them didn't.

The year after the Iranian embassy siege the number of candidates on Selection was six times what it had been in previous years. Everyone wanted to be James Bond, abseiling off roofs and swinging through windows in black kit. After a couple of days it was Platform 4 for most of them: the Regiment's way of saying: 'Thanks for coming. Now fuck off.'

Platform 4 was the platform at Hereford station where the train left for London. If you were on it, you were no longer on Selection.

And that's because the Regiment wasn't looking for

James Bonds. Still isn't and never will be. What the Regiment looks for is people who can lie cold, wet and hungry in a ditch for a week, shit into a bag and eat packet soup, and then get up and fight as if they've just done a stint at Richard Branson's £39,000-a-night Caribbean eco lodge. That's a different kind of person altogether.

That's a person who is obsessive about their craft; who can focus on a goal no matter what and see it through to the end; and who can crawl the extra mile on their bellies if they're already on their knees.

Yes, as part of the Regiment, of course you get to do all the exciting stuff. But it's just another part of the job. That job is to be the best Special Forces soldier you can be. Self-discipline and personal responsibility are one half of the Special Forces equation. Attention to detail and the pursuit of excellence, the other.

It takes all sorts. There is no special 'SAS personality'. I know men who are the life and soul of the party and others who had about as much personality as a crash test dummy. It didn't matter. Four things everyone had in common were these:

- **Self-discipline**
- **Personal responsibility**
- **Attention to detail**
- **Pursuit of excellence**

As a member of the Regiment you know what you've got to do. So you do it. You crack on. You get on with it. You say: 'Yes, I'll have some of that!'

And that's why I felt at home pretty much from the word go. Because that kind of philosophy fitted my personality to a T. I mean: why wouldn't you? Think about it. You've got the Tora Bora cave complex in Afghanistan. The Taliban are in there. You know they're in there. And they know that you know they're in there!

It's pitch black, so you need night-vision goggles. Plus, the confined spaces of the caves and tunnels mean that the assault teams' movements are going to be slow and very restricted.

You've got to be thinking that if the Taliban had even two brain cells between them they would rig up explosive devices, gas on trip wires or some shit like that to fuck you up. They know every nook and cranny! But so what? You are going in there to sort them out so all you can do is fix your bayonet, 'bomb up' with grenades and ammo, and crack on with it.

Close-quarter fighting in such a confined and dark battle space means the Taliban will be right on top of you before you know it. So clearing the caves is going to be down to good old-fashioned hand-to-hand stuff. You know, with knives, bayonets and two-pound ball hammers.

But the lads love it. They can't wait. It's what they train for. Hour after hour after hour. There's this ruthless pursuit of excellence in the Regiment. An absolute focus on getting the job done no matter what the odds or circumstances. The fact that lives are being taken isn't an issue. It's the craft, the profession that's the juice. Not the killing.

The enemy are called players because that's what they are – in whatever game they're 'playing' at the time.

Now, funnily enough, that kind of thing isn't everyone's idea of a fun day out. But you just crack on. Why wouldn't you? That's what you are getting paid for.

If you don't like it, get out of the SAS.

You train and train and train and focus on the end result: VICTORY! You never, ever, *ever* think of defeat.

Who Dares Wins!

TARGET PRACTICE

Practical Tips for Aiming, Reaching and Exceeding Your Goals . . .

OK, so storming an underground cave complex behind enemy lines in Afghanistan is not the kind of thing that most of us are going to face on a Monday morning after we've dropped the kids off at school. But even so, if this kind of mindset can help flush out the Taliban from the heartlands of Kandahar and Helmand, think of what YOU might be able to do with it in the brutal suburban deltas of Kidderminster and Hemel Hempstead!

To help you get your head around it, Andy and I have sat down and quantified precisely what it is that makes it up – and we've succeeded in identifying SIX KEY FEATURES which, if used in the right way, will make a huge difference to your life no matter where you are.

Not only will they help you get you what you want, they'll also help you clarify the brief. Was what you GOT really what you WANTED in the first place?

1. Work out what it is you really want

This may sound obvious but you'd be amazed at how many people don't succeed in reaching their goals because they don't know what the goal is to begin with!

The bottom line is this:

Before you GET you first have to KNOW. And it's nowhere near as easy as it sounds.

There are two components to accomplishing any goal:

- **DOING, and**
- **THINKING**

But a heck of a lot of DOING actually takes place to UNDO the effects of lazy or inappropriate THINKING. David James, the ex-England goalkeeper, once told me something very interesting.

If the keeper was in the perfect position every second of the ninety minutes, you'd never get the flamboyant, spectacular, eye-catching saves the crowd loves to see. They'd all be a matter of routine.

The great goalkeepers are the ones who are in the right place at the right time most often. Not the ones who have to hurl themselves across the goal to make a fingertip save because they were out of position to start with.

It's true, isn't it? The more a goalkeeper uses his brain, the better he is at reading situations, anticipating the actions of opposing players and optimally adjusting his own position accordingly, the less he will need to rely on outstanding physical ability.

Andy tells me about an old mate of his in the Regiment. Tony was a plastic Jock whose grandmother was born in Skye but who grew up himself in the 'Scottish quarter' of Margate.

'That was basically his house,' says Andy. 'Funny, he couldn't quite get over the fact that he was a Sassenach. Probably because every time he got out the tartan and went down the pub we'd sneak into his room and stick St George's crosses up all over the place!'

Anyway Tony, bless him, was always banging on about getting a dream cottage on a remote sea loch in the Highlands of Scotland.

'"Five acres when the tide's out, three acres when it's in," he used to say. He had visions of candlelit New Year's Eve dinners, roaring fires, cigars, whisky, all the lads telling stories about the good old days . . . the works. Eventually, when he came out, he got what he wanted – bought a cottage just like the one he'd been rabbiting on about all those years – and spent months doing it up. Problem was, once it was finished, he hated it! Not only that, but it was too far away for any of us to make the trip up there. We went on the piss in Hereford instead!'

'So what happened?' I ask.

Andy laughs.

'He ended up selling the fucking thing and getting a flat in Led-bury,' he says, 'where we *did* have a few good nights. At one of them I asked him what that cottage thing was all about. And he goes, "Well, in hindsight I reckon what I was *really* after all along was just, you know, that feeling of being with your mates. And I can get that anywhere. I don't need to disappear into the middle of fucking nowhere!"

'I could see what he meant. It's an easy mistake to make. But if he'd just sat down and thought it all through before he picked up the phone to the estate agents; if his brain – to use your goalkeeping example – had just managed to get its footwork right and anticipated where the cottage ball was coming from, then he could've saved himself a lot of hassle. I mean, I've done it myself. We've *all* done it. Take my first big car purchase, for example. When most people splash out on a flash motor they do it properly. They conduct a bit of research – check out the glossy mags, compare prices online, that kind of thing. Me? Nooooo! I go and buy a brand new Porsche purely because some sales guy in a showroom pisses me off!'

'Yeah, Andy,' I say. 'We've all done *that*, mate.'

'No, look, straight up, I wandered into this Porsche showroom one morning just to kill some time before meeting a friend and hitting the gym. I had my tracksuit bottoms and trainers on and the receptionist clearly thought I was there casing the joint. I mean, she didn't even bother to say hello. Anyway, I spend five minutes or so eyeing up all the shiny lumps of metal when this young bloke with greased-back hair and cufflinks the size of plasma TV screens finally pipes up from behind a desk. He doesn't come over, he just shouts across the room: "Can I help you?" It wasn't a question. It was more like an accusation. I think the only reason he sparked up was because I'd started to help myself to the complimentary coffee. I waited for the fancy coffee machine to finish sputtering out a cappuccino before pointing to a blue one with a glass sunroof. Yes, mate, you can, I said. I want that one!

'You should've seen him then, Kev. He sprinted across the showroom faster than Usain Bolt. Even delivered the fucking thing to my house! And that was how I ended up with a Porsche 911, all-wheel-drive Targa.

'I suppose in one way, looking back on it, the dickhead was the world's best salesman. I mean, he'd touched a nerve without even trying. People who make snap judgements about the way you look or what you happen to be wearing really piss me off.

'I loved the car for precisely two weeks. But then the shine of its dark blue exterior started to wear off for me. There was no way I was going to scoff bacon sandwiches and ruin the leather upholstery. I got stopped three times by the police in the first week. And then, to cap it all, I was given the name Herbal Henry by the village we'd just moved to because, well . . .

'The tin lid on it was the boot. It was so small I actually wrote off to the Porsche head office asking if they did special miniature luggage sets to go with it. Christ, if I couldn't even get a suitcase in there how the fuck was I supposed to cram in dead bodies?

'I kept it for less than a year before getting rid of it. It was a classic case of exactly what you're talking about: DOING and not THINKING.

'I didn't want the car. I just wanted to fuck the sales guy off.

'Well, I suppose one out of two ain't bad!'

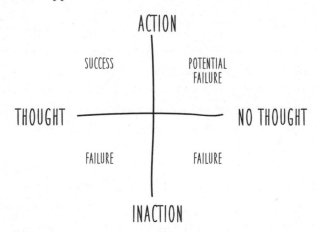

BEING SUCCESSFUL DEPENDS ON A COMBINATION OF DOING AND THINKING

2. Once you've worked out what you really want . . . truly commit to it

When you've figured out what it is that you really want – when you've done all the self-talk, been ruthlessly self-honest with yourself, then gone through it all again just to make sure! – the next thing you need to do is to TRULY commit to your goal.

No – not commit to it.

TRULY commit to it!

It's not the same thing at all.

Sure, both STANDARD CLASS and PREMIUM CLASS commitment will help your plans arrive at their destination. But one is way more effective than the other and ensures a far greater likelihood of those plans arriving intact.

So what's the difference between committing and TRULY committing?

Well, let's take three everyday goals – losing weight, giving up smoking, and being the best at what you do:

- **Being committed to GOING ON A DIET means watching what you eat.**

Being TRULY committed to going on a diet means watching what you eat, exercising regularly, cutting down on meals out, and having no high-fat foods in the house.

- **Being committed to GIVING UP SMOKING means gradually reducing the number of cigarettes you smoke over the course of, say, a week.**

Being TRULY committed to giving up smoking means cutting down on cigarettes, wearing a patch, having a disgusting collection of old cigarette butts floating in a jar of water on your desk, taking up some form of exercise to act as a positive counterbalance, and avoiding key smoking 'triggers' such as going out with friends who smoke or frequenting places that you associate with smoking (e.g. bars).

- **Being committed to BEING THE BEST means putting in the hours.**

Being TRULY committed to being the best means putting in the hours AT THE EXPENSE OF EVERYTHING ELSE and being prepared not to see a return on your investment for many years.

When the boxer Sugar Ray Leonard was a kid at school he didn't get there by jumping on the school bus with all the other kids. He ran behind it.

'The other kids thought I was crazy, because I would run in the rain, snow – it didn't matter,' he says, looking back. 'I did it because I didn't just want to be better than the next guy, I wanted to be better than all the guys.'

Crazy commitment can lead to crazy success.

And it's not just the things you DO that make the difference between commitment and true commitment. The way you THINK also has a bearing. Top sports and business people, for example, just like Special Forces, NEVER CONTEMPLATE FAILURE before a crucial competition or deal.

Why would they – is it going to help them win? Of course not!

Just the slightest flurry of high-altitude doubt is enough to trigger a devastating confidence landslide at lower elevations. So, instead of thinking to themselves: 'What if it all goes pear-shaped?' they think to themselves: 'What does it take to WIN?'

In true GOOD PSYCHOPATH fashion, they focus on the prospect of GAIN rather than that of LOSS.

And it is this simple difference in focus that separates the Ben Ainslies and the Steve Redgraves and the SAS from . . . well, whoever it is that they're up against.

Seven-time world snooker champion Stephen Hendry was once asked whether he felt even a modicum of sympathy for Jimmy White's catalogue of near misses at the Crucible.

'I feel no pity at all,' he said. 'If he's not up to the job that has nothing to do with me. Sport is a ruthless business.'

On another occasion, he enunciated the motivation under-lying his own stratospheric success:

'It's nice when you're beating an opponent and you're kicking him when he's down. That's what sport is all about, the only reason for playing.'

In the back of yet another London taxi, Andy and I are on our way to the Royal Society of Medicine. He wants to check out the library – oh, and the bacon sandwiches. But not, as he's quick to point out, necessarily in that order.

'A friend of mine's son has just started playing rugby at school,' I tell him, knowing he's played a bit in the past. 'Got any advice for him?'

'Yeah,' says Andy, with one eye on the meter and the other on the route. 'Tell him to go into every tackle fully committed. If you go in fully committed, then you're way less likely to get hurt. Rugby is like life. You're going to feel pain – there's nothing you can do about it. It's part and parcel of the game. But it's funny. The people who feel it most are the people who try most to avoid it.'

We jump out on Wimpole Street and Andy coughs up.

There's a first time for everything.

He nudges me.

'Shall we?' he asks.

'Would be rude not to,' I say.

'Hey, mate,' we go. 'How's business?'

3. Streamline

Swimmers shave their bodies. Cyclists wear funny-shaped helmets. And sprinters squeeze themselves into figure-hugging lycra jumpsuits. Why? To cut down on even the most infinitesimal resistance to their forward motion.

In top-level sport (as in top-level soldiering), even a fraction of a second can make the difference between gold and silver; between a world record and missing out; between being on the plane and watching the Games at home; between a successful head shot and, well . . . the loss of thousands of innocent lives.

So the main contenders leave no stone unturned. When they hit the track, the pool, the velodrome or the embassy, every move they make propels them towards the finishing line with maximum efficiency.

YOU NEED TO DO THE SAME!

We're not suggesting you start waxing or wearing lycra of course (unless, like Andy, you want to). But in order to give yourself the best chance of crossing *your* finishing line in gold-medal position you need to make sure that EVERYTHING YOU DO is as aerodynamic as it can be – that it is carrying you towards your goal as directly and as speedily as possible.

'One of the ways I learned to do that in the Regiment in the early days,' Andy says, 'was to get into the habit of asking myself the question: is what I am doing RIGHT NOW THIS MINUTE moving me measurably closer to my goal – to be the best soldier I can be?

'You know what happened? After a while, when you start doing that, you find that even the simple act of asking yourself that question at regular intervals during the course of a day will have a big impact on how you spend your time.'

Andy's right.

If you're serious about standing on your own individual podium humming your personal national anthem while the dignitary of your choice puts a medal round your neck – or throws you a sand-coloured beret with a winged dagger on it – why mess about doing stuff that's not DIRECTLY RELATED to getting you there? It's simple. If you're doing something that is not specifically geared to moving you forward towards your goal – or, worse still, is actively preventing you from reaching it – here's what you do.

Or rather, ahem, here's what Andy says you should do:

BIN THAT SHIT!

And bin that shit RIGHT NOW!

What Andy is trying to say, I think – far more eloquently than I could ever put it – is this: think of your actions and behaviours as being the different players in TEAM YOU. If one of them isn't pulling their weight you need to give them their marching orders and get someone else in. In SAS-speak, you need to cut them away and send them packing to Platform 4.

TODAY!

4. Be results driven

One of the toughest lessons you learn in life is this: it doesn't matter how hard you work if you are not working EFFICIENTLY.

We all know someone who puts in every hour God sends BUT NEVER GETS ANYTHING DONE! They always seem to be on full throttle but at the same time appear incapable of DELIVERING AN END PRODUCT. Well, you can be certain of one thing. If you want to be successful, that someone had better not be YOU!

The football manager Brian Clough was once interviewed at half-time during a crucial game. The opposing side had played his team off the park and the interviewer wasn't slow in pointing this out.

Cloughie smiled and gestured behind him.

'Look at the scoreboard, young man,' he said.

It read one–nil to Clough's lot.

This simple exchange contains a profound truth that transcends football and can be applied to any walk of life. You can stroke the ball around the park as skilfully and as gracefully as you want. But if you can't stick it in the back of your opponent's net you may as well stay on the bus.

Ever bought a new outfit, got a new hairdo, wangled adjacent seats at the company away day . . . and NOT asked the guy or gal out?

Ever spent months getting in before eight, leaving after five, adding more and more frills to your CV . . . and NOT put in for that pay rise or new job?

Ever spent days, weeks, months even, preparing your pitch and then NOT asked for the crucial concessions at the negotiating table?

Of course, we're all guilty of this to some extent. It's in our nature. Psychologists even have a term for it – it's called *approach-avoidance conflict.*

Approach-avoidance conflict describes the growing feeling of anxiety that we experience when an important goal approaches. When it's a long way off we can't wait for the day to come. But when it's right there on top of us we want to put it off.

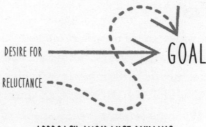

DESIRE FOR ⟶ **GOAL**

RELUCTANCE

APPROACH-AVOIDANCE DYNAMIC

Except, of course, if you're a GOOD PSYCHOPATH!
Here's Andy:

In the 1980s a guy called Terry Waite was the Archbishop of
Canterbury's special envoy and became quite good at negotiating with hostage takers and getting captives released. So, in
1987, Waite goes to Beirut to negotiate with the Islamic Jihad
Organization for the release of some western hostages. To cut
a long story short, it all goes pear-shaped and Waite ends up
being taken hostage himself.

Scroll forward four years and, in 1991, the SAS are hit
with a 'fast ball' job. Downing Street know where Waite is being held and we are tasked to rescue him. So we fly to Cyprus
where helicopters will then take us into Beirut.

It was a simple smash-and-grab job. We reckoned we
would have no more than 45 minutes in total – to land the
helicopters, fight our way to where Waite was being held, grab
him and then leg it back to the choppers that would ferry us
back across the Med to Cyprus.

If it took any longer we were royally fucked and quite likely
to end up chained to a radiator next to the man himself. I, for
one, wasn't particularly enamoured with that possibility as it was
less than a year since I'd come off radiator duty in Baghdad.

So 45 minutes was the plan.

Anyway, we get to Cyprus but then it's all hurry up and
wait. We spend days running around the compound's perimeter
trying to keep our fitness up while waiting for the green light.

When it came, the plan was leap into body armour, jump on a helicopter, all bombed up with gas and smoke, and just get on with it. This was a great job as it was short, sharp and full on.

Unfortunately, it never happened. Turned out we had more green lights than a Tesco's checkout. Downing Street gave us hundreds of them! Each time, we'd leap into our gear, jump into the heli, then clamber back out an hour or so later with the rotors powering down and the job cancelled. We would then all go for another run around the compound, totally pissed off.

What the fuck was happening back in London? Why didn't the top brass just get their fingers out of their arses and get on with it?

Anyway, this shit went on and on until the job was finally aborted for good and we all flew back to Hereford. That, of course, really pissed us off. But not as much as a month or so later when we all saw our Terry getting released on TV.

If only those secret negotiations hadn't taken place behind our backs . . .

Next time you're watching Andy Murray at Wimbledon, remember this: the player who wins a tennis match isn't necessarily the player who wins the MOST points. It's the player who wins the CRUCIAL points.

Anyone can play well and look good when they're two sets up and at forty–love on their opponent's serve. But how well can you play when you're two sets down and at break point on your *own* serve?

5. Think metaphorically

In case you're wondering, it's no coincidence that we've been using a number of sporting metaphors recently to 'tee up' what we're talking about.

Studies have shown that finding a good metaphor that WORKS FOR YOU and using that metaphor to REFRAME YOUR GOAL and the potential obstacles that might get in the way of your achieving it significantly boosts your chances of success.

If you're into horse racing, for example, you might want to replace the word 'obstacles' with HURDLES, make a chronological list of precisely what those hurdles are and where they are situated on the COURSE, and JUMP them one by one taking care not to LOSE YOUR MOUNT.

If you've recently been on the wrong end of a series of negotiations with a competitor that appear to be going nowhere it might help to recast the situation as a game of TUG-OF-WAR. You have two options to avoid being dragged into the MUD PIT. One is to get your finger out and PULL HARDER. The other is to LET GO OF THE ROPE.

If you love CARS but hate PLANES you might want to think of TURBULENCE in the air as being like POTHOLES on a road.

A year or so ago a very good mate of mine died unexpectedly. Coming, as it did, out of the blue I was a bit cut up about it. A week or so later a card came through my letterbox.

It was from Andy.

This is what he wrote:

Life is a difficult mission. We are all Special Forces soldiers, expected to make split-second decisions – big and small – under extreme pressure, behind enemy lines, every single day.

Most of what happens is out of our control and we operate on a need-to-know basis – surrounded on all sides by danger, madness, grief and disappointment – as missile tracers that might well decide our future light up the skies above us.

Being the best you can be is the same for anyone no matter who you are. You have to suffer, endure pain, grit your teeth, take it on the chin, smile, laugh, and press on through the shit bent double under all your baggage as the things and the people that mean most to you are captured, gunned down or go missing in action.

Life doesn't come with a safety catch.

Told you he was a GOOD psychopath – and it worked. I got on with the piece I was meant to be writing with him and we made our deadline.

But if it doesn't work for you: no problem. Find out what does, find whatever analogy means most to you, and try rebooting your goal within that format. Look at what you're setting out to achieve, quite literally, in a different way. You'll be surprised at how much 'staying power' it gives you!

6. Time it right

There's a time and a place for everything, right? At least that's what the old cliché tells us. But now we've got the science to prove it.

Most people have the common sense to realize that asking the boss for some time off just after her pet Labrador has been run over probably isn't the best moment to do it.

'Especially if it was you that ran him over!' adds Andy.

But what a lot of people *don't* know is that every 24-hour period may be divided up into an infinite number of peak TIME WINDOWS which, depending on what it is that you want to achieve, offer the optimum conditions for success.

Getting the best out of yourself means calibrating your efforts so that they coincide with these windows – whichever of them are open and most relevant to your aim. Going back to our sporting metaphors, it's not enough just to go for your shots. You have to go for them at the RIGHT TIME.

If your job revolves around CRITICAL THINKING and DECISION MAKING, for example, you're best maxing out in the morning.

Any time before noon is the optimal period for maintaining focus because concentration requires willpower, and willpower, just like a muscle, begins to weaken and fade as we get progressively more tired throughout the day and build up an excess of psychological lactic acid.

One study, for instance, had volunteers enter a room filled with the aroma of freshly baked cookies. They were then sat at a table on which were presented two gastronomic alternatives: a plate of those sweet-smelling cookies or a bowl of radishes. Half of the volunteers were asked to munch the cookies, while the other half were asked to nibble the radishes. Afterwards, both sets of volunteers then had 30 minutes to complete a fiendish geometric puzzle.

Guess who gave up quicker?

Exactly!

The volunteers who were asked to sample the radishes (and to thereby resist the mouthwatering cookies) gave up on the puzzle after an average of just 8 minutes, while the lip-smacking cookie-chompers kept going for nearly 19 minutes.

Moral of the story?

Willpower is a limited resource.

Or, as Andy puts it: 'If you're going to say no to the cookies, make sure you don't have something more pressing to do later on!'

Sometimes, of course, there is more at stake than at other times. A more recent study, for example, found that judges making parole decisions were likely to give the thumbs up around 65 per cent of the time *after* a meal break – but almost never right before one. But those in positions of power, the key influencers and decision-makers in society, know this only too well. Do you know, for instance, why you only ever see Barack Obama in grey or blue suits?

It's because deciding what to wear in the morning is one decision – among the many more important ones that he has to make during the course of a day – that he doesn't have to worry about. He wants to keep his head as clear as possible, and his energy levels as high as possible, so as to maximize his performance on the BIG shots. And he'll leave no stone unturned to achieve that.

Did you also know that 12 noon to 4 p.m. is the prime time for workplace distractions? To be honest, neither did we! But it makes sense in light of what we've just heard. Especially if you skip lunch.

A warm shower just before logging on in the morning (or after lunch) will help. A small rise in body temperature has been shown to stimulate both working memory and alertness – the two key ingredients of sustained cognitive performance.

'So make sure you stick the body wash in your briefcase before you leave for work,' suggests Andy. 'Plus a couple of Mars bars!'

On the other hand if CREATIVITY is your thing, peak INSPIRATION tends to coincide with peak DROWSINESS – which in most working adults occurs at around 2 p.m.

As your brain becomes tired your thought processes become more diffuse – think a wide arc of light as opposed to a narrow beam – drifting from one idea to the other and forming associations that a more focused mind might not.

Then there's email.

Think it's a simple case of just drafting a message and pressing 'send' whenever you get a spare moment?

Think again!

Studies have shown that email is a black art.

As a case in point, research suggests that the best time to send a BUSINESS-RELATED message is during what is known as the POST-WORK PEAK – on average, between 5 p.m. and 6 p.m. – when most people are starting to wrap things up and head home.

Twenty-six per cent of marketing emails that are dispatched during this period are opened compared to an average of just 17 per cent – though, as can be seen from the table below, the optimal time zone varies from business to business:

INDUSTRY	OPTIMAL TIME ZONE
FINANCE	7–10 a.m.
HOTELS	10–11 a.m.
RETAIL	10–11 a.m. or 4–6 p.m.
LEISURE	10 a.m.–12 noon or 10–11 p.m.
TECHNOLOGY	12 noon–3 p.m.
GREEN/ENERGY	12 noon–3 p.m.
TRAVEL	3 p.m. or 10–11 p.m.

INDUSTRY	OPTIMAL TIME ZONE
CHARITY	4–6 P.M.
MARKETING	5–7 P.M.
PUBLISHING	7–8 P.M.
EDUCATION	7–9 P.M.
AUTOMOTIVE	7–9 P.M.
EVENTS	8–9 P.M.

BEST TIME TO SEND AN EMAIL ACROSS VARIOUS INDUSTRIES

If you are in any doubt, here are some GENERAL PRINCIPLES:

- Just 4 per cent of ALL EMAILS sent between midnight and 7 a.m. are opened.
- FINANCE and HEALTHCARE are two primary concerns that tend to keep people awake at night. So to ensure maximum receptivity to your message, send emails relating to these types of issues in the MORNING.
- One third of RECRUITMENT emails sent between 6 a.m. and 7 a.m. end up being read – a 16 per cent mark-up on the average. Why? 'Because this is the time,' as Andy rightly observes, 'that many prospective employers are busy weighing up the logistics of the day ahead.'
- Just under a quarter of HOTEL OFFERS distributed between 10 a.m. and 11 a.m. are opened. Reason? Fun and relaxation are uppermost in many people's minds as they ease themselves into their work!
- There is an email-opening HIATUS between noon and 3 p.m. – the peak period for workplace distractions, if you recall from a little earlier – the exception being when it comes to environmental

issues such as conservation, sustainability, energy and technology. 'Do these guys have greater willpower?' wonders Andy. Worth a look, I reckon!

- The period between 3 p.m. and 5 p.m. sees a gradual INCREASE in email opening rates – this being especially the case with the TRAVEL INDUSTRY. There is a 41 per cent probability that travel emails sent at 3 p.m. will be opened – significantly higher than average.
- A SMALLER SPIKE in activity occurs between the hours of 7 p.m. and 9 p.m. Emails on issues demanding CAREFUL CONSIDERATION – such as CARS, EDUCATION and INSURANCE, for example – are most effective at this time as people are able to give them their full attention without the distractions of work-related matters.
- Email opening rates TAIL OFF dramatically after 9 p.m. LEISURE and TRAVEL related messages are the exception, however – with over a third being opened between 10 p.m. and 11 p.m.

'I suppose,' as Andy rather ruefully points out, 'at the end of the day we're all escapists at heart!'

QUESTIONNAIRE
HOW GOOD ARE YOU AT LAYING IT ON THE LINE?

Assign a rating to each of the following statements, then add up your total and check it with the scores on the next page.

		strongly disagree	disagree	agree	strongly agree
		0	1	2	3
1.	I know what I want and I'm not afraid to go for it.	○	○	○	○
2.	Pressure brings out the best in me.	○	○	○	○
3.	I recover from setbacks quickly.	○	○	○	○
4.	I can sacrifice short-term pleasure for long-term gain.	○	○	○	○
5.	When I set my mind to something I achieve it.	○	○	○	○
6.	I'd prefer to be an unpopular winner than a popular loser.	○	○	○	○
7.	I can focus on what's important and block out everything else.	○	○	○	○
8.	If my success comes at the expense of others, so what? That's their problem.	○	○	○	○
9.	If it's fifty-fifty I'll go for it.	○	○	○	○
10.	Criticism doesn't knock my confidence.	○	○	○	○
11.	I am not easily intimidated.	○	○	○	○

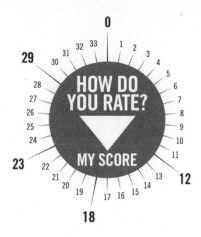

0–11 You have trouble nailing your colours to the mast because there *is* no mast! You need to tighten up and toughen up fast.

12–17 No one would describe you as the most competitive person in the world. You prefer easy compromise over hard-fought victory. More heaven-sent than hell-bent.

18–22 You're doing OK pootling along in the middle lane. You occasionally put your foot on the gas when you need to but don't take undue risks.

23–28 You spend a fair bit of time overtaking but don't hog the fast lane and are prepared to move over when you absolutely have to.

29–33 A born racer – foot to the floor all the way! When the chips are down you nail it. No matter what.

 CHAPTER SIX

BE YOUR OWN PERSON

All that ever held me back, I think, was fear. But then I went into the dressing room and shot it in the face.

Lady Gaga

THE PENNY DROPS

I'm going to start this chapter off with a little magic trick. Magic tricks don't really work very well on paper. But anyway. Here goes.

In front of you are five coins – a 50-pence coin, a 20-pence coin, a 10-pence coin, a 5-pence coin and a penny.

I am going to predict, in advance, which one you are going to hand me in a minute or so. In fact, I have already written my prediction down at the bottom of page 167.

Step One

OK, so what I want you to do first is to pick THREE coins and push them towards me. Let's say, for the sake of argument, that you choose the 50-pence, 20-pence and penny coins – discarding the 5p and 10p.

Happy with that? Good!

Step Two

So next what I want you to do is choose ONE of the three coins and discard it. Let's say, again for the sake of argument, that this time you choose the 20p.

So now we are left with just two coins on the table.

Step Three

For your next move I want you to choose ONE of those coins and push it towards me. Let's say it's the 50p.

This means that you should be left with just ONE coin in front of you – the penny.

Step Four

Pick the penny up and hand it to me – and now turn to page 167 to see if my prediction was correct.

That's magic, folks!

GIVE ME FIVE

Actually, folks, it isn't magic at all. But then you knew that, didn't you? Instead, it's a very clever piece of psychology called the *Principle of Forced Choice*.

And I've just done it on Andy.

'Forced choice? Yeah, I had a bit of that in Baghdad!' he says, looking out the window across the Deer Park. 'Bit different to this, though. Go on, then – let's have another bash.'

Andy has come up to Oxford to visit me in Magdalen College and we're sitting in my office at the Calleva Research Centre in the New Building. It's called 'new' because it was built in the 1730s and the rest of the college dates back to the late fifteenth century. As does some of the plumbing.

'Don't know about Baghdad,' I say, trying to bang some water out of the tap into the kettle. 'But forced choice actually forms the basis of most "demonstrations" of mind control and is extremely powerful. That's because when it's done well, it's the mindreader's equivalent of carbon monoxide. Colourless, odourless, and virtually undetectable. But it's also extremely simple.'

Oddly enough, I figured that you – like Andy – might want another 'bash' so I've made a second prediction that I've written down at the bottom of page 200.

Let's say that this time, in STEP ONE, you push the 50-pence, 20-pence and 10-pence coins towards me – leaving behind the

5-pence and the penny. This actually makes my job easier and cuts out a step!

Because in STEP TWO all I now need to ask you to do is to remove the three coins you have pushed towards me and to pick up one of the two coins left behind. If the coin you pick up is the penny, I will ask you to discard it on to the pile with the other three.

That just leaves the 5-pence coin on the table.

But if, on the other hand, you pick up the 5-pence coin, leaving the 1p coin on the table, I will simply ask you to hand it straight to me.

Now check to see if my second prediction was correct.

That's not magic, folks. That's psychology!

CHARITY BEGINS UPSTAIRS

At this stage you may be wondering where we're going with this. Why start off a chapter on having the courage of your convictions, on being your own person, with a two-bob magic trick that, in reality, operates by actively *removing* any semblance of free will from the decision-making process?

(Which, as I'm sure you're aware by now, is how it *does* operate: I make up my mind in advance which coin I want you to end up with and then work backwards adjusting the protocol accordingly.)*

Well, the answer to that question may surprise you. One of the things that we all have in common is that we make decisions. All day. Every day. There is no way around it. No decision-making concessions. For any of us.

You might *think* that you can go a whole day without making a decision. But in truth you've made thousands.

In fact, every single second of every single day packs a decision:

---

*For instance in *TRIAL 1, STEP 2* – if my prediction had been 20p, as soon as you had picked up the 20p to 'discard' it I would've asked you to hand it to me and declared my prediction correct. In *TRIAL 1, STEP 3* – if my prediction had been 50p, I would've framed your pushing it towards me as evidence of you 'selecting' it, not discarding it.

- The decision to sit in this position.
- The decision to sit in that position.
- The decision to scratch your leg.
- The decision to scratch your nose.
- The decision to move in.
- The decision to move out.
- The decision to buy this book.
- The decision to stop reading this book.

True, many of these decisions are unconscious. You may not be aware that you're putting in any effort to make them. You may not feel that you've had to *decide* to make them. But you've still 'made' them.

Now, scientists are beginning to uncover something very interesting about the way we make decisions. Something which is causing them – and should be causing *us* – to take a long, hard look at how we live our lives:

OUR UNCONSCIOUS MINDS PLAY A FAR GREATER ROLE IN THE CHOICES THAT WE MAKE THAN WE MIGHT THINK.

Not just when it comes to trivial decisions such as whether we cross our legs or take a sip of our tea. But when it comes to bigger decisions, too. Such as whether we give to charity. Or whether we find an action morally right or wrong. Even when it comes to how anxious or confident we feel.

'Moreover,' I say to Andy, as we give up on the plumbing and head out to the Senior Common Room instead, 'it takes just the simplest and subtlest of nudges to change the way we act – touches which, through centuries of unconscious exposure, we have unwittingly coded into the language of everyday life.'

Studies have shown, for instance, that:

- We really do *'take the moral high ground'* – that we
  are more likely to put money in a charity box if it is at
  the top of an escalator than at the bottom.

- We really do *'wash our hands of it'* – that we make harsher moral judgements with clean hands than with dirty hands.
- We really do feel *'weighed down'* by anxiety – that in virtual simulations of everyday life we feel way less confident in our surroundings if our height, unbeknownst to us, is shortened by a head (around 25cm).

'Which is why, I guess, we say we "look down" on people,' Andy comments.

In other words, a lot of the time when we *think* we're making up our own minds, we are in fact being swayed by influences that are operating completely outside of our awareness. The Principle of Forced Choice may well have us fooled when we're performing a simple coin-choosing task. But that's not the half of it.

Once we've chosen those coins, it may also have a say in what we do with them.

WHAT'S MY LINE?

Back in the 1950s an American social psychologist called Solomon Asch conducted a now classic experiment which demonstrated the effects of the most powerful influence of all on our behaviour and our decision-making: THE BEHAVIOUR AND DECISION-MAKING OF OTHERS.

What Asch did was incredibly – and worryingly – simple.

He assembled a group of nine volunteers in front of a slide projector and presented them with a series of line judgement tasks like the one shown overleaf.

Trial one: 1p.

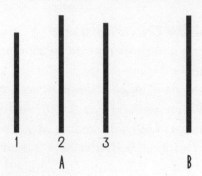

The volunteers' job was easy. They had to state out loud which of the three vertical lines shown in diagram A was the same length as the one in diagram B.

'It's a doddle, right?' says Andy. 'You'd need your eyes *and* your brain tested if you got it wrong. Unless, of course, it's another of your tricks . . . ?'

'No, no trick,' I say. 'But you know what? As it turned out that's exactly what over three-quarters of the volunteers ended up doing at least once during the course of the study. They got it wrong!'

'Why?'

'Because,' I say, 'on closer inspection the experiment wasn't quite what it seemed. In actual fact, eight of the nine volunteers in each trial were fiendishly "in on the act" and had been instructed by Asch to give the same predetermined *wrong* answer on some of the comparisons. Crucially, these eight flunkies gave their answers *first* so the pressure was on the ninth guy – the *real* volunteer – to follow suit. Which 76 per cent of them did – ignoring, into the bargain, the evidence of their own eyes so as not to appear stupid.'

The bottom line is chilling.

So intent are we on fitting in that most of us are prepared to bin our own opinions and recycle the viewpoints of others. So hell bent are we on not standing out that we're prepared to side with complete strangers against ourselves.

'Even when we "know" that we're right and they're wrong,' as Andy points out. The gravitational pull of the group is, it would seem, one of the most powerful forces in the universe. Few of us can hold out against it.

SAFETY IN NUMBERS

It's not difficult to appreciate the power of the group. You only have to look around you. Football matches, pop concerts, political parties, religious faiths, Facebook . . .

'Oxford colleges,' interjects Andy, as we pour ourselves a coffee.

. . . the group is everywhere.

'But why?' he asks. 'What's the fascination?'

'Actually, the answer to that question is really quite simple,' I say. 'Basically, our brains still think that they're back on the plains of East Africa, some two million years ago in our evolutionary history.

'The brain we had in those days is in many ways pretty similar to the one we have now and the primeval neural infrastructure that governed our lives back then – the pipes and wires of simplicity, subsistence and survival – still run the show today, creaking and clanking under the infinitely more complex demands of modern society.'

'Sounds like the taps in your office!'

'Now think about it. In prehistoric times, in the wilds of the African savannah or the depths of the Mongolian steppes, being ostracized from the group usually ended in tears. Predators, climatic conditions and starvation were all better dealt with within a group setting than they were singlehandedly.

'Today, that's not the case. We've got the benefit service, social housing schemes, the NHS . . . all of which safeguard against a pitiless prehistoric demise.'

'It's basically the old-fashioned tribal system, isn't it?' says Andy. 'The army's another example. Ask any soldier and he'll tell you the same thing. The regiment he's in is the best in the army and the battalion he's in is the best in the regiment. It's funny, but deadly serious at the same time. On the one hand the set-up promotes competition between units. And that's a good thing. But on the other hand, even more importantly, what it gives you is lots of tightly knit tribes that aren't fighting for Queen and Country but for *each other*. You know, studies have even shown that the more cohesive fighting units are, the less they are at risk of PTSD.'

'Good shout,' I say. 'And the Ghost of Ostracization Past is still with us. Everywhere! We go along with what the boss says even though we know it's crap. We spend Christmas with the in-laws *again* even though every year it's the same old shit.'

'We cop the same hairdo as Harry Styles even though it makes us look like a dick?' Andy cuts in.

I take a slurp of my coffee.

'Ahem, anyway,' I continue, 'we're terrified of standing out, of being on the "outside". And it's incredible how deep this feeling goes. One study, for instance, showed that the brains of African-Americans registered hurt when they were given the cold shoulder by none other than a group of Ku Klux Klan. Another showed that even if you *pay* people to get the group elbow it *still* stings. Every culture has their own way of blackballing someone. Jehovah's Witnesses disfellowship; Catholics excommunicate; Mennonites shun; clubs, fraternities and social groups expel . . .'

'And in the Forces it's a dishonourable discharge,' says Andy. 'Stays with you for life.'

'Exactly,' I say. 'And it's all to maintain standards. Keep things ticking over. Enforce a moral code. It's all to make sure that everyone sticks together. Because all it takes is one person to go off and start doing their own thing . . .'

' . . . and the curtain comes down on everything,' says Andy.

'Everyone starts leaving the cave.'

HOW TO CURRY FAVOUR

Just how subtle the pressure to conform can be in everyday life may be seen from a brilliant study which attempted to do the impossible: get hotel guests to reuse their towels.

The study was very simple. Basically, the researchers placed five different recycling request cards in over two hundred hotel rooms and totted up the number of guests from each room who bought in.

The cards were distributed randomly and each room got one of the following:

- Help the hotel save energy
- Help save the environment
- Partner with us to help save the environment
- Help save resources for future generations
- Join your fellow guests in helping to save the environment. (In a study conducted in Fall 2003, 75 per cent of the guests participated in our resource savings program by using their towels more than once . . .)

Which one do you think came out best? If you think it's the last one then you're not alone. Forty-four per cent of the guests who saw this card in their room reused their towels.

The least effective was the first one – the one that benefited the hotel. Less than 16 per cent of guests bought that.

And that's not all.

When the successful request was *personalized* to read as follows:

- Join your fellow guests in helping to save the environment. (In a study conducted in Fall 2003, 75 per cent of the guests who STAYED IN THIS ROOM (e.g. #123) participated in our new resource savings program by using their towels more than once . . .)

. . . compliance increased even more. To almost half.

'I guess if you're in two minds about something,' Andy points out, 'you're always going to go with the flow. You'll just follow the rest of the herd.'

Which is true. And which is great if the herd is doing the right thing – like helping to save the environment. But not if its motives are vague or misguided or harmful and no one is any the wiser.

'One of the funniest examples of this I've ever come across,' I tell Andy, 'although it wasn't funny at the time – happened when I was a boy.'

One evening, when I was around nine or ten, my father took me out to an Indian restaurant. As he's paying the bill, he turns round to me and says:

'Kev, if there's one thing I want you to remember in life, it's this. Persuasion ain't about getting people to do what they *don't* want to do. It's about giving people a reason to do what they *do* want to do. Watch and learn.'

So he picks up a spoon and tinkles it against his glass. The room falls silent. Dad gets to his feet.

'I'd like to thank everyone for coming,' he announces. 'Now I know that some of you have come from just around the corner and some of you have come from a little bit further afield. But I want you to know that you're all very welcome, and that it's very much appreciated . . . Oh, and there's a small reception in the King's Arms across the road after this. It'd be great to see you there!'

With that, he starts to clap . . . as, of course, does everyone else.

You can picture the scene. A restaurant full of strangers who we've never seen before, who've never seen *each other* before, all applauding wildly because *they* don't want to look like the gatecrashers to the party!

As we make our way out I can't help myself.

'Dad,' I ask, 'we're not really going to the pub, are we?'

He puts his arm around me.

'Course not, son,' he laughs, gesturing back towards the restaurant. 'But you know what? That lot are – and my old mate Malcolm has just taken over as landlord. He'll make a few quid tonight!'

FROM CON-SENSUS TO NON-SENSUS

My father's little wheeze in the Indian restaurant all those years ago might well have made a few quid. Who knows how many bewildered diners traipsed across the road to the King's Arms to raise their glasses at a non-existent party? If half as many people followed each other over as gave him a round of applause, then Malcolm, or whatever the hell his name was, would've done all right for himself that night.

But there are other, equally instinctive yet infinitely more injurious ways in which our deep-rooted tendency to follow the crowd can cost us money. Foremost among these is the perilous phenomenon of groupthink. Groupthink is what happens when groups – committees, task forces, think tanks, families, you name it – fail to critically evaluate the ideas they come up with because of a desire to minimize conflict.

We've all been there.

The pitch everyone thought ticked all the right boxes . . . but which turned out to tick all the wrong ones. The practical joke everyone agreed seemed a great idea at the time but which ended up a total disaster (stand up Messrs Ross and Brand).

'The Iraq invasion in 2003?' Andy offers. 'There was certainly a lot of what you're talking about going on after 9/11.'

Maybe.

The result is less than optimal decision-making – sometimes on a disastrous scale – facilitated by the members of whichever group is in question setting aside doubts and personal reservations in favour of smooth, swift, unanimous consensus. The causes are well documented. The process has been studied extensively by psychologists over the years and a number of contributing factors have been identified.

These include:

- A dominant, charismatic leader.
- Bombardment with positive pointers (especially those which are difficult to verify or debate).
- External pressures to 'get the job done'.
- The discouragement, or active snuffing out, of dissenting perspectives and viewpoints.

No group is immune to the paralysing psychological nerve agent that is groupthink. But in some groups, of course, it can be way more costly than others.

Investment bankers, security analysts, business leaders, technological innovators, and political and religious alliances all have a bit more to lose than a bunch of diners in an all-you-can-eat Indian restaurant if they fail to think independently of each other and instead protect, reinforce or exaggerate their group's prevailing mindset.

'You wonder why fund managers can't beat the S and P 500?' our old friend Gordon Gekko asks in *Wall Street*. 'Because they're sheep. And sheep get slaughtered . . . Gimme guys who are poor, smart, and hungry – and no feelings. You win a few, you lose a few, but you keep on fighting. And if you need a friend, get a dog.'

No danger of *him* getting swallowed by the group!

Fortunately, however – though unfortunately, perhaps, for Mr Gekko – groupthink may be remedied by a very simple antidote: the incidence of one, lone dissenting voice in the ranks.

The presence of a Devil's Advocate.

'When Asch ran his study a second time, for instance,' I tell Andy, as he picks up Robert Robinson's 1947 Nobel Prize for Chemistry from the mantelpiece over the fire, 'all it took was one of his eight co-conspirators to break rank and blurt out the correct answer and the power of the group was gone.

'The real volunteer made the right choice every time.'

But, in everyday life, it's easier said than done.

To stick your head above the parapet; to risk being bollocked, or barracked, or belittled by the boss, or the chairperson or the 'acknowledged expert in the field' takes considerable fortitude – as Ed Snowden and any number of whistleblowers and contrepreneurs before him have discovered to their cost.

Added to which you may, in fact, be wrong. And *they* might actually be right. At the time you just don't know. All you have to go on is the courage of your convictions.

'You know, the intelligence services operate along exactly these lines in the fight against terrorism,' Andy points out, putting the Nobel gong back carefully into its case and returning it to the mantelpiece. 'At grass roots level it's a psychological struggle, not an armed one. It's a piece of piss to radicalize someone. Even the IRA found it easy to get young guys to become suicide bombers. But both politically and tactically it was an outrageous no-no, so in the end they decided not to use them.

'But the recruiting job itself was easy. They just got a group of like-minded people in a room, showed them some propaganda, told them a bit about the cause and, over time, their positions hardened and they became more extreme.

'You can do it anywhere to anyone. It's not just a hardline Islamist thing. Sure, some of the recruits will fall by the wayside and decide they want a life. But others won't and before you know it they're sniffing round the rucksacks in Black's. Mind you, it's also easy to throw a spanner in the works – though the secret's knowing where and when to throw it. If you get it right, all you have to do is plant someone in the group, organization or whatever it is who questions the cause or the propaganda, and that's it. Then the whole thing goes down like a pack of cards.'

You can drown in a group.

Until it springs a leak.

CHEAT, THINK AND BE MERRY

Andy and I are walking around Cloister Quad, the ancient sepulchral heart of Magdalen College. It's a beautiful spring morning and the sun is lancing across the upper slopes of the bell tower – the Hillary Step of the Oxbridge Himalaya. We pause as Andy peruses the Wall of Remembrance, the names of the Magdalen alumni who lost their lives in the two world wars.

For a moment, he seems lost in thought.

'It's funny,' I say as his eyes move from column to column. 'No one knows for certain how the psychopathic personality might have got started back in evolutionary history. Or, in fact, how it's stood the test of time. But there's no shortage of theories – and I wouldn't mind betting that the capacity to be unpopular, to put your neck on the line and stick two fingers up to what other people might be thinking without batting an eye, might well have had something to do with it.'

'How's that?' asks Andy, back in the land of the living.

'Well,' I say, 'in the days of our ancestors, when just about every communal decision had an immediate bearing on survival, the presence of groupthink had the potential to wipe families, small groups and even entire communities clean off the face of the planet. Having the instruments to puncture it would, quite literally, have been a lifesaver.'

As we continue around the quad, I explain to Andy in a little more detail what I mean.

'Perhaps the most obvious theory concerning the origins of psychopathy,' I say, 'is what I call the *popular demand* theory. Research has shown that individuals who score high on psychopathic traits such as confidence, charisma, ruthlessness, fearlessness, mental toughness and risk-taking – the "James Bond" profile, you might say – have more sexual partners than those who score lower on such traits.'

'So purely on the law of averages,' Andy butts in, 'psychopathic genes are going to get around a bit!'

'That's right,' I say. 'But other theories, ironically, focus on the more dubious aspects of psychopathy. There's a study just out, for instance, which reveals an intriguing link between creativity and cheating – both, you might say, examples of rule-breaking behaviour, one admirable and beneficial to the team or the group, the other not so admirable and downright harmful to it. Anyway, the results of the study have shed an interesting new light on the pros and cons of thinking outside the box. The researchers found that volunteers who cheated on a problem-solving task not only did better on a subsequent task involving creative thinking but also reported feeling less constrained by rules and regulations in general.'

'Funny that,' says Andy. 'Even as a kid I never believed rules applied to me. I decided not to worry about them but just let everyone *think* I did. As far as I was concerned, they were for other kids who were a bit slow on the uptake! So, go on then. What's the bottom line? What does this experiment say about *me*?'

'Well,' I say, 'let's put it this way. What it shows is that rule-breakers are rule-breakers. People who break social rules are also more likely to break other kinds of rules too – like thinking and problem-solving rules. They're more likely to come up with creative solutions to problems, be innovators, inventors, to think originally about things. In the days of our ancestors, people like that would've been invaluable. As they are now. The fact that you maybe couldn't trust them might well have been a price worth paying.'

'So let me get this right,' says Andy, as we stop by the entrance to Addison's Walk. 'Are you lot now saying that cheating is good for us?'

I cough.

'If we're lucky,' I say, 'we might see some deer in here.'

LOVE AND HATE

The findings of this latest study are actually in line with my own personal hunch about the origins of psychopathy: that 'it' didn't evolve at all but rather the individual personality traits that comprise the psychopath mixing desk beefed themselves up on evolutionary steroids over time as they gradually became more useful.

These traits, by pure random chance, then happened to wind up in the same primeval individual one dark Darwinian day who, in the brief, basic, brutal few years that followed managed to keep their head above the floodwaters of natural selection for a sufficient – and productive enough – length of time to start the genetic ball rolling down through all future generations.

'OK, so that might be simplifying things a tad!' I tell Andy.

But the point I am making is one that goes right the way back to our mixing-desk analogy of earlier.

To Kierkegaard's concept of the 'dizziness of freedom'.

To Sartre's dream of being everything we can be.

And to Nietzsche's incitement to challenge the status quo.

It goes right the way back to the fundamental difference between being a GOOD psychopath and a BAD psychopath.

Ever since the days of our prehistoric ancestors, there has always been a need for risk-takers in society. There has always been a need for the ruthless in society. There has always been a need for the charming, the charismatic and the deceptive in society. And there has always been a need for the emotionally robust in society.

These are the people:

- Who *don't* need to be liked.
- Who *don't* need to belong.
- Who have no need for validation or affirmation.
- Who aren't afraid to challenge prevailing norms.

Remember, the key to success is to deploy these personality traits – as Andy does – with both discretion and restraint:
- At the right LEVELS
- In the right COMBINATION
- In the right CONTEXT

And having the courage of your convictions to go against the grain, to be your own person and do your own thing regardless of what other people may think of you, is no exception.

'You know,' I say to Andy as we set off around Addison's Walk, 'whenever I ask someone: "If I could turn you into a psychopath for half an hour, with total impunity, what would you do?" most people fall into one of two camps. They either immediately come up with a catalogue of gleeful revenge against all those bastards who've pissed them off down the years. Or they say that they would tell the person they had never told they loved . . . that they loved them. Or something along those lines.

'Now the key phrase in what I just said there is "with total impunity". As soon as the thirty minutes is up, everything returns to normal as if nothing has happened. No regrets. No embarrassment. Nothing.'

'Which is, of course, the primary difference between us psychopaths and the rest of you,' Andy points out. 'We couldn't give a damn about what anyone else thinks of us.'

We pass Oscar Wilde's seat.

'I agree,' I continue. 'And right there, I think, lies the allure of the psychopath to most people. I think in a world where our behaviour is coming under closer and closer scrutiny – did you know that in the UK there's roughly one CCTV camera for every twenty people, and what are we up to now on Facebook: almost a billion users? – we long more than ever to be free from the shackles of societal restraint, from the burden of our own self-consciousness, though we know, deep down, that we probably couldn't handle the moral and emotional fall-out if we were. But you guys – you psychopaths – *can*! And I think in that sense we envy you your existential freedom. You fan the flames of our feverish libertine fantasies.'

'Fan what?' asks Andy.

'Never mind,' I say. 'In fact, I think if Freud were alive he might say we have "psychopath envy"!'

LEAD, FOLLOW OR GET OUT OF THE WAY

Andy and I have retraced our steps and are sitting in Oscar's seat. The meadow in front of us is in full bloom – a magic carpet of white and yellow haze that would've changed very little since Wilde's day.

Who knows what odes, what secret golden verses this timeless little vista might have inspired? Andy says:

> You know, I've never understood this reluctance to throw down the gauntlet. The hesitation to go for life's jugular. Even as a kid I never had any problem making decisions. When I was about 13 and starting to think about girls, I realized I had acne and a 36-inch waist. Something had to be done.
>
> Not having a clue about healthy diets (my breakfast would normally consist of a can of Pepsi and a Mars bar), I went to my local doctor and asked him. He gave me a sheet of paper telling me to eat apples and tomatoes, things like that, so that's what I did.
>
> I lost a stone over the summer holidays and still stay away from sugar even now. I made the decision and that was that. Job done.
>
> Then there was all the gang stuff. Like most of the kids on our estate, I ran about with one lot or another. But I was never the leader of any of them. Far from it. I never wanted to be a leader because gang leaders were always getting the piss taken out of them – or even worse, getting the shit kicked out of them – when they fucked up.

So what was the point? Absolutely jack shit! I preferred to stay in the background watching and listening and then making up my own mind what I wanted to do instead of being told by some knob who didn't know his arse from his elbow.

I never did anything I didn't want to do. No one could make me and if they tried they usually wished they hadn't. I never smoked, for example. The gang started when we were about nine or ten. But it never made any sense to me so I just didn't do it.

The other kids stank of tobacco, it cost more money than any of us had, and smoking dog ends picked up from the estate's stairwells just didn't do it for me. If that meant that I didn't fit in, well, fuck it.

Mind you, all this being in the background stuff ended when I was 16 years old and joined the army. I was sent to the Infantry Junior Leaders Battalion and was told on day one that as well as being trained to *take* orders as a basic infantry soldier I was also going to be trained to *give* them.

So whether I liked it or not, I was going to have to be a gang leader after all – and do all of the things that went with it. I was going to have to make decisions that would affect not only *my* life but also the lives of others. But in a much bigger way than I was ever going to do in Peckham.

Then again, some things never change – and just like the kids in the gangs back home, I soon learnt that every other Junior Leader always had a better plan than yours. And whether they did or whether they didn't – and, to be fair, some did! – always jumped up and down like Blakey from *On the Buses* ramming it down your throat if yours went tits up.

Funnily enough, though, you never saw those people stand up and be counted in the planning phase of a project, at the time when opinions and decisions were actually needed.

Nooo . . . they only piped up afterwards!

'Like you were saying,' Andy continues, 'people seem to have this fear of failure, this automatic self-protection module built into them. When the finger is pointed they don't want it pointing at them.'

'So how do *you* actually go about making decisions?' I ask. 'What kind of thought process goes on in *your* head?'

Andy leans back and gazes up at the comatose blue sky. Magdalen airspace is cloudless. This is what he says:

> Well, as I see it, there are two ways to make a decision. The first is when it's calm and there is time to learn more about whatever situation you're making the decision about. That's when you seek opinions and get ideas from whoever is involved in the outcome. Everyone should be encouraged to share their opinions. And everyone should be encouraged to listen to them.
>
> In the SAS this is a tried-and-tested system because you work as part of a four-man team and everyone involved in carrying out the plan has their own individual skills and their own individual input – and so all are part of the process.
>
> It's a useful system because at the end of the day everyone wants to stay alive!
>
> But out here in the real world, where the emphasis isn't always on staying alive, I've discovered things work a bit differently. Just like in the Junior Leaders Battalion all those years ago, if a plan is successful everyone's suddenly a part of it.
>
> But if the plan turns to rat shit and everything goes tits up exactly the same people will turn round and tell you: 'I told you!'
>
> Fine by me!
>
> From their point of view – from the coward's point of view – it's a win-win situation, isn't it?
>
> But that's not the way *I* operate. Never has been and never will be.
>
> I like to put my neck on the line. After listening to everyone, I'll make a decision and stick to it. I mean, when all is said and done – and as someone once said, there's a lot more said than done! – coming up with a plan isn't exactly rocket science, is it? All you can do is make the best decision you can based on your experience, your training and your knowledge.

Everyone else then either falls in behind me and gets on with it. Or they step aside and let the ones who *do* want to move forward get going.

The second decision-making process kicks in when you have to make an *instant* decision. This is when the shit's hit the fan and everyone is looking for an immediate answer to a problem.

In the past, I've had to make life and death decisions within seconds – the shepherd boy in Iraq, for instance. That's just the way it is.

Sometimes I've had my experience, training or knowledge to call on. And that's great. But sometimes I haven't – and that's also great! If something has to be done, then it has to be done no matter what you know or don't know. Any delay just ends up making things worse. You just have crack on and do it.

Lead, follow, or get out of the way!

'Simple as that?' I ask.

Andy looks at me blankly.

'Yeah, simple as that,' he says. 'Any plan or decision I make immediately becomes my mission. And nothing else matters apart from that mission. Nothing diverts me from it because I am one hundred per cent confident that the mission will work. It dominates everything else going on inside my head.'

'But where does that confidence come from?' I ask. 'Have you always had it or is it something you've learned over the years?'

Andy stands up.

'I've always had it,' he says. 'I've had it for as long as I can remember. Even as a kid I knew I'd get out of trouble. OK, I might end up in a little bit of shit. You know, I might only get 80 per cent out of trouble. But that didn't matter. I just knew I'd get out in the end. I'll give you an example. During the BTZ patrol my eight-man unit was, as you know, exposed in the desert. As the Iraqis started advancing on us in their armoured vehicles, all we had were our assault rifles and one disposable anti-tank rocket per man.

'We could hear the armoured vehicles' tracks about to come over the high ground to our left. There was nowhere to run, nowhere to hide – we'd already established that! – and we were in the middle of the fucking desert. If we ran what difference would it make? All it would mean is we'd die out of breath.

'Now it was as clear as crystal in my mind that as soon as those armoured vehicles came over the rise we were history. So anything we did was a bonus. I had to make an instant decision. What would it be? Surrender? Run? Fight? Fight! It had to be! I decided to face the Iraqis head on and attack!'

'And is it the same now?' I ask, 'on Civvy Street? Are you as decisive in everyday life as you were on the battlefield?'

'Absolutely!' says Andy. 'Once I left the SAS and joined the real world, I found that exactly the same thought processes work in business. I'll give you another example.'

At the time when mobile phones were in the process of becoming smart phones with all the geeky gadgetry and shit, a friend and I were convinced that there would be an explosion in the digital book market. So we came up with a plan to get books on mobiles – you know, to provide the software and that – and then to sign all the publishers and mobile phone companies up to subscribe to it.

That became my mission. And if a publisher or phone company knocked us back to begin with, so what? I just kept ploughing on with the mission because in my head I was certain that both sides would 'get it' in the end and come round to our way of seeing things.

As it turned out – they did! And so did Tesco's as a matter of fact, the UK's biggest booksellers. They ended up buying our company in a multi-million-pound deal as part of their digital empire. Of course, we're talking here about 'professional' contexts, Kev. About making a stand for a living. Or in my case to *keep on* living!

But it's also important just to *stand up for yourself*. You know, in everyday life. If you're always being pushed around, if you're always doing what other people want and not what *you* want, then you're never going to know who you really are – and neither will anyone else.

You'll be everybody and nobody.

Your whole personality will be a patchwork quilt of everyone else's – stitched together by the need to be liked or the need to fit in or the need to *be someone*.

But the irony is: you'll never be *anyone* if you live like that. You'll just be an alias. You'll be a temporary Word file that keeps on appearing and disappearing but which actually has nothing in it.

Andy's right, of course. And his observations won't come as a surprise to too many of you out there, I'm sure. But what might well come as a surprise is the fact that by being a bit more curmudgeonly you could do a bit better for yourself in life.

A recent study entitled *Do Nice Guys – and Gals – Really Finish Last?*, for instance, comes up with an answer to that question: a resounding, if rather unpalatable YES!

Male employees who score below average on the personality trait 'agreeableness' earn around 18 per cent more per annum than those who chill out at the smilier end of the scale. Tougher-minded women, on the other hand, fare a little worse, but still come out on top: earning around 5 per cent more.

One of the reasons for this differential, the researchers suggest, is surprisingly simple. Ball-breakers are more likely to secure higher salaries for themselves across the negotiating table. Either to begin with, when offered the job. Or later, when getting a raise.

But there are other, less proximal reasons.

Ballbreakers are also more likely to:

- **Be respected (if not exactly liked).**
- **Give it to you straight (even if it hurts).**
- **Push both themselves and their employees harder.**

In short, you're more likely to know where you stand with a ball-breaker.

And that, in modern-day business culture, is a way more valuable asset than simply being liked.

THE MOUSE MAN

'Talking of being liked, I once heard a story about one of the world's most successful hedge fund managers,' I tell Andy, as we come out of Addison's Walk and double back on ourselves to the New Building.

> In the middle of the night, around 3 a.m., he dials up his secretary and gets her out of bed.
>
> 'What's the problem?' she mumbles, half asleep.
>
> 'I need a mouse,' he replies, casually. 'Could you pop out and get one for me?'
>
> The woman is gobsmacked.
>
> 'Er, I don't wish to be rude,' she stammers. 'But do you have any idea what time it is? I mean, do you really need to have one *now*? Can't you just wait until the computer guys get in in the morning?'
>
> There's a moment of silence.
>
> Then a moment of horror as the awful realization dawns.
>
> 'I'm afraid you don't understand,' says her boss. 'I'm not talking about my computer. My computer is working fine. No, when I say mouse, I mean a *real* mouse. You know, for my cat. She's bored.'

Back in my rooms Andy opens the wardrobe. Ever since I told him it was C.S. Lewis's old pad when he was here back in the 1920s he's been hell bent on it.

It's one stonker of an anti-climax. No lions or witches to speak of. Just a West Ham scarf.

He pulls it out. Then tosses it back in.

'You know, your story about the Mouse Man doesn't surprise me one bit,' he says, closing the door on the magic of Narnia for ever. 'Guys like him are actually more common than you might think in the city. And you know what? The reason we don't hear more about them is precisely because they're SUCCESSFUL.

'The moment things go tits up – that's when the skeletons come tumbling out of the closets.'

I think Andy may well have a point and I tell him about an exercise I once ran to demonstrate precisely how willing we are to cede ruthlessness to success.

The idea was pretty simple.

I handed the following fictitious description of a company CEO to a bunch of first-year psychology students and asked them to indicate, on a scale of 1 to 10, how good a boss they rated him:

> Paul Jones is 38 years old and is the head of a major city investment corporation. He is a maverick nonconformist with an explosive temper who is prone to pushing boundaries and who occasionally operates on the borders of ethical practice. He is a flamboyant risk-taker and is ice-cool under pressure but is known for his tendency to reduce senior colleagues to tears and to fire them on the spot if their level of performance fails to match up to his own remorseless standards. Last year, under his stewardship, the bank's annual pre-tax profit stood at a record-breaking £8 billion.

On the basis of this description, Paul's average rating weighed in at a commendable 8.3 out of 10.

That's a point for every billion!

Yet when I showed the profile to another group of students his share price plummeted to a diminutive 0.6 on the key substitution of just a single, significant detail:

> Paul Jones is 38 years old and is the head of a major city investment corporation. He is a maverick nonconformist with an

explosive temper who is prone to pushing boundaries and who occasionally operates on the borders of ethical practice. He is a flamboyant risk-taker and is ice-cool under pressure but is known for his tendency to reduce senior colleagues to tears and to fire them on the spot if their level of performance fails to match up to his own remorseless standards. Last year, under his stewardship, the bank MADE A RECORD-BREAKING PRE-TAX LOSS OF £2 BILLION.

'If you're going to be ruthless you'd better make it count!' I say to Andy.

He smiles. 'That's one way of looking at it, I suppose,' he says. 'But another way might be this: if you want to count, you'd better make sure you're ruthless!'

I grab my jacket and we head back across the cloisters to the dining hall.

Lunch then punting then something cold by the river is the order of the rest of the day.

'You going to let me have a go?' asks Andy.

'At drinking by the river?' I say. 'Not sure, mate. They're nice people round here. To be honest, they just don't need it.'

Suddenly, Ray Winstone joins us. 'I'm not talking about your poncey Pimms,' he snarls. 'I mean punting!'

I smile.

'Oh *punting*! Yes, of course mate,' I say. 'Why wouldn't I? In fact, you'll be doing more than just having a go. The old back's starting to play up. You'll be at it all day.'

YES-TERDAY'S NEWS

While Andy and I were writing this chapter Carla, a friend of mine, took a particular interest. Carla is a secretary at a top London law firm and, on first impressions at least, seems – or should I say, seemed – like the poster girl for job satisfaction.

She was outgoing, intelligent, had a good sense of humour – all the things you get in the personal ads – but if you scratched beneath the surface the picture was a little less rosy. Beneath the veneer of sassy sophistication, Carla was exhausted, depressed and run off her feet – and all because of a simple glitch in her personality.

She couldn't say no. To anyone. This one single character flaw was ruining Carla's life. It had already cost her a relationship (when she was getting in from work she was switching on the computer and putting in another shift at home); at least one good friend (having got hold of some tickets for a Bruce Springsteen gig two months in advance she'd then stayed in the office preparing the company audit); and also, ironically, an unblemished employment record (mistakes were beginning to creep in and she'd been given an official warning).

She was desperate for something – anything – to stem the flow of 'yes'.

Could befriending her inner GOOD PSYCHOPATH possibly help?

Andy and I had a long chat with Carla and afterwards put our heads together. What we came up with was a three-month programme based on the principles laid out below. When the three months were up we had another chat with Carla. But this time a much shorter one. In just that brief period of GOOD PSYCHOPATH training she'd managed to get her life completely back on track.

She'd become her OWN PERSON. Not everyone else's. She had a new job, a new boyfriend, and a new life. But this time one that *she* was in control of. She was still the same 'old' Carla: warm, friendly and outgoing. But it was no longer just a façade. She now felt that way for real.

In fact, her inner GOOD PSYCHOPATH actually *enjoyed* saying no. Each time she said it, it felt like a pat on the back.

Carla the doormat was suddenly YES-terday's news.

'Well, it certainly works!' she told us when we met up with her the second time. 'It really has made a difference. And if it's done the trick for me it's definitely going to work for other people.'

Sounds like an ad, doesn't it? Which it is! But it really *won't* be long before you start to notice a difference.

'And if you don't,' says Andy, 'so what? You're not exactly going to do anything about it, are you?'

THE ART OF NO-ING IS KNOWING

Remember Andy's mate Tony, the plastic Jock, in Chapter Five – the Regiment guy who bought the Highland cottage only to discover he never really wanted it in the first place?

Well, here's the deal.

The Number One principle for getting what you want is also the Number One principle for avoiding what you *don't* want:

Work out precisely what it is that you want to do with your time – because if you don't know what you DO want to do with it, you won't know what you DON'T want to do with it!

In other words:

- **Before you can become your own person, you first have to know who that person is.**
- **Before you go your own way, you first need to know exactly where that way leads.**
- **Before you turn people down you, first need to know that you *want* to turn them down.**

'A good way of starting the ball rolling,' says Andy, 'is to keep a diary of all the times when you say yes when you mean no. Or better still, all the times when you *should've* said no but said yes. That way you'll be able to identify triggers – feelings, situations, people – which will then give you a heads-up for the next time you find yourself in that position. I guarantee two things will happen:

'First, you'll be surprised at how many times you do it.

'Secondly, once you start keeping a record of all your unnecessary yeses – all your "unyecessaries"! – you'll start cutting down on them anyway.'

TREAT PRESSURE AS A COMPLIMENT

'If people are putting pressure on you to do something,' says Andy, 'you should treat it as a compliment. It means they value what you've got to offer – otherwise they wouldn't bother.'

He's right. And this way of looking at it – unusual though it is – allows you to do something you may never have thought of before. It allows you to RESPOND from a position of STRENGTH as opposed to REACTING from one of WEAKNESS.

This distinction between RESPONDING and REACTING is fundamental to becoming your own person.

RESPONDING is:

- **Measured**
- **Authoritative**
- **Empowering**

REACTING is:

- **Knee-jerk**
- **Defensive**
- **Exhausting**

So how does this difference between RESPONDING and REACTING pan out in your dealings with others? Well, it enables you to do a number of things that make it easier to stay true to yourself.

1. It helps you cut short the guilt trip

By RESPONDING to REQUESTS as opposed to REACTING to PEOPLE, you depersonalize interactions and draw an important line between REJECTING WHAT A PERSON IS ASKING and REJECTING THE PERSON THEMSELVES.

How many times have you found yourself saying something like this:

'Well, under ordinary circumstances, no, but seeing as it's you.'
Or: 'I wouldn't normally. But because he's a mate . . .'

When the messenger becomes part of the message, it's easy to feel outnumbered. It's easy to feel that it's suddenly two against one.

'It was exactly like that in Northern Ireland,' says Andy. 'If I'd grown up on the Bogside instead of an estate in Peckham I'd probably have been one of the players. I know it seems hard to believe but some of them were actually all right. At the end of the day it wasn't the lads *themselves* that we were fighting against. It was what they were doing. And that's exactly why we called them "players".

'There wasn't anything personal about it. It was all strictly business. Everything was just a "game" – albeit a very unpleasant one.'

2. It allows you to justify your rejection

Research has shown that the simple act of providing a reason for your behaviour – even if it's utter nonsense! – makes it far more acceptable than if you don't give one at all.

One famous study, for instance, showed that if people barged into a photocopier queue without explaining why, they were quickly sent packing. But if, on the other hand, they asked if they could go to the front because they 'really needed to use the photocopier' – duh! – that was fine. They got away scot free!

3. It gives you the opportunity to frame your refusal in the other person's self-interest (and therefore your own)

'Imagine that your boss asks you to do something but you're already up to your neck in it working on a crucial presentation for next week,' says Andy. 'Instead of saying "yes", invoke the Perceived Self-Interest principle of persuasion and say something like this:

> I'd love to help but I really want to make sure next week's presentation is streets ahead of our competitors' and I need to devote all my resources to ensuring that's the case.

'Not only have you got off the extra work – you've gone up in your boss's estimation!'

WORK ON YOUR BASE-LEVEL CONFIDENCE

Everyone knows what happened to the guy who built his house on sand: the first storm and the house collapsed.

Well, what's true for houses is also true for people. If you want to stand up for yourself – and you want to *remain* standing – you need to have a solid foundation.

The bedrock of that foundation is CONFIDENCE.

Confidence is integral to standing on your own two feet because it builds SELF-ESTEEM. People with HIGH self-esteem feel GOOD about themselves and people with LOW self-esteem feel BAD about themselves – and the problem with feeling bad about yourself is that it sets off a vicious circle.

If *I* don't feel good about myself, low self-esteem sufferers think, then why should anyone else? And in an attempt to give them a reason they do anything they can to please.

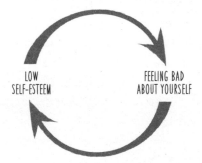

LOW SELF-ESTEEM   FEELING BAD ABOUT YOURSELF

So how do you go about building up your confidence? How do you put an end to this cycle of self-despair? A number of simple pointers may help.

1. Confidence is hard work

Quite literally, according to Andy.

'Confident soldiers,' he says, 'and, of course, I'm not just talking about soldiers here, are those who put the hours in. That's why in the Regiment confidence is always sky high. You have to work your bollocks off in the first place to get in. And then you have to work them back on again to stay in! Give me two soldiers of equal ability – one who gives his all in everything he does and another who just goes through the motions – and I'll tell you who's the more confident.

'Confidence doesn't just come from doing a good job. Confidence comes from knowing you've done a good job.'

Andy's observations have significant implications for the way we conduct not just our interactions with other people but also our lives in general.

Core confidence comes from:

- **Facing up to our responsibilities on a daily basis.**
- **Discharging them judiciously.**
- **Overcoming the challenges they bring.**

If you're a performer – an athlete, musician or actor, for instance – you should be practising every day otherwise, deep down, you'll realize that you're 'burying your talents' and your self-esteem will suffer.

If you're a working mum (or dad) who's not spending enough time with your kids, then again, deep down, you may have the sense that you're 'not quite up to it' . . . and that nagging sense of falling short as a parent will translate into low self-esteem.

At the same time, of course, as we saw in Chapter Four, it's important not to go down the perfectionist road. All of us fall short on an impressively regular basis and goading ourselves, kicking ourselves and beating ourselves up about it is not going to change that any time soon.

The answer lies in finding the right balance – and maintaining that balance – as opposed to scampering like crazy from one end of life's manically teetering seesaw to the other, REACTING to the ups and downs.

In balance you find control.

And in control you find confidence.

And in confidence you find YOURSELF.

2. Don't just BE the part – LOOK the part!

We've all heard the saying: 'You can look the part but can you be the part?' But research suggests that there's more to 'looking' than meets the eye.

One study, for instance, has shown that adopting an authoritative pose for two minutes (legs a couple of feet apart and hands on hips) can raise testosterone (the body's confidence hormone) levels by as much as 20 per cent.

'So next time you're facing a difficult meeting,' says Andy, 'shut the door, put up the "Do Not Disturb" sign, and bung on a couple of *Wonder Woman* DVDs.'

But the way you look doesn't just boost your *own* confidence. It can also inspire confidence in others.

'I know a German arms dealer who wears a made-in-the-USA suit, button-down-collar shirt and understated watch when he is selling in the US,' Andy tells me, 'but cargos, same shirt and a chunky Breitling when he's working in Kabul.

'Everywhere he goes, he carries a manicure set with him at all times, to make sure his nails are immaculate. As he says, "When you look like your customers they warm to you because their unconscious tells them that you are one of them. But being just that little bit more smartly dressed than them tells them I am the same, only just a little better. So then they want a piece of the action.'

Of course, it's also important to look the part during the meeting itself – and anything that conveys anxiety, regret or discomfort to other people should be hunted down to extinction and ruthlessly put out of its misery:

- Avoidance of eye contact
- Fidgeting
- Nervous tics
- A hunched, submissive posture . . .

. . . they've all got to go.

Find out what it is that gives YOU away – and give IT away!

Because the more you *look like* what you're saying, the more it'll look like you mean business.

'A few years ago I worked on the action film *Heat* as a technical advisor,' says Andy. 'The film starred Al Pacino and Robert De Niro along with an arsenal of automatic weapons in downtown LA. What's not to like?

'Anyway, while I was there I learned a lot from the film's director, Michael Mann. One thing he taught me, during a show-and-tell session at the production office, was how important it is to get the details right. In the meeting, we had all the main characters' minor accessories spread out on a table – rings, watches, tie pins, stuff like that. Michael was checking that he was happy with the final selection. As it turned out one of the items – one of the actors' watches that was only ever going to appear in the film for ten seconds max – took up an hour's discussion. I just couldn't figure out what all the fuss was about. Who cared if it was a Rolex or a Timex? Did it really mean anything in the grand scheme of things?

'You bet it did! It meant everything. The character being discussed was called Nate, a sophisticated underworld middleman played by John Voight. The scene in which we see the watch is when he's on the phone, drinking a glass of champagne. Now, this guy is über-cool. He just wouldn't wear a chunky, flashy bit of bling. Instead, he'd wear something much more understated – and so that's what Michael chose for him.

'I learned a big lesson that day from Michael Mann. And it was this. In life, it's not just people in the know who get things. It's all of us. Whether we're aware of it at the time or not. I guess, from my own line of work, I kind of knew that anyway – you know, all the little details I was telling you about when you're working undercover and blending into local communities and shit. But—'

'But when it's *not* a matter of life and death, the level of detail surprised you?' I interject.

Andy shakes his head. 'You don't know Michael Mann, Kev,' he says. 'To him making movies *is* a matter of life and death! But yeah, you're right I suppose. So anyway, if you're sitting in the pictures munching popcorn when Nate takes his drink and you see a big lump of bling on his wrist, your unconscious is instantly going to scream at you that something is wrong. And just that one, small, seemingly insignificant detail can fuck up your enjoyment of the film.

'But if, on the other hand, Nate wears a cool, sophisticated, understated watch, we don't care if we don't know how expensive it is. Or what make it is. Instead, what matters is that our brains recognize that it *is* expensive. And that it *is* cool. Just like Nate. We then gain even more satisfaction from the film because our unconscious gives us a little pat on the back to tell us how clever we are in appreciating this detail.'

I stare at Andy in stunned silence.

If I'd closed my eyes there for a moment I could have been forgiven for thinking there was another psychologist in the boat. Not only that but, much to my annoyance, he'd also managed to punt us up and down the Cherwell without so much as a single drop of water entering our craft.

As we enter the shade of the moorings under Magdalen bridge, I have to admit the temptation is overwhelming. One quick shove and the bastard's in the lilies!

But much to my regret, and unlike Oscar Wilde perhaps, I manage to resist it.

'Quite the psychologist, aren't we?' I mutter instead.

'Well, we need at least one,' he says.

He secures the boat and jumps out.

A leg goes in.

I pretend I haven't noticed.

But I know he knows I have.

Now we know the above is a lot to take in, so while you're working on it . . .

. . . we're going to end with an emergency course in assertiveness first aid just in case you need to say 'NO!' tomorrow!

1. Summon up your courage

If you're used to saying 'yes' or not sticking your neck out, then, let's face it, like any habit you're going to find it difficult to give up.

'But just being aware of that fact,' says Andy, 'should make it a little bit easier. Once you realize that you need to be a little bit brave . . . it's amazing how often you can be!'

2. Remember that it's all relative

Next time you find yourself in a position where you're being put under pressure to do something you really don't want to do, just think to yourself: 'There are some people in life who actually enjoy saying no!' Then see if there's anything in it!

'Or just imagine you're one of the dragons in *Dragon's Den*,' says Andy. '"Thanks for coming but this time I won't be investing. Good luck!" You'll be surprised by the reaction you get from the other side. It'll be nothing compared to what you thought it was going be. What you have to remember is this: they have just as much going on in their lives as you do in yours. They'll quickly move on.'

3. Ask yourself what's the worst that can happen

You may feel like a bad friend, a lousy colleague, an uncaring partner. But that's all it is: a feeling. It'll pass – and quicker than you might think. In fact, any awkwardness or anxiety you feel is a good thing. It's a healing, healthy pain as opposed to a malignant, malevolent one.

It's the pain of you getting your life back.

So what if your boss, or friend, or workmates are inconvenienced, disappointed or surprised by the fact you've knocked them back?

'That's *their* emotions,' says Andy. 'And their responsibility. Not yours. You've got absolutely no control over what they think. So why worry about them? If they find what you are saying is unreasonable, that's their problem. Get over it.'

So what if you miss out on an opportunity this time? There'll be others. And again, as Andy rightly points out:

'It's not all or nothing. When you close the door on something you don't want to do, you open another on something you do want to do.'

4. Strategically withdraw

If you're caught in an influence ambush, and discover, to your horror, that your 'no' gun isn't loaded, retreat to a safe position under the pretext of checking your diary (or some other such reason appropriate to the context) and quickly slot in points 1, 2 and 3!

Then it's safety catch off and ALL SYSTEMS NO!

Giving yourself that vital bit of breathing space puts any decision you might suddenly have to make on a functional, emotional bypass, enabling you, as we said earlier, to surgically remove the request from the person making it and to evaluate its merits calmly, rationally and under a local psychological anaesthetic.

5. Start practising

Today! Pick some soft targets and start off with those, then gradually build up to some harder ones. Go into a shop, for example, and when the sales assistant asks if they can help you say: 'No.' On a train, if someone asks you if you mind if they open the window say: 'Yes.' Or in a restaurant, if the food or the staff fails to measure up, don't leave a tip or ask that the service charge be deducted from your bill.

Just like any other muscle the 'no' muscle needs to be toned.

Andy suggests working out on cold-callers.

'Don't just put the phone down on them,' he says. 'Why would you want to do that? You're passing up a free training session! Tell them straight that you're not interested in whatever shit they're trying to flog you and then stay on the line to hear what they've got to say. If you're not match fit and need a bit of a warm-up, it's just what the doctor ordered. And you don't even pay for the call! I think cold-callers should be available on the NHS.'

'Is that what you do?' I ask, as the sun puts its feet up over Christ Church meadow and the first beer of the evening hits the spot. 'Give them the run around?'

He wrings out his sock. 'Nah,' he says. 'Where's the fun in that? I just ask them if they've let Jesus into their lives. Nine times out of ten the next thing you hear is a dial tone!'

Trail two: 5p.

QUESTIONNAIRE
TO WHAT EXTENT ARE YOU YOUR OWN PERSON?

Assign a rating to each of the following statements and then add up your total and check it with the scores on the next page.

		strongly disagree 0	disagree 1	agree 2	strongly agree 3
1.	If someone is doing something that annoys me I let them know it.	○	○	○	○
2.	I like to speak my mind.	○	○	○	○
3.	Disagreeing with a group of my peers doesn't bother me.	○	○	○	○
4.	I am good at coming up with creative and innovative ideas.	○	○	○	○
5.	If something is important to me I fight for it.	○	○	○	○
6.	It doesn't bother me if my opinions offend or upset others.	○	○	○	○
7.	It's not important to me that others like me.	○	○	○	○
8.	I am immune to sales patter.	○	○	○	○
9.	I feel comfortable complaining about poor service.	○	○	○	○
10.	I like to stand out from the crowd.	○	○	○	○
11.	It isn't important to me to keep up with the latest trends.	○	○	○	○

0–11 You possess about as much individualism as an ant colony and a profile so low it's almost subterranean. No wonder no one knows who you are. *You* don't know who you are!

12–17 You have little appetite for conflict and a strong need to fit in. Time to get out more!

18–22 You're no pushover but prefer not to upset the applecart if you can help it. You are affable and easy-going. Ish!

23–28 You can give as good as you get and don't take crap from anyone. A psychological street-fighter!

29–33 Thinking outside the box? What box?

CHAPTER SEVEN

BECOME A PERSUASION BLACK BELT

Don't raise your voice.
Improve your argument.

Desmond Tutu

BELT UP

'I heard a story once about Bono and Sophia Loren,' says Andy, hoisting his holdall off his back and slinging it down on the shiny terrazzo floor in front of him. 'They're on this flight together and it hits a storm. Loren's shitting herself with all the bouncing around and then, to cap it all, the plane is struck by lightning. By this stage she's going obviously mental . . . until Bono turns round to her and says: "Don't worry – it's just God taking your photograph."

'It completely transforms things and she actually starts to laugh.'

We're at the airport queuing up to check in. Andy's doing a book tour in Belfast and I'm tagging along for the ride.

A bloke in front of us is on his mobile phone. We're not sure who he's talking to but from the way things are going there's an outside chance it could be his therapist. He's sweating, white as a sheet, and muttering stuff about take-off and landing being the times when things are most likely to go pear-shaped. He's not exactly enthused about the next couple of hours and has clearly done his research. So much so that he's beginning to make *me* nervous.

'Reminds me of a story I heard about Muhammad Ali,' I say. 'He's on a flight and as they're taxiing out on to the runway, the cabin steward suddenly notices that he hasn't fastened his seatbelt. So she goes over to him and asks him to do it up.

'"I'm Superman," Ali says to her. "Superman don't need no seatbelt."

'She doesn't miss a beat. "Superman don't need no aeroplane!" she says.'

SPICE PEARLS

Now wouldn't it be great if persuasion always worked like that?

Immediately. Incisively. Instinctively.

But, of course, it doesn't, does it? Instead, most of our attempts to get other people to do things are about as effective as an exfoliating shampoo. In everyday life, persuasion is often a matter of trial and error. Of due process and negotiation. We get it right as many times as we get it wrong.

But clearly there *are* times when influence works first time. And clearly there *are* people – psychological cat burglars who are able to trick, charm and schmooze their way at will past our brains' defence and security systems – who are better at persuading than others:

- Who can convince the boss to give them the pay rise they asked for.
- Who can convince the traffic warden not to write out the ticket.
- Who can convince the Champ to buckle up.

Is such deadly, black-belt persuasion licensed only to a chosen few? Or are we all able to do it – once we've decoded and mastered the secrets?

As a social psychologist—

'Geek!' honks Andy, as the queue starts moving again and we scuff our bags along the floor with our feet.

– in a world of ever increasing complexity, in a world placing ever greater demands on our attention, this was a question that I badly wanted to answer – even if Andy had already got there before me.

'Of course we can all do it,' he laughs. 'I'll give you a few lessons if you want.'

Did you know, for instance, that the brains of modern-day Western city-dwellers like us take in as much information during the course of a twenty-four-hour period as the brains of those who lived in rural medieval Britain would've taken in . . . during the course of an entire lifetime?

If we want to stand out we need to make ourselves count!

So I'll tell you what I did.

I started to collect stories exactly like the one about Ali and the cabin steward.

I started to put together an influence 'curiosity shop' – exhibits of persuasion at ten when usually it's at three or four.

Then, when I'd collected about two hundred or so, I subjected them to something called 'factor analysis' – a statistical technique that allows psychologists like myself—

'He means geeks,' Andy remarks to the girl on the check-in desk.

– to extract the key ingredients of whatever it is that we're looking at.

I wanted to sequence the genome of this militant strain of persuasion. Uncover its DNA. And tantalizingly my analysis revealed FIVE CORE COMPONENTS which, when combined in unison in the one persuasion message, don't just knock on the door of success, but kick it in, recline on the sofa with a nice cold beer and flick on the flat-screen telly.

And which also, rather handily, form the acronym SPICE!

And SPICE stands for:

- **Simplicity**
- **Perceived self-interest**
- **Incongruity**
- **Confidence**
- **Empathy**

And on the way to Belfast we're going to talk you through each of these components in turn and their critical importance in getting you what you want.

'I bet you a tenner you can't get us into Business!' Andy whispers to our long-suffering check-in girl.

'Don't listen to him,' I say. 'He's a psychopath. They're top-level psychological code-breakers. They can hack into your brain's emotion servers and before you know it you'll be doing everything he tells you!'*

Andy looks at me, then back at the girl.

He winks at her.

'Double bluff,' he says.

SIMPLICITY

'I've got a joke for you,' I say, as we shovel down handfuls of peanuts.

We're sitting in Business – and Del Boy's looking smug. I've known some fast talkers in my time but this guy takes the biscuit. I'm not saying he's bent but he could sell shaving soap to the Taliban.

Probably has, knowing him.

A nurse is doing the rounds of an intensive care unit when she's called over by a man in a respirator.

'Nurse!' whispers the man hoarsely. 'Are my testicles black?'

'The nurse starts to panic. She whips up the sheet, takes a quick look underneath, but thankfully everything's fine.

'No, sir,' she says. 'I've just taken a look and everything is perfectly OK. You've got absolutely nothing to worry about.'

It doesn't do any good.

'Nurse!' whispers the man even more urgently. 'Are my testicles black?'

Now the nurse really starts to panic.

'Sir!' she says, 'I've just taken a look and everything is perfectly OK. You've got absolutely nothing to worry about. Now please – time costs lives in medicine! Just spit it out in simple language: what seems to be troubling you?'

*To find out how persuasive you are, why not take our test at the end of the chapter?

With his right hand, the man grasps the nurse weakly by the arm, while with his left slowly removing his oxygen mask.

He draws her gently towards him.

'Nurse!' he whispers, with seemingly the last vestiges of strength left in his body:

'ARE MY TEST RESULTS BACK?'

Our brains have a preference, a hardwired preference, for SIMPLICITY over complexity. And nowhere is this more true than in the chaotic, cacophonous cauldron that we call persuasion. But precisely how powerful a spell the magic of simplicity casts over the influence process isn't always immediately apparent.

We glimpse its handiwork in all walks of life . . . from politics to poetry to oratory. When President Roosevelt wanted to persuade a traditionally isolationist America to bail Britain out during her darkest hours of the Second World War he precision-engineered the simplest of phrases to do it. He called his policy: *Lend-Lease*.

And he described it in the simplest of language:

Suppose my neighbour's home catches fire, and I have a length of garden hose . . . if he can take my garden hose and connect it up with his hydrant, I may help him put out the fire . . . I don't want to say to him before that operation, 'Neighbour, my garden hose cost me $15; you have to pay me $15 for it' . . . I don't want $15 – I want my garden hose back after the fire is over.

The rest is history.

When John Keats wrote the first verse of his famous poem *La Belle Dame Sans Merci*, he could've written something like this:

What is the matter, armed old-fashioned soldier,
Standing by yourself and doing nothing with a pallid expression?
The reed-like plants have decomposed by the lake
And there are not any birds singing.

But he didn't.

Instead, he got out his sharpie and knocked out the following masterpiece:

> O *what can ail thee, knight-at-arms,*
> *Alone and palely loitering?*
> *The sedge has wither'd from the lake,*
> *And no birds sing.*

Beautiful, isn't it? The right combination of words tapped skilfully into the brain cracks open a safe deep within its vaults of rich and ancient emotion. And isn't it precisely *because* of its propensity to say more with less that great poetry enjoys such unrestricted access to our hearts?

When Winston Churchill delivered his immortal, 'Hostilities will be engaged with our adversary on the coastal perimeter . . .' address in the summer of 1940, he could've put it differently. Instead of going down in history as the author of one of the greatest speeches ever made, he might have considered something less wordy:

'We shall fight them on the beaches . . .'

'Haha, yeah right!' Andy laughs. 'Someone once told me a story about an advertising exec in New York. One morning he's walking to work through Central Park when he sees a blind man begging. The man is holding up a sign that says: "I am blind." But his bowl is empty. On his way back from work the ad man passes the blind man again and notices that his bowl is *still* empty. So he picks up the sign, gets out his pen, and makes a simple change:

'He writes: "*It is spring* and I am blind." A couple of hours later and the blind man is raking it in.'

Nice.

But the evidence for simplicity's hold over us isn't just anecdotal. There's science in the mix as well.

Research on the psychological principle of COGNITIVE FLUENCY, for example – how easy or difficult an object, argument or concept is to think about – demonstrates time and again that the easier something is to understand the more profitable, the more pleasurable, the more persuasive – in general, the more *positive* – we seem to find it.

Which of the following two food additives, for instance, would you say sounds the more dangerous: *Hnegripitrom* or *Magnalroxate*?

Most people say *Hnegripitrom*.

How about this?

Which of the following two amusement park rides do you think is scarier: *Chunta* or *Vaiveahtoishi*?

Most people say *Vaiveahtoishi*.

But you know what? All four of these names are made up. The reason the majority of people go for *Hnegripitrom* and *Vaiveahtoishi* is purely on account of the fact that *Magnalroxate* and *Chunta* are easier to *say*, and therefore easier to *think about*, than *Hnegripitrom* and *Vaiveahtoishi*. And, in general, we tend to equate simplicity with safety.

The same principle works on the stock market.

One famous study conducted several years ago found that if you invest in companies with pronounceable ticker codes (like GOOG for Google), you stand to make 10 per cent more profit after *just one day's trading* than if you invest in companies with unpronounceable codes (e.g. RDO).

Companies you can *say*, *pay*!

In a similar vein, another study listed the features of a product in either an easy-to-read or a difficult-to-read typeface. Guess what the researchers found? Easy-to-read typefaces pretty much doubled the number of people willing to purchase the product.

Little wonder, then, that every time you walk into an Apple store it's like having your senses scrubbed clean with a gigantic cognitive wet-wipe!

In fact, if you chart the evolution of virtually any consumer technology you'll find the same pattern. You start out needing an IQ the size of Donald Trump's hair to use it and end up a tech-ho without necessarily even being able to *spell* IQ. And the irony is that our forensic pursuit of the minimalist ultramodern is portentously depicted in ancient neuronal cave art scored deep within the gorges of our brains.

Things that are easy to process give us a momentary pleasure fix.

When we look at objects that are easy to pick up, for example, we produce microscopic smiles invisible to the naked eye. These imperceptible changes in facial muscle tone can be measured by a technique called electromyography* – and are *not* present when we look at objects that are difficult to pick up.

The take-home message is clear.

When considered in the context of websites, phones, cars, arguments – or anything else for that matter – the power of simplicity is absolute.

As we learned from Epicurus in Chapter Three, we have an inbuilt preference for pleasure over pain. And for anything that enables us to indulge such a preference, our brains roll out a big red chemical carpet.

'But you still haven't explained *why* our brains prefer simplicity over complexity,' Andy says, taking off his go-faster Timberlands and pressing the 'recline' button on his seat. 'I mean, all this geek stuff is great and all that. But what's it *for*? The gun goes bang. But *why*?'

He sinks beneath the horizon.

'Yeah, OK,' I say. 'Fair point. But you know what? Our intensive-care nurse of earlier has already kind of answered that for us. Time doesn't just save lives in medicine. It was also very much of the essence during the course of our evolutionary history.'

I scrabble around in the seat pocket next to me for some paper – the sick bag will do – and pull out a pen.

'Don't worry about that, mate,' says Andy. 'In Business someone comes and holds the thing for you. You just have to press the call button.'

'Any more of your jokes and I just might,' I say. 'Now, come back here.'

---

*Electromyography is a technique for evaluating and measuring the electrical activity of nerves and muscles.

I smooth the bag out and write down the following sum while the seat whirrs and Andy jerks back into view. Then I get the in-flight menu and cover it up.

$$
\begin{array}{r}
1000 \\
40 \\
1000 \\
30 \\
1000 \\
20 \\
1000 \\
+\ 10 \\
\hline
\end{array}
$$

'OK,' I say. 'On the back of this bag I've written out a very simple sum. Now what I'm going to do is I'm going to reveal each of the numbers one by one to you and your job is to add it up out loud as we work our way down. You got me?'

Andy looks doubtful.

'It'd help if you put pound signs in front of them,' he says. 'But OK, let's give it a go.'

'Right,' I say, and reveal the first number.

'One thousand,' says Andy.

'You're on a roll,' I say, and reveal the second number.

'One thousand and forty.'

'Genius!' I say, and move on to the third.

'Two thousand and forty . . .'

A few seconds later, Andy comes up with the total:

FOUR THOUSAND ONE HUNDRED!

'They wanted me on *Countdown* instead of Carol Vorderman,' he crows. 'But I turned 'em down. I fancied a bit more of a challenge.'

'Some people reckon you *are* Carol Vorderman,' I mutter.

'What was that?' he says.

'Nothing,' I say. 'Anyway, I don't believe this but you've actually got it *right!*'

Andy looks at me like one o'clock half struck.

'What do you mean, I got it right? Of course I got it right. Why wouldn't I?'

'Well,' I say, sheepishly. 'When 99.9 per cent of people get to the penultimate calculation – 4090 + 10 – their brains instantly reach for the nicest, roundest, cuddliest whole number that they can think of. And they come up with . . . 5,000. Even Cambridge maths professors get this wrong. But you . . . ?'

'Maybe they could do with a few more psychopaths in Cambridge?' Andy laughs.

I'm not so sure. I shove the bag back into the seat pocket and grab a glass of champagne from the cabin steward who's doing the rounds. I feel like I've earned it.

'Anyway,' I say, taking a sip, 'that, to answer your question, is why our brains love simplicity. You see, whenever our prehistoric ancestors faced a difficult situation – let's say a predator, for instance – it would've been those who came up with the correct solution to such a predicament, be it fight or flight, that would've been most likely to survive and to pass on their genes to future generations. But even more likely to survive and to pass on their genes to future generations would've been those who came up with the correct solution *most quickly*.

'Imagine, for instance, if every time you were faced with a sabre-toothed tiger you had to weigh the situation up from scratch: black, orange, stripy, fangs, drooling . . . creeping towards me slowly—'

'What do you mean, "every time"?' Andy butts in. 'There wouldn't be an "every time". There would just be the one, mate.'

'Exactly,' I say. 'Life happens way too fast for it to be any other way. So over the years, the millions of years of our evolutionary history, our brains have learned to take short cuts; to use mental rules of thumb to make decisions; to employ learned associations; to assimilate millions upon millions of bytes – talking of sabre-toothed tigers! – of previously stored information to generate response outcomes.

'Remember what that QC told me that time? Information travels round the brain like electricity around a circuit. It takes the path of least resistance. And the simpler you can make your argument, the more simply you present your case, the faster and more powerfully that information flows.'

'Which is odd, isn't it?' says Andy. 'Because most people think that by dressing things up, by using long words and flowery language, they're making themselves sound more intelligent. I mean, that's what that business bullshit chart was all about, wasn't it? But actually, from what you're saying it's the complete opposite. The more complicated you make your argument the more likely it is to run into a mental roadblock in people's heads.

'You know, it's exactly what you're taught in the Regiment to do if you're caught and interrogated. Be the "grey man". Be the simple victim of circumstance who just happened to be in the wrong place at the wrong time. Make it as easy as possible for your captors to dismiss you as a worthless bag of shit. If you can be the grey man you don't stick out in the crowd.

'Even when planning operations we are always told, KEEP IT SIMPLE STUPID. I still use KISS in my writing and even in business. So when the shit hits the fan my brain can work out very clearly what I need to be doing because it isn't filled up with irrelevant information.'

Of course, we're not saying that by keeping things simple we should in any way be dumbing things down. In fact, we're saying exactly the opposite. It's often remarkably easy to complicate matters – and inestimably more difficult to simplify them.

As Samuel Johnson famously once quipped: 'I don't have time to write you a short letter so I've written you a long one.'

Instead, what we *are* saying is this. There lies great beauty in simplicity – and such essential, elemental elegance is a honey trap for the brain.

Mathematicians constantly strive to find the shortest possible formula to describe a complex phenomenon. It's called, in their language, 'algorithmic irreducibility'.

We should do the same when we're setting out to try to persuade.

'Is it me or is there a funny smell around here?' I ask Andy, as one of the cabin crew drops by with some hot towels.

'Just you, mate,' he says, slipping his feet back into his Timberlands.

PERCEIVED SELF-INTEREST

'Hey look,' says Andy, jabbing me in the ribs. 'Here he is – the poster boy for your Bad Good guys!'

We're somewhere in the air between Birmingham and Liverpool and Andy is clicking through the film collection on his Mac.

Sure enough, there on the screen in front of him is Gordon Gekko, hair slicked back, white-collared shirt, braces, cufflinks, the whole nine yards.

I lean over and take a closer look as Andy unplugs his earphones and turns up the volume.

Bang on cue he delivers the line: 'It's not a question of enough, pal. It's a zero-sum game. Somebody wins, somebody loses.'

Andy smiles, before clicking on to the next film. He's got the attention span of a goldfish on crystal meth.

'It was all about him, all right,' he laughs. 'He didn't give a shit about anyone apart from himself. As long as the money came rolling in, that was all that mattered.'

He's spot on, of course. For Gekko, it *was* all about Gekko. But actually, unlike assets in the world of high finance, naked self-interest is not, as the man himself might put it, a zero-sum commodity. Sure, some of us might have more of it than others. But all of us own shares in ourselves – and like any corporate trader we're keen to see their market value rise.

I once heard a story about King Louis XI of France. Louis was a staunch believer in astrology and so wasn't exactly surprised when a fortune-teller correctly predicted that a certain member of his court would die within a week.

Mindful, however, that such a powerful clairvoyant as this

might pose a considerable threat to his authority, he decided to send for him – having secretly arranged that he subsequently plunge to his death from a high window ledge.

'You claim to be able to interpret the heavens,' Louis addressed him gravely, 'and to know the fate of others. So tell me: what fate will befall YOU? And how long do you have to live?'

The astrologer thought carefully about this for a moment. Then he smiled.

'I shall meet my end,' he replied, 'just three days before Your Majesty meets his.'

Now, folks, we wouldn't dream of telling you to do anything underhand in this book.

I mean, would we?!

But what we *will* tell you is this.

If, when you are trying to persuade someone to do something, you can frame your message so that it appears to be in THEIR INTERESTS as opposed to your OWN, you are going to have a much better chance of getting whatever it is that you want than if it's the other way round.

Someone once asked a very pertinent question: what's the best way of riding a horse?

Answer: in the direction in which it is going!

Well, from leading *reins* to leading *brains*. THE BEST WAY OF CHANGING SOMEONE'S MIND IS TO GET *THEM* TO CHANGE IT FOR YOU!

'When I was writing *Flipnosis*,' I tell Andy, 'I hung out with a couple of the world's top con artists both here in the UK and across the pond in the US. And while I was with them I posed each of them a question: "What, in your opinion, is the single most important factor in getting someone to do something for you?"

'And you know what? Both of them, pretty much verbatim, gave me the same answer. Ninety-nine per cent of people make the same simple mistake when it comes to persuasion. Ninety-nine per cent of people think that the fundamental secret of persuasion is exactly that: TO GET SOMEONE TO DO SOMETHING FOR YOU.'

'I can believe it,' says Andy, flicking on to Angry Birds. 'But . . . it isn't, is it? The fundamental secret of persuasion is to GET SOMEONE TO DO SOMETHING FOR *THEMSELVES*.'

He zaps off his Mac and shoves it back into the arm of his chair. 'I'll give you an example,' he says.

My wife had a friend who was one of your lot. She worked in some university up north somewhere. Anyway, as well as being one of the geek brigade, she was also one of the green brigade, and started up a campaign to get people cycling to work or taking the bus instead of driving in. She put up posters, flyers, sent round emails – you name it, she did it.

Nothing happened. Didn't make a blind bit of difference. The car park was as rammed as it had been before she started. One night she came round for dinner and started blabbing about it. The main problem seemed to be that her head shed, who was also some bigwig on the university board or something, wasn't interested and hadn't got behind it and backed her.

'Why not?' I asked.

'Well,' she said, 'he's a self-centred, slimy little man and there's nothing in it for him. He's got other fish to fry.'

'What other fish?' I asked.

'Revenue generation,' she said.

Apparently, the big bee in his bonnet – or rather the big bee in the bloke above him's bonnet – was the fact that the university finances were going tits up and they needed to make some money. Fast!

Ahhh! I thought. So that's the way in, is it? The bastard's strapped for cash.

'I've got an idea,' I told her. 'Why don't you tell him you've come up with a cunning little plan to swell the coffers? He'll nick it, pass it off as his own at the next committee meeting – because that's what slimy little gits like him do – and if they like it and give it the thumbs up, he'll be flavour of the month.'

She looks at me as if I've just handed her a turd!

'Why the hell would I want to make *him* look good?' she shouts. 'I've just told you he didn't support me. Why on earth should I help *him*?'

'Because,' I tell her, 'if it all goes according to plan you'll get exactly what you want. You see, your brilliant idea to raise money is to introduce a hefty increase in car parking charges. Local councils do it all the time – it's the easy option.'

Anyway, to cut a long story short, six months or so later when we see her, she's beaming from ear to ear.

'How's the campaign going?' I ask.

'Couldn't be better,' she says. 'The senate approved a hundred per cent increase in the annual car parking tariff and since then everyone's been cycling or busing it on to campus!'

'Bet your boss looks a right dickhead!' I say.

'Yes,' she says, 'he does!'

'Funnily enough, it's a trick I learned from my Northern Ireland days, Kev. If you want to get an informer to do something you find out what's important up the chain of command and play on that. People always want to impress those above them – even when they're fucking them over!

'Basically, if you want to get your boss to do something, find out what's important to THEIR boss and piggyback what YOU want on that.'

Andy's right. The best way of riding a horse is, indeed, in the direction in which it is going.

But the trick, when it comes to persuasion, is just a little bit more subtle than that. The trick, when it comes to persuasion, is to give that horse the impression it's not being ridden at all.

INCONGRUITY

Andy and I are standing at the baggage carousel in Belfast airport. As usual, the thing has been chuntering away for God knows how long and there's still no sign of our bags.

A bunch of lads are here on a stag-do. They've got personalized T-shirts, green curly wigs, a life-size cardboard cut-out of – presumably – the groom, and the obligatory blow-up doll.

Their bags come round immediately and they roar off laughing into the Belfast night.

Sod's Law.

'Here,' says Andy, tapping me on the arm. 'Listen to this. A young bloke is in the final stages of getting things ready for his up-coming wedding and everything is going fantastically smoothly apart from the slightly tricky issue of his fiancée's extremely hot younger sister. One day, he finds himself alone in the house with her and she creeps up next to him on the settee and suggests they, you know, slip upstairs for a couple of hours before the big day rolls round.

'Anyway, the young man starts to panic and, rushing through his options, storms out of the house into the front garden where, unbeknownst to him, a reception committee awaits consisting of his fiancée, his father-in-law to be, his mother-in-law to be, and all the extended family.

'They all give him a huge round of applause, his fiancée plants a big kiss on his cheek, and his father-in-law to be declares, in public, that he's delighted to give him his daughter's hand in marriage as he's finally proved himself a man of honour.

'Moral of the story?'

'Dunno,' I say. 'You never know what's round the corner?'

'Always leave your condoms in the car!'

The role of incongruity in the influence process is twofold.

On the one hand it forms the basis of pretty much everything we find funny. Our brains love to be wrong-footed, to have the rug of expectation whipped unceremoniously from beneath their feet. And when that happens, in the right context, we laugh!

But alongside humour incongruity also has another psycho-active property, namely that of distraction.

Unusual, surprise or unexpected events jolt our brains into a micro-hypnotic trance during which all our usual neural security systems are scrambled and all our cognitive surveillance equipment disabled. And it's at times like that that we're at our most suggestible.

Let's deal with each of these two properties of incongruity in turn: humour and distraction.

Humour

OK, so it's no use beating around the bush. There have literally been hundreds of books on persuasion written down the years (and I, of course, include my own one in that – ahem, £8.99 on Amazon!).

But the one big take-home message that we want you to re-member above all others from this chapter is, as Andy puts it, this:

'Persuasion ain't rocket science!'

And here, again as Andy puts it, is the first lesson from the Good Psychopath school of the bleeding obvious:

'If, when you are trying to persuade someone to do something, you can make them feel GOOD as opposed to feeling BAD, then you are going to have a damn sight better chance of getting what you want than if it's the other way round.'

'When I was writing *Flipnosis*,' I tell Andy, 'I interviewed a bunch of New York traffic cops and I asked them whether anyone had ever said anything particularly memorable down the years that had succeeded in getting them off a ticket. Anyway, one of the cops told me about a guy he'd pulled over for speeding.

'Did you know you were doing eighty in a fifty-five zone?' he asked him.

'Sure,' said the guy. 'Yes, I did.'

The cop was dumbfounded.

'Then why the hell didn't you pull over as soon as you saw me?' he asked.

Quick as a flash, the guy turns round and says:

'Well, officer, three weeks ago my wife left me for one of you guys and when I saw your lights in my rear-view mirror I thought you were bringing her back!'

That guy got off a ticket that day! And the reason for that is pretty simple. He'd given the cop pretty much all he *could* give him under the circumstances. He gave him a feel-good factor. He put a smile on his face.

And the cop, through the law of reciprocity – a very powerful law of influence – had felt the need to do the same, had felt the need to reciprocate. And he'd given the motorist pretty much all *he* could give him under the circumstances.

He let him off a ticket.

Distraction

But as we were saying, there's more to incongruity than just humour – than just a feel-good factor. Incongruity also has another psychoactive property – namely that of distraction.

Unusual events or novel situations shunt our brains into an auto-suggestive state during which we're able to *take in* information but aren't necessarily able to consciously *process* it. And it's at times like that that we're most at the mercy of those who are trying to persuade us.

'Several years ago,' I tell Andy, as we stand watching a near-empty conveyor belt continue to take the piss, 'a colleague of mine conducted a fun study on how incongruity, distraction and micro-hypnosis pan out in the influence process in what's probably *the* most unforgiving persuasion known to man – and I say "man" with good reason – because the study he did was on chat-up lines.'

'Oh yeah,' says Andy, peering down the delivery ramp. 'What, purely in the interests of scientific advancement, he wanted to know if chat-up lines actually work, did he?'

It's hard to keep a straight face.

'Well, yes,' I smirk. 'I mean, if they *don't* why the hell do we bother with the bloody things, right?'

Andy moves away from the delivery ramp and over to one of the baggage reclaim monitors. He squints up at it suspiciously.

'I'm beginning to wonder why we're bothering with *this* bloody thing!' he mutters, pacing up and down.

'Anyway,' I say, 'what he did was this. First, he sampled a load of chat-up lines at random from the web. Secondly, he grabbed a bunch of students. Thirdly, he divided the chat-up lines equally among those students. And lastly, he let the students loose in some bars and clubs with the explicit instruction to try each of their lines out five times and then to report back to him with the data.

'What he wanted to find out, of course, was whether any of the lines were foolproof – whether any of them would work five out of five times.'

'And did they?' asks Andy, suddenly sparking up.

'Well,' I say, 'six months or so later when the dust had settled and the students *did* report back to him with the data, it turned out that only *one* of those lines was foolproof, only *one* of them worked five out of five times.'

'What was it?' asks Andy.

'I'm not telling you,' I say.

He moves a bit closer.

'OK,' I say. 'You've twisted my arm. What you do is, you go up to a girl in a bar and you say this:

'My mates bet me twenty quid that I couldn't start up a conversation with the best-looking girl in the bar. So how about I go and buy some drinks and we spend their money?'

Andy looks unconvinced. 'You sure?' he growls.

'I agree, it doesn't sound all that great in the cold light of day, does it? But actually, the plot thickens. The line only works if, immediately after it, you insert a compliment. It could be anything. It could be "I like your hair", "I like your shoes", "I like your dress" – anything, so long as it's a compliment.'

'Now, you're *really* beginning to take the piss,' says Andy. 'Now, you're going into Derren Brown territory.'

'I know,' I say. 'It sounds odd, doesn't it? But actually, once you start to get your head around the pretty rudimentary psychology that's at work here, everything, rather quickly, starts slotting into place. You see, what's happening here is this.

'What this left-field, labyrinthine approach strategy does is it throws completely offline the woman's primary response to encountering a pick-up artist in a bar, namely, caution and circumspection. And so as she's desperately trying to get her head around the terms and conditions of this crazy, complicated deal, in slips the compliment sub-radar, ducking unseen beneath the razor wire of her consciousness and immersing itself undetected in the emotional, reward centre of her brain.

'The result? When she's come round from her micro-hypnotic trance – a residual feeling of wellbeing. And she's a bit more likely to take you up on your offer of a drink!'

There's still no sign of our bags so I get out my laptop and give Andy a first-hand demonstration of what I'm talking about – the power of incongruity to throw a spanner in the works of our usually articulate thought processes.

'Ah, no,' he mutters. 'You're not going into white-coat mode, are you?'

'Sssh!' I hiss, holding my finger up to my lips. 'This is a lab, mate. No talking!'

I locate the file I'm looking for and open it. The display opposite pops up on the screen in front of us.

'In front of you is a series of squares,' I intone. 'In each of these squares you'll notice a word appears in a different location. Going from top left to bottom right along each row, I want you to say out loud, as quickly as you can, which position each word appears in, OK? It's either left, right, up, or down.'

Andy nods.

'So, just to be clear, you don't *read* the word, you just *state its position*. Got it?'

He nods again. 'Yes, doctor.'
'Right, let's go . . .'

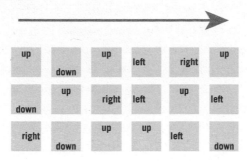

Andy rattles through the list.

Twelve seconds.

'How was that?' I ask.

'Piece of piss,' he says.

I take back the laptop, turn it towards me and hit the space bar. Another display flashes up on the screen.

'OK,' I say, handing it back to him. 'Now you've got the hang of it I want you to do exactly the same thing again for this next lot of words, OK? Remember, don't read them, just tell me where they appear in the boxes. With me?'

'Sorted,' says Andy.

And off he goes again.

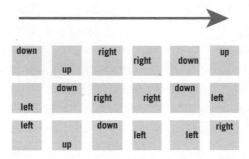

Seventeen seconds later it's a different story.

'Fucking hell!' he goes. 'Feels like I've been on the piss for a couple of days! Weird! What's going on there, then?'

I laugh.

'Let me tell you something, mate,' I say. 'You've got no idea how well you just did on that test! Most people screw this second list up big time – it can take some of them over a minute longer. In fact, some of them can't even finish it! A five-second difference is pretty much next to nothing. But exactly what I'd expect of someone like you.'

'What do you mean: someone like me?' asks Andy.

'A psychopath,' I say. 'It's all about focus. You see, the reason for the time lag – as you're now only too well aware – is that on the second list the *conscious* instruction to *state the position* of the words crosses swords with the *unconscious* expectation of simply *reading* them: a battle made much worse because of the INCONGRUITY between the words and their positions. All of a sudden, what you are *expecting* and what you actually *experience* don't match up – and your brain gets tied up in knots.

'But this – what we call – *interference effect* between two competing urges, the natural instinct to say the words versus the instruction I gave you *not* to say them and to instead state their position, doesn't just apply to reading. It happens pretty much everywhere. Whenever, for instance, we find ourselves in unfamiliar surroundings. Or, as with the chat-up line, are surprised by the unexpected.

'For a split second or two, our brain switches off from the immediate situation – does a double-take – and concentrates instead on whether it's got its facts right. Our brain, in other words, *blinks*.

'Now, this change of gear may last only a matter of milliseconds but even such a brief departure as this from the issue in question makes a huge difference. First, it sparks what is known in the trade as a *cognitive reframing* of whatever is going on. It inserts a minuscule degree of separation between us and our immediate reaction – a psychological local anaesthetic, if you like – that invites us to re-evaluate whatever it is that we're looking at.

'Secondly, it creates an infinitesimally short time window of cognitive confusion through which any incoming information – such as compliments, for example – can slip, unchecked and unopposed, into the deepest recesses of our brains.'

'Bit like a psychological stun grenade then?' says Andy.

'Yes,' I say. 'Exactly.'

He nods. 'So this interference effect you were talking about between expectation and reality,' he says, 'do you get it in airports?'

'Happens everywhere, mate,' I say.

'Thought so,' he sneers. 'Because all the time we've been standing here waiting for our bags and jabbering on about bloody chat-up lines, they've been sitting over there by that pillar!'

CONFIDENCE

'Queen Street,' says Andy in a broad Belfast accent.

We hand the taxi driver our luggage and he sticks it in the boot.

'Been anywhere nice?' he asks.

'Kandahar,' says Andy. 'Makes a change to get away for a few days' peace and quiet.'

We exchange glances.

'How's business?'

The role of confidence in the influence process is fairly self-evident from the eponymous label 'confidence artist'. In fact, one of the con men I spent some time with and interviewed summed it up rather succinctly.

'Whoever heard of a confidence man who wasn't confident?' he asked.

Which, when you think about it, is a pretty good question. But in everyday life, the part played by confidence in persuasion is a little more subtle, perhaps, than first it might appear.

Sure, on the one hand it's important that you as a persuader make the recipients of your influence – the person or people you are trying to persuade – feel confident in YOU.

In other words, that you establish CREDIBILITY.*

But on the other hand it's equally important that you as a persuader make the people you are persuading feel confident in THEMSELVES; feel confident that they are as much a part of the influence process as you are; feel confident that they are making up their minds of their own volition.

Because – as every parent knows! – the more a person feels pressurized or bullied or coerced into making up their mind, the more resistance that you as a persuader are going to have to overcome.

Credibility

Let's park the CONTROL aspect of confidence up to one side for a moment and deal with the CREDIBILITY side of things.

Now the story we're going to tell next doesn't exactly show our emotional intelligence skills in the best of lights. But it's such a brilliant example of the transformative power of raw confidence that it's very difficult to leave it out. (Though, we do have to admit, we did think about it!)

One sunny afternoon in the Cotswolds a couple of years ago, Andy and I and our immeasurably superior other halves decided to have a picnic in the countryside. After hiking across the fields for a couple of hours, we entered a belt of woodland in the middle of which was a beautifully manicured green. There was a pond in the middle of the green, and a bench. And sitting on the bench having their own little picnic were a nice young couple with a baby.

'That looks a good spot,' Andy pronounces cheerily. 'And here, if we squeeze through this gap in the fence, we can cut straight through.'

All four of us clamber through the gap in the fence and lope on to the green. As we pass them, the couple on the bench look up at us and nod.

---

*This, incidentally, is why medical experts wear white coats when being interviewed on telly and why business analysts appear against a backdrop of share indices and computer monitors.

We nod back.

We shake out our blanket, open up our basket, and spend the next three-quarters of an hour munching cucumber sandwiches in the glorious Oxfordshire sunshine. We peer into the little ornamental stream that flows through the miniature rockery. We examine the flowers. And my wife, as an afterthought, even picks a few to take with her.

'Fantastic!' pronounces Andy, as he fires up the gas-powered BBQ. 'I'm going to get some of that chicken.'

When, eventually, we decide to make a move, the couple on the bench call us over.

'Excuse me,' says the woman rather tentatively. 'I don't wish to be rude but, erm, would you mind telling me how you got in here?'

'*In* here?' says Andy. 'In *where?*'

I take over.

'Sure,' I say, gesticulating airily towards the woods. 'Same way you did, I guess. The gap in the fence?'

The man and the woman glance at each other nervously. Then the woman puts down her salad bowl and quietly scoops up the baby.

'Er, no,' says the man. 'You see, actually, this is our garden.'

Very slowly, as if we've just walked in on an Al-Qaeda cell, Andy and I put down our picnic paraphernalia and turn around. Briefly, through some trees at the back, I suddenly get a glimpse of a house.

And a car.

And a washing-line full of clothes.

'We didn't want to say anything,' the man continues, 'because we thought you were the owners of the, er,' he smiles and nods smugly behind him, 'holiday cottage?'

'I've seen it!' says Andy.

'We've just moved here,' says the woman, 'and in the bumpf that went with the house it said that the owners sometimes drop in to, you know, check the place over once in a while.'

'Right,' I say. 'Well, nice to have met you. We'd, er, better be making a move.'

THE GOOD PSYCHOPATH'S GUIDE TO SUCCESS

The four of us back away into the undergrowth, grinning idiotically. We wave when we get to the fence.

'Nice spot for a picnic!' Andy's missus mutters under her breath as her T-shirt snags on a branch.

It's a terrible thing to walk in absolute silence!

Control

Now there's no doubt whatsoever in mine and Andy's minds that we, well . . . got the rub of the green that day! It was raw, *misplaced* confidence that earned us that picturesque picnic spot. But as we were saying, there's more to confidence – even misplaced confidence – than just establishing credibility.

Sure, on the one hand it's important that you as a persuader make the recipients of your influence – the person or people that you are trying to persuade – feel confident in YOU.

But on the other hand it's equally, if not even more important that you as a persuader make the people you are persuading feel confident in THEMSELVES; that you push, as far as you possibly can, the *illusion* that they are as much a part of the influence process as you are; that they are making up their minds of their own free will.

Because, folks, as Andy rightly points out: 'The best way of getting someone onside is to convince them, as soon as you possibly can, that there *are* no sides!'

'There's a great story about Winston Churchill which demonstrates exactly that,' I tell him, as the taxi pulls up outside our hotel.

One evening, at the end of a lavish party for Commonwealth dignitaries in London, Churchill spots a fellow guest about to steal a priceless silver salt-cellar from the table.

Now, caught between the desire on the one hand to avoid an undignified contretemps and the equal and opposite desire on the other hand not to let the bounder get away with it, what is Churchill to do?

Well, what he does is this.

He picks up the matching silver pepper pot, puts it inside his own coat pocket, wanders over to his 'partner in crime', takes it out, sets it down on the table in front of them, and whispers conspiratorially in his ear:

'I think they've seen us. We'd better put them back . . .'

'Problem resolved simply, elegantly and without any further ado.'

'Class!' says Andy, appreciatively.

'In fact, this is just one of the talents,' I continue, 'if you can really call it a talent, that the world's top con artists have over the rest of us. They are brilliant exponents of the art of getting us to *think* that we're making up our own minds when in reality they are there behind the scenes pulling the decision-making strings like genius psychological puppet masters.'

One of the con men I spent some time with and interviewed even had a term for it. He called it the 'Hot-In-Here' effect.

Think about it. There are two ways in which you can get some-one to open a window. You can either ask them straight: 'Would you mind opening the window?' A direct request.

Or you can go the indirect route and say something like this: 'Phew! Hot in here, isn't it?'

Now, nine times out of ten in this latter scenario whoever it is will get up and open the window – BELIEVING IT TO BE THEIR OWN IDEA.

And that is where things start to get dangerous. Because the research shows that as soon as we do something once for someone VOLUNTARILY – and the key word here is VOLUNTARILY – we are way more likely to acquiesce to future requests. We slip secretly and unknowingly into their power.

'Exactly the same principle of mind control works in magic,' I tell Andy, 'through the application of the technique I showed you with the coins that time: "forced choice".

'And it's probably no coincidence that one of the con men I hung out with was, in a previous incarnation, a rather accomplished stage magician. Tell you what, after you've settled up with Jeeves here, I'll show you!'

While Andy and the driver exchange tips about the quickest way of getting from the airport to Belfast city centre, I fire up the laptop again. When their heart-to-heart has concluded, I call them both over.

'Right,' I say, 'Andy, the first thing I want *you* to do is to think of an *odd* number between one and ten. Don't tell me what it is, just keep it in your head. OK?'

Andy nods.

'And what I want *you* to think of,' I say to the taxi driver, 'is an *even* number between one and ten. You got it?'

He nods too.

'OK,' I say. 'What's going to happen now is this. On the computer screen in front of us here a list of words is going to appear one by one and your task is to remember the word or pair of words that goes with the number that you've got in your head. You with me?'

They both nod.

'OK,' I say. 'Let's start . . .'

I press the space bar and the following list appears item by item on the screen. It's funny seeing the two of them there hunched over the computer on the bonnet of the cab. Usually I do this in a bright, warm lab in Oxford. Not a blustery hotel car park in the middle of Belfast.

1.   Precious metal
2.   Wool
3.   Cutlery
4.   Golden colour
5.   Highly polished
6.   Ball
7.   Sharp
8.   Cat's toy
9.   Kitchen utensil
10. Round

'Good,' I say, when the words finish flashing and the screen goes blank. 'Both of you should now have a word or phrase in your head. Right?'

'Yep,' they both say.

'Great,' I say. 'So what I'm going to do now is I'm going to throw another list of phrases at you one by one and this time your task is to remember the phrase that you think goes best with the one you've got in your head at the moment. Happy with that?'

They both mumble something and I press the space bar again. More flickering and flashing:

Blue felt-tip pen
Penny postage stamp
Carving knife
Yellow ball of yarn
Original oil painting
Old felt hat
South Sea island
Western stage coach
Antique clock
China coffee cup

'Right,' I say, when the list phases out. 'Have you both now got a phrase in your head?'

They look first at each other and then at me.

'Yes,' they nod.

'OK,' I say. 'With the aid of my fiendish mindreading powers I am now going to demonstrate to you that, although you may believe yourselves to be in control of your own thought processes, they can at times be manipulated by superior psychological powers. In other words, on this occasion—'

'Get on with it!' raps Andy. 'It's starting to fucking rain!'

'Er, sorry,' I say. 'OK, Andy – you're now thinking of a CARVING KNIFE. And you –' I turn to the taxi driver – 'are thinking of a YELLOW BALL OF YARN.'

'For Christ's sake,' says Andy. 'I've fucking had enough of this!'

He slings his bag over his shoulder and starts marching across the car park to the hotel. I close up the laptop, chuck it into mine, and follow him.

'Next time go by Nutt's Corner not the Antrim Road!' he yells back at the taxi driver. 'You might get a tip.'

We check in, freshen up, and twenty minutes later meet back downstairs in the bar.

'You know,' says Andy, 'I didn't mention it earlier for obvious reasons but over here in the old days confidence was very much the name of the game. When you're working undercover you've got to have the confidence to convince people you are who you say you are and not who they think you might be. When I was in Derry during the Troubles my job was to gather information about terrorist Active Service Units or ASUs: their weapons, hides and known associates – that sort of thing – so we could pre-empt attacks, make arrests, and save lives.

'It took about six months before I felt well and truly bedded in. Mind you, by that time I was a local. I didn't have a shave until Friday night. I wore market jeans and cheap trainers. And I did simple, silly things like always crossing the road where a lollipop man or woman was standing.

'I was after continuity – you know, a smile, a nod, sometimes a hello, it didn't matter which. What I wanted was human contact, some normal and everyday happening that people would see. I needed to be moving about the city like a local and being the Grey Man I was telling you about earlier, someone who doesn't warrant a second look.

'I mean, the reason people like me were "asked" to join this undercover group in the first place was because we grew up in places like Peckham – and an inner city is an inner city wherever you are. We'd feel at home in that kind of environment. I'll give you an example. The Bogside Estate in Derry was, and still is, a hard Republican area. So as an outsider, to even have the confidence to walk in to begin with, you have to fill your head with a reason to be there.

'If you don't feel it in your head, you don't look as if you feel it physically. And that's when the people around you start to sense that something is wrong.

'It's almost like method acting – so much so that, after a while, I genuinely started to believe the reasons I came up with myself. I used to pretend I was going to see a mate, or sometimes, for no particular reason, a brother-in-law. The real world didn't have a clue who I was. And that's what you've got to hang on to. They wouldn't be thinking: "Ah, look – there goes a Special Forces undercover operator."

'They'd just be thinking: "Who the fock's he? Has he come down from the Shantello or Creggan? Or has he come over from one of the Protestant estates the other side of the river and is going to try to kill someone?"

'If you feel confident it takes just seconds to bluff it and make them feel comfortable that you're one of them. A quick *What the fuck are you looking at?* would usually do the trick. Sometimes you didn't even have to open your mouth – a look was enough.

'That was the general attitude I liked to embody. One of the tribe. That way – as they used to say back home in Peckham – "Everyone's a winner!" *They* felt safe and *I* could then get on with whatever it was I was doing.'

We finish our drinks and head into the restaurant for a bite to eat.

'By the way,' Andy says as we sit down. 'That mindreading stunt you pulled earlier. How did you do it?'

'Haha! I knew you couldn't resist it. It's actually quite simple.

'The odd numbers on the first list – not that you would've noticed – were all on a shiny pointy theme: precious metal, cutlery, highly polished, sharp, kitchen utensil. So you picked one of *them*. But the even numbers followed another theme, a knitted cuddly one: wool, golden colour, ball, cat's toy, round. And the taxi driver picked one of *them*.

'Now, when we get to the second list – the one from which I asked you to select the phrase that best matched the first one you chose – well, there were only two that were really in with a shout: carving knife for you and yellow ball of yarn for him.

'None of the others – South Sea island, Western stage coach, antique clock – had any connection with either sharp and pointy *or* knitted and cuddly. So without realizing it both of you were *forced* into the choices you made – hence, as I said, the name of the technique: "forced choice".

'You might've been under the impression that you were making up your own mind. But, brilliant mentalist that I am, I was one step ahead of you all the time.'

Andy shakes his head.

'Go on,' I say. 'Admit it! Pretty cool, isn't it?'

He scratches his neck.

'It's not bad,' he says. 'For a geek.'

EMPATHY

It shouldn't come as too great a surprise that empathy makes up the final ingredient of SPICE.

The previous four ingredients – simplicity, perceived self-interest, incongruity and confidence – all roll a psychological red carpet out for the brain, make us feel good in some way. And empathy arguably does that more than all of the other four put together.

Empathy may be characterized from a variety of different perspectives. But here, we're going to carve the definition up three ways.

Empathy is the ability to:

- **READ** another person.
- **BOND** with another person.
- **SPEAK** another person's language.

Or, to use a communications analogy, empathy is the ability to tune into another person's emotional wavelength and to broadcast your message on that frequency as opposed to within a more general psychological bandwidth.

In a study conducted in a telephone call centre, for instance, sellers were given a choice of wearing left-ear or right-ear headsets. Results showed that sellers who chose left-ear headsets made more sales than those who chose right-ear headsets – possibly because they took a naturally more 'intuitive/emotional' approach to customers as opposed to a 'logical/intellectual' one.*

The more skilled you are at psychological comms the more successful you'll be at persuading people to do things.

'One of the lads in the Regiment had a bit of a problem with his temper,' Andy tells me, as we scoff down spaghetti bolognese. The kitchen has shut but luckily the chef managed to find some in a pot somewhere.

'It had gradually got worse, starting with smashing things up and fighting on nights out to kicking off at home – you know, slapping his wife about and that. It got to the point where he was on his final warning and something needed to be done. He'd seen some people, been to an anger-management class in town, and they'd suggested meditation. That didn't go down too well. I think he demolished the place when he heard that. Meditation was something that sandal-wearing lentil-eaters did. Not a rufty tufty SAS trooper.

'Then one day one of the other lads who was big into karate was talking to him in the pub and slipped into the conversation that at the higher levels of the martial arts it all becomes less physical; the emphasis is more on getting your body and mind in tune than it is on the technical side. He mentioned meditation.

'And that was it. All of a sudden meditation was something that fitted with who he was. It was on his wavelength. He started a course and got really into it. He never looked back after that.'

That lad in the pub was a clever guy. Who knows whether he

*In the same way that our eyes are connected to opposite hemispheres of the brain (right eye – left hemisphere / left eye – right hemisphere), hemispheric lateralization also occurs for auditory stimuli too. Traditional conceptions of hemispheric specialization suggest that the left hemisphere is logical, analytical and rational while the right hemisphere is intuitive, emotional and holistic.

knew what he was doing? Maybe he did, maybe he didn't. But what he managed to pull off in that conversation was a brilliant rebranding job on the whole meditation 'thing'.

By repackaging – or, to use the technical term, REFRAMING – it, he dragged meditation out of what we call his mate's LATI-TUDE OF REJECTION (the decision-making zone ruled by 'No!') and into his LATITUDE OF ACCEPTANCE (the decision-making zone ruled by 'Yes!').

And the light went from red to green.

LATITUDES OF REJECTION AND ACCEPTANCE

The art of branding, or framing, is a dark art indeed!

It's incredible how much more you can achieve with just a simple turn of phrase; how powerful your message can become by tuning your influence dials in to PERSONAL as opposed to GEN-ERAL frequencies.

The American florist Max Schling once ran a brilliant ad in the *New York Times*. The copy, composed entirely in shorthand, was ripped out by thousands of curious businessmen who inevitably went to their secretaries for a translation.

The ad (unbeknownst to the businessmen, of course) turned out to be addressed . . . yes, you've guessed it . . . to the secretaries *themselves* – asking them to put a bit of business Schling's way next time the boss wanted flowers for his wife!

And we've all got languages that we understand better than

others. Where Schling used shorthand, other skilled persuaders use metaphor. Imagine I was your boss and I wanted you to put in a couple of hours extra after work on an urgent presentation. Imagine that I also knew (good bosses always do their homework!) that you were training for the London Marathon.

If I transmitted my request on a GENERAL INFLUENCE FREQUENCY it might sound something like this:

I was wondering whether you could stay behind after work tonight for a couple of hours to help finish the presentation.

And my chances might be fifty-fifty.

However, if I transmitted my request on a PERSONAL INFLUENCE FREQUENCY it would come out a little different:

I know it's a tough part of the course right now but I was wondering whether you had the stamina to push through the wall and go the extra mile tonight to help finish the presentation.

And my chances would increase significantly.

The power of metaphor, as we saw in the previous chapter, isn't just confined to the act of persuading ourselves. It can also be harnessed to influence other people.

'You know, when you work undercover you use a lot of these kinds of skills,' says Andy, shovelling in the last of his spaghetti.

I look up from my own bowl and it's not a pretty sight. There's so much sauce on his face it looks like a very bad fake tan.

'I'll give you an example,' he says:

The Bogside I was telling you about earlier is a maze of two- and three-storey tenements interconnected by dark alleyways. Some alleys lead to other alleys. Some just come to a dead end. The architect, if there was one, must have been high on LSD and playing with Jenga blocks when he drew that place out.

But you know what? Some things never change. Just like

where I grew up in London, it had a Spar shop, kids running about with mothers shouting for them to get the fuck inside as it was tea time, and groups of blokes hanging about drinking, smoking and generally making too much noise.

The only real difference between a Derry estate and one in London was that in Derry these men were at war. There was no gangster-style, pretend-shooting hand gestures from these lads. They had explosives, machine guns and grenade launchers and could kill you for fucking real.

Anyway, one evening I found myself in the Bogside looking for some players who had just brought a couple of assault rifles on to the estate. The plan was for their snipers to take out a Brit army patrol later that night. Kids shouted and screamed as they chased a football through the puddles. Scabby dogs skulked in the doorways. The few street lights that still worked started to flicker on.

As I passed the Spar shop – an old freight container with a heavily padlocked door – the kids stopped playing football and stared. That wasn't unusual. Children as young as five or six got paid as dickers – to give an early warning signal of any potential problem that might be coming the estate's way.

It didn't bother me. Why should it? After all, I was going to see a mate, wasn't I? That's why I was there. I did my normal routine and stared them out.

Who the fuck are you looking at?

I had no idea what time it was. You don't wear a watch in case someone comes up and asks *you*. With an empty wrist, you can just shrug them off and keep moving.

Adults were looking at me now as well. They all knew the weapons were being moved into position, and in one or two kitchens faces were pressed up against the glass, trying to see through the condensation.

I looked right back and stared them out.

Who are you looking at? Get back to boiling your cabbage!

Anyway, by this stage a couple of male voices had piped

up behind me. But I wasn't turning back to look. Why should I? I just kept walking. If they challenged me, I'd front it out. My accent was just about passable in short bursts. But why *should* they challenge me? My mate lived on this estate and I'd been here many times before. So they could just fuck off.

There was no hesitation in my stride. I made sure of that. Like I said, I had every right to be there. I knew where I was going. I turned left down the next alley to see if they carried on following.

Shit, dead end!

There was no way I could now just turn back around and come out again. How natural would *that* look? I mean, if you knew where you were going you knew where you were going. You wouldn't just suddenly get it wrong.

The mumbling voices stopped at the mouth of the alley. Not surprisingly, the fuckers were checking me out. Everything in this part of the world that was unknown and moved was deemed a threat. The wall at the end of the passage was approaching fast and when I reached it I stopped. Surprise surprise, the ground was littered with dog shit, old Coke cans and a burnt mattress.

I could hear the voices still murmuring to each other behind me and it was easy enough to guess the conversation. 'What the fuck's he doing down there?' Then I could hear windows being opened for others to join in the chorus.

I unzipped my jeans and went to take a piss. But it wasn't happening. I started counting. How long does a piss take? It was all going on behind me but I couldn't exactly turn round to have a look, could I? If I did that, it really *would* kick off.

One thing was for certain. They weren't about to come down the dead end after me. Way too risky. If they did that they'd have no idea what would happen. But that didn't help me get over the anger I was feeling with myself. It's hard to explain unless you've been there, Kev. But it's all to do with fucking up and not having control.

Anyway, thirty seconds passed. I jumped up and down on the balls of my feet to get rid of any imaginary dribbles, zipped up and turned round. The guys had gone. It was weird. I walked to the end of the alley and it was like nothing had ever happened. The only people in sight were children on rusty old bikes.

I turned left to carry on with the job as kids threw cans at dogs and the cabbage cookers checked me out.

But now wasn't the time to fuck them off. Now was the time to smile at them, to be embarrassed for pissing under their kitchen windows. I mean it wasn't exactly nice, was it?

So that's what I did. I shrugged, gave them a sheepish grin, and went on my way.

And fuck me, wasn't one of the faces looking down at me the old lollipop guy from the Strabane road that I always gave a nod to when walking past!

So you know what, mate? You're right. At the end of the day, no matter where you come from, what you look like, or how much homework you do, you've got to have the ability to get on with people. To build up a bit of rapport. To fit in.

I mean, if you can't do *that* no one's going to tell you *anything*!

And you've also got to be able to read people; to gauge how they might be feeling, guess what they might be thinking.

The right word – or the right piss! – at the right time can potentially save hundreds of lives while the wrong word at the wrong time can potentially cost you your own.

At the end of the chapter Andy and I have put together some handy hints to help you build rapport in *all* aspects of your life – not just if you happen to be wandering around undercover somewhere on some inner-city housing estate.

But I'm intrigued by what he says about reading people – and before we crash out I fire up the laptop one last time and give him a little test.

It's the 'Reading the Mind in the Eyes Test' developed by the

Cambridge psychologist Simon Baron Cohen to assess how good we are at judging other people's mental states from limited information. The idea is to choose which emotion you think a person is expressing simply from looking at the eye region of their face.

If he's any good he'll get at least three out of five, I think, as I show him the pictures below:

Playful, comforting, irritated, bored

Aghast, fantasizing, impatient, alarmed

Terrified, amused, regretful, flirtatious

Content, apologetic, defiant, curious

Joking, insistent, amused, relaxed

He gets all five. (See page 245 to check.)

'I'm impressed!' I say. 'Want to do another five?'

He saunters off down the corridor to his room.

'I'd take a lesson out of Ali's book if I were you, mate,' he calls back over his shoulder. 'Quit while you're behind!'

GOOD PSYCHOPATH TIPS

HOW TO PUT A STRANGER AT EASE/BUILD INSTANT RAPPORT

1. Smile

Smiling is infectious. Researchers in Sweden presented volunteers with subliminal pictures of smiley and angry faces and monitored activity in their own facial muscles. Even though volunteers had no idea what they were looking at, the smiley faces stimulated the *zygomatic major* muscle (involved in smiling), and the angry faces the *corrugator supercilii* (which moves the eyebrows when frowning.)

2. Make eye contact

Every motorist knows they are more likely to be let into traffic if they make eye contact with an approaching driver than if they don't. Research shows that eye contact can account for as much as 55 per cent of information transmission in a given conversation – the rest being apportioned between 'nonverbal auditory' (e.g. intonation) at 38 per cent, and 'formal' verbal content at just 7 per cent.

3. Pay them a compliment

Compliments are like Viagra for the brain. Positive validation not only makes us feel good, it can also serve as a natural conversation starter. But make sure the compliment is genuine. Insincere flattery is as welcome as a turd in a swimming pool – and just as easy to spot.

4. Call them by their first name

Top salespeople and politicians have a genius for 'instant intimacy'. But asking a stranger's name, and then using it, can give any of us a head start. First names personalize an encounter, and make those we speak to feel valued. In fact, studies have shown that if you ask a person a favour they are more likely to oblige if you begin by using their name.

5. Lighten up

'I made myself homeless to sell this!' a *Big Issue* seller once told me. I bought a copy on the spot. Humour instantly disarms – which is why 'GSOH' appears in over 80 per cent of personal ads. You don't need to go into stand-up mode, but don't stand on formality either. A great way of building rapport is to loosen up.

6. Offer them a hot drink

Ever wondered why estate agents can't wait to put the kettle on? Thanks to a team of psychologists we now know the answer. Researchers in the US tricked volunteers into holding either a hot or a cold drink before rating how 'warm' or 'cold' a stranger was. Guess what? Those who held the hot drink rated the person as more caring and generous than those who held the cold drink.

7. Mirror

Researchers in the Netherlands asked students to give their opinions about a bunch of advertisements. Unbeknownst to the students, a member of the research team mimicked half of them while they spoke, roughly mirroring the posture and the position of their arms and legs, and taking care not to be too obvious. Minutes later the experimenter dropped six pens on the floor, making it look like an accident. Guess which students were *three times* more likely to help pick up the pens – you got it, the ones who'd been mimicked!

8. Touch

Studies have shown that waitresses who touch diners on the arm a couple of times during their meal earn considerably more tips than those who don't. Touch stimulates the production of the 'love' hormone oxytocin – important not just in forging romantic relationships but also friendship bonds. But don't overdo it. Too much touching is just plain creepy!

9. Find common ground

In the early 1970s, a group of researchers in the US approached students on a university campus and asked them for a dime to make a phone call. Some of the researchers looked like the students – they were dressed in hippy clothing and had long hair – while others dressed 'straight'. It turned out that the 'hippy' researchers had a 2 out of 3 strike rate whereas the 'straight' ones got lucky less than 50 per cent of the time. Appearances count. And the ones that count most are the ones most similar to our own. Why else do you think that guy who sold you the car the other week took such an interest in where you were from? Coincidence that his friend also happens to live there? And what about the guy in the electrical store who sold you that tumble-dryer? The one who got you talking about the football and who also supports West Ham . . . ?

How did you get on? Correct: playful, fantasizing, regretful, defiant, insistent

QUESTIONNAIRE
HOW GOOD ARE YOU AT PERSUASION?

Assign a rating to each of the following statements and then add up your total and check it with the scores on the next page.

		strongly disagree	disagree	agree	strongly agree
		0	**1**	**2**	**3**
1.	I am good at reading people and finding out what makes them tick.	○	○	○	○
2.	I have no trouble walking into a roomful of strangers and socializing.	○	○	○	○
3.	I have a knack for getting myself off the hook.	○	○	○	○
4.	I am good at negotiating bargains and discounts.	○	○	○	○
5.	I have no trouble seeing things from another person's perspective.	○	○	○	○
6.	People have said I have a powerful or magnetic aura.	○	○	○	○
7.	At a party or gathering I often find myself in the middle of a lot of different conversations.	○	○	○	○
8.	I would fancy my chances of talking a potential jumper off a ledge.	○	○	○	○
9.	I am good at telling jokes.	○	○	○	○
10.	People are putty in my hands.	○	○	○	○
11.	I am skilled at constructing powerful and cogent arguments when fighting my corner.	○	○	○	○

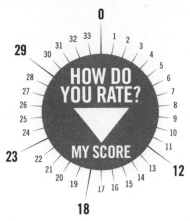

0–11 You couldn't sell fire to a caveman! But now you know the secret it's time to start practising.

12–17 You'd probably manage fire but would struggle with the warranty. Definite room for improvement.

18–22 You win some, you lose some. For every time you get it right, you get it wrong. You need to raise your game to join the pro ranks!

23–28 You definitely know your way around other people's brains. You have a pretty good hit rate for getting what you want – and it's more judgement than luck.

29–33 You say, 'Jump!' Others ask, 'How high?'

CHAPTER EIGHT

TAKE IT ON THE CHIN

What other people say about me
is none of my business.

Michael J. Fox

ON THE BALL

The road to the goalkeeper David James's house is a long and winding one and ends at the top of a hill in rural Hertfordshire. In the drive you're greeted by a life-size, multi-coloured, fibreglass bullock which looks like an Emo version of its corporate concrete cousins down the road in Milton Keynes.

'It went AWOL once,' David tells me, 'while I was away. Then there was a sighting of it along the M38. I went down there and picked it up. It's famous!'

We wander into the kitchen and David sticks the kettle on. I haven't seen him for six months, since he went to play on a primeval lump of rock called Iceland on the goal line of the Arctic Ocean.

He looks fit. As good as he did in his heyday when he was Liverpool – and England – number one.

'Get yourself a cheap white suit and you could've been on the Duran Duran yacht in 1981,' is his verdict on my new haircut.

'Just milk, thanks, David.'

I check out *his* hair which, over the years, has changed more times than a drag queen with multiple personality disorder. Unless I'm mistaken, there's a whiff of a quiff going on.

I've come with a film crew who are setting up in the living room. We're shooting a piece on psychopaths and David has agreed to be interviewed.

A few weeks ago, in his column in the *Guardian*, he wrote an eerily intriguing article based largely around my book. 'Psychopaths Haunt the Beautiful Game – And I Might Be One of Them' was the alluringly saturnine title, and in it he talked about the benefit of psychopathic personality traits in high-level, competitive sport.

Now I'm here to get the *real* story!

I'm not disappointed. As the morning unfolds I learn something rather interesting. Goalkeepers, within the footballing fraternity, are traditionally regarded as mad. They are the beautiful game's answer to drummers: on their own, at the back, the last line of defence.

But while there is no particular reason for drummers to be mad, there is, it would seem, for goalkeepers.

They have to spend long periods of the game 'up the other end' on their own, for instance, isolated from play and their teammates. But then, quite literally at the kick of a ball, must possess the ability to switch their long-distance focus back into immediate action mode (this, incidentally, as Andy points out, is similar to the ability required by Special Forces soldiers to rapidly shift from a 'hearts and minds' mindset to one of 'conflict' – and then back again – when working on the ground among native communities abroad).

They have to dive at the feet of oncoming strikers, actively placing themselves at risk of getting a shoeing. How many evolutionary caveats does *that* fly in the face of?

As Andy, once again, points out: 'The first thing you learn when you're taught the noble art of street-fighting in the Regiment is that under no circumstances should you go down. Hardly anyone can throw a decent punch but everyone can kick.'

And as if that isn't bad enough they have to hurl themselves through the air to impede the progress of a ballistic missile that, at the right feet, can travel at speeds of 60mph and upwards. (Bullets, Andy observes, travel considerably faster – but the general idea is *not* to impede their progress.)

But there is one other difference that marks goalkeepers out from everyone else on the pitch: their ability to tolerate insults.

Standing in goal for long periods of time in such close proximity to the crowd affords, as David puts it with characteristic understatement, ample opportunity for 'good-natured banter'.

'Yeah,' I say. 'I can imagine.'

'You get used to it,' he says, smiling ironically. 'You have to. If you can't handle having the piss taken out of you, then my advice is: don't become a goalkeeper. Yeah, you get all the usual stuff about your parentage, the way you look, who they want to shag. But at the end of the day you just have to think to yourself: if it wasn't me standing here they'd be dishing out exactly the same shit to some other fucker.

'The bloke up the other end – he's getting the same as you. It's nothing personal. As soon as you start thinking it is, you might as well hang up your gloves.

'You just take it on the chin. And some of it's actually quite funny. I remember an incident once with the Everton keeper Tim Howard, who's got Tourette's. As he ran up to take a goal kick the crowd started going "Ooooooooh", you know, in a kind of crescendo. Then, when he kicked it, they all shouted out: "Shit, fuck, cock, bastard, wanker!"

'Another time was with the Rangers keeper Andy Goram. When it came out that he had schizophrenia a chant went up: "There's only two Andy Gorams." As I say, you just have to let it wash over you. Don't give it a second thought. Because if your mind's on *that*, it's not on the game. You're literally not on the ball.'

ANYBODY HOME?

I mention this because Andy and I are sitting in the stands at Edgar Street watching Hereford United play a game that loosely resembles football.

It's painful to watch. The Bulls were doing all right for the first half hour and seemed to be on top. But then one of their players was on the receiving end of a badly mistimed tackle and, rather than let the referee deal with it, decided, for a crazy couple of seconds, to police the game himself. He squared up, lashed out and was lucky to stay on. It's been downhill ever since.

'I just can't understand it,' Andy mumbles through a bacon sandwich that's shipping even more fat than Hereford's chances of winning today. The pig that went into it must've been so dense it bent light. 'It's madness. It's probably the first time those two players have ever set eyes on each other. And at the end of the ninety minutes they'll probably never see each other again. They'll be on different buses heading in different directions.

'So why get involved? First of all, chances are it wasn't deliberate. And secondly, even if it was, why give him the satisfaction of letting him know that he's got to you? The slightest reaction and you're just rubber-stamping what he's done, showing him it's registered.

'If a boxer takes a right-hander in the ring the last thing he's going to do is signal to his opponent it's a good shot. Instead he grins at him. So why is this any different? Pick yourself up, smile, and get on with the game. That's got to be better than a bit of Morris dancing and telling him his mother's an old slapper or whatever. If you're on the pitch, expect to get singled out for a bit of treatment every now and again.'

Andy and David are both at what we might call the business end of the psychopathic spectrum.

But both are GOOD PSYCHOPATHS.

They've used the settings on their respective psychopath mixing desks to enhance not just their own talents and careers but also the lives of others. In that respect, their attitude to dealing with the shit life sometimes throws at us is fairly typical.

Whereas the rest of us might get hot under the collar if we're personally slighted, treated unfairly or have our dreams dashed, psychopaths possess a rather desirable capacity – if they wish to call on it* – just not to give a damn.

---

*BAD PSYCHOPATHS often tug on our emotional heartstrings by acting crestfallen or hard done by in order to manipulate us into feeling sorry for them, taking their side, and doing what they want. But the evidence, for the most part, is that these emotions are simply that: an act. BAD PSYCHOPATHS also use anger in a similarly instrumental fashion – to intimidate, as opposed to cajole us into line.

They have an irrepressible bounce-back-ability quality about them, a 'no quarter given, none taken' perspective on life which, yes, on the one hand can sometimes make them appear too laid-back for their own good, but which, on the other, can be hugely beneficial.

'I get to meet leaders from all walks of life, including politicians, business CEOs, and many in the entertainment business,' Andy tells me. 'The vast majority of them are great to work with: smart and open to new ideas. I guess that's why they're at the top of their game.

'But a few of them have definitely been blinkered and held pre-conceived ideas of who they thought I was, and what they thought I should or shouldn't be doing. One CEO of a company I was trying to do business with, speaking to his board referred to me as a "barrow boy" and told them that that was the reason he didn't want to do business with me. Did it bother me? Did it fuck!

'For a start, I've got no control over what anyone thinks of me. And besides, that kind of attitude can be turned to my advantage. It's easy to get under the wire of those kind of people and do what I need to do without them even realizing. Or better still, leave them thinking it was all their idea in the first place!'

Let's consider, for example, the following three scenarios common in everyday life:

- You're at a set of traffic lights and a guy pulls up next to you shaking his fist through his car window because he thinks you cut him up at the roundabout back there.
- You apply for promotion at work and think you deserve to get it. But your boss passes you over for someone you don't get on with.
- A good friend can't make your party because she's ill. But you later discover that she actually went to another party instead.

Typical reactions to these three situations might include the following:

- You wind your own window down and become embroiled in a heated argument with the guy in the other car.
- You seethe with inner resentment and, consciously or unconsciously, become passive-aggressive at work – undermining your newly promoted colleague by providing them with neither the moral nor technical support that they need in their new position.
- You cut your friend off – refusing to return her phone calls, emails or Facebook messages and bad-mouthing her behind her back.

Now, all three of these reactions are completely understand-able. The territorial instinct that we inherited from our distant evolutionary cousins doesn't just surface when it comes to matters of *physical* sovereignty – issues such as national borders, picket fences and tray tables, for instance. It also comes to the fore when we feel that our *psychological* territorial waters are being encroached upon.

'In fact,' I tell Andy, 'studies have shown that the same areas of our brains that light up when we feel *physical* pain, the dorsal anterior cingulate and the anterior insula, are also the two regions that light up when we feel *mental* pain – like when we're excluded from a group, for instance, or when we're dumped by our partners.

'So getting the elbow metaphorically can hurt just as much as getting it literally.'

But at the same time, one of the major evolutionary selling points of the modern human brain is its adaptability: the ability that it confers on us – via the swish new state-of-the-art thinking mall that we visited in Chapter Four called the prefrontal cortex – to pile up the sandbags of reason against ancient tsunamic surges of emotion.

So with that in mind let us ask you this:

If you could CHOOSE – coolly, calmly and collectedly – your response to the aforementioned scenarios, would you go for the three that were mentioned?

Or would you seek out some better alternatives?

- Would you, if you had the option, enter into a slanging match with the other driver and then screech off cursing, scalping your back tyres? Or would you look at him, smile and look away . . . and then when the lights go green, pull away slowly as if you hadn't even noticed him?
- Would you, if it were down to you, compromise both your own performance and that of your team by bearing a grudge at work? Or would you prefer to knuckle down, show your boss and your colleagues that you can take it on the chin, and think: 'Fuck it, better luck next time'?
- Would you, if you could make the decision freely, really cut your friend off? Or would you give her, perhaps, the benefit of the doubt – there might've been some guy at the other party that she'd been trying to hook up with for ages and she didn't want to offend you by turning your invitation down?

Now guess what? We've got some news for you! The choice, the option, the decision is TOTALLY up to you!

Don't believe us?

OK then, who *is* it up to?

The crazy motorist?

Your short-sighted boss?

Your misguided friend?

Are you really going to hand these people the keys to your feelings and allow them to let themselves in and crash out in the spare room whenever they happen to be passing? Or next time are you going to put up the 'No vacancies' sign?

Because every time you do one of the following:

- bear a grudge
- harbour resentment
- feel sorry for yourself

- take offence
- think someone's got it in for you
- sulk
- feel put out
- take something to heart
- try to get your own back
- assume the role of the victim
- blame other people for making you feel bad

. . . you're doing exactly that. You're renting out your emotions to tenants who are just going to trash them.

Not only that, but by letting people get under your skin, you're putting yourself at risk of losing deals, friends and all sorts of other opportunities. You are allowing other people to direct the motion picture of your life.

All you have to do is NOT TAKE IT PERSONALLY.

All you have to do is shout: CUT!

And it's easier done than said!

THE POWER OF CHOICE

The secret to putting up the 'No vacancies' sign is actually quite straightforward. It begins, as do most life-changing revelations, with a single, simple question.

Next time you find yourself in a potentially inflammatory situation don't go into it without a plan.

'Victorious warriors win first and then go to war, while defeated warriors go to war first and then seek to win,' says Andy, as we shuffle out of the football ground and contemplate what to do next. 'Sun Tzu – *The Art of War*.'

On today's showing, I reckon, someone should stick that up over the door of the Hereford United dressing room.

So, next time you're in a position where you think you're being given the shaft, go through the following routine:

1. Notice the fire hazard signs.
2. Feel the heat.
3. Take a step back.
4. Understand that if you stand too close you're going to feel hot.
5. Understand that if you stand too close *for too long* you're going to get *burned.*

And then: ask yourself this:

- **What would I do if I didn't take this personally?**
- **What would I do if I *didn't* feel the heat?**

The very act of asking this of yourself accomplishes two things:

1. It creates a momentary fire-break between yourself and the situation, which gives you time to THINK as well as FEEL.
2. It takes CONTROL of the situation away from the other protagonists and hands it over to YOU by giving you a CHOICE. You are either IN and open the door. Or you are OUT and the door is locked.

Simple as.
End of.
IN or OUT.
Having a choice, or BEING AWARE that you have a choice, makes all the difference you need.

'In the Regiment this is one of the fundamental techniques they teach you to resist torture and interrogation,' says Andy, as we follow the crowd south to where, he tells me, the old cattle market used to be – and which is soon to become Hereford's answer to Westfield. 'It doesn't matter how good a shot you are: if you don't have a target, you're not going to hit it!

'So the number-one priority when you're captured is to not let them break you *mentally*. They might be able to do whatever they want to you *physically*, you've got no control over that. But what you *do* have control over is what they do to your mind. Just like you say, you have a choice.'

'You can either let the bastards in or you can keep the bastards out?' I suggest.

'Well, yes,' says Andy. 'But if you're thinking of them as bastards you've already got the door on the latch. You think of them as players, like I was saying about Northern Ireland. You think of it as a game that both sides are trying to win. That way there's nothing personal.' He went on:

> During my time in Baghdad, the military interrogators who tortured me were very much of the same mind as me. One of them actually said to me as he took out a pair of pliers: 'I understand that it's your job not to tell us what we need to know. But it's my job to make you talk. So I will begin.'
>
> Fair enough. I was OK with that. And to be honest, playing stupid has always come very easily to me, so I went for that option and told them nothing!
>
> On the other hand, the secret police that I got handed on to later *did* piss me off. They weren't just getting on with their job. They were positively fucking enjoying it. But even there I had a little trick up my sleeve to make myself believe that I was winning – that I was still in control. I focused on the fact that they hadn't killed me yet.
>
> As far as I was concerned, if I was still breathing, I was still winning. Simple as that.
>
> During the interrogations themselves, of course, I didn't think of anything because I had no control over the situation except to say nothing. But I'd use my 'still breathing, still winning' mantra in my head during cell time. Especially when the guards popped their heads round the door to dish out the routine beatings.
>
> I'd focus on my mantra, curl up to minimize the damage, and just take it. It was pointless resisting because then even more of them would pile into the cell and join the party.

At the end of the beating if I was still breathing, I was still winning!

What made me feel even better was moving my arms and legs around to check that there was nothing broken. If I was breathing and could still crawl – that really *was* a great feeling. That wasn't winning. That was a whitewash!

But at the same time, however, I also knew that these same guards who were kicking the shit out of me might also turn into my saviours if I could manage to make a connection with them – if I could somehow get them to think of me as a human being rather than the bloke who'd been killing their mates. So whenever I was given food or water by any of them I would always attempt to make eye contact and thank him. Not in a begging way. But by trying to be as normal as possible.

I was winning!

I'd never complain about my injuries, either. But again, I always knew that if any of them ever asked me to show him my wounds I was making a connection.

Get in!

Of course, the connection thing was an uphill battle because they were constantly changing the guards to stop any relationship forming. But that didn't matter. Just gaining a bit of eye contact, however brief, was enough for me to know that I had some control over the situation. That I was still in the game.

THICKER SKIN = THICKER WALLET

Andy's mention of games and players reminds me of a study that was conducted several years ago by a team of researchers in Japan.

The team pitted a bunch of psychopaths and non-psychopaths against each other on something called the *ultimatum game* – a simple procedure designed to test how good we are when it comes to making decisions about money.

The game involves two players and works like this.

Player 1 is handed a sum of money and must decide how it should be split between themselves and Player 2.

Player 2 must then make up their mind whether or not to accept Player 1's decision.

If Player 2 is happy with Player 1's offer and decides to accept it, then the money is split accordingly.

But if – and this is where it starts to get interesting – Player 2 is *not* happy and rejects Player 1's deal then both players come away empty-handed. Neither of them gets anything.

Take a look at the diagram below you'll notice something rather obvious about the ultimatum game.

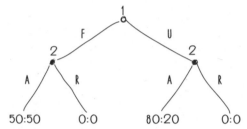

THE ULTIMATUM GAME (1 = PLAYER 1: 2 = PLAYER 2: F = FAIR: U = UNFAIR: A = ACCEPT: R = REJECT.)

Player 1 can either be a dealmaker or a ballbreaker.

On the one hand they can go 50:50.

Or on the other hand they can go 80:20.

'Of course, given the rules of the game,' I tell Andy, 'they'd be mad to go 80:20. Or even, for that matter, 70:30.'

Results show that when offers start approaching the latter kind of ballpark, most of them are kicked into touch. That, it would seem, is the point where it starts to get personal.

Except when you play with a psychopath!

Because the team from Japan who did exactly that discovered something rather interesting.

Not only did the psychopaths accept more unfair offers than their non-psychopathic counterparts – therefore ending the game with more money – but physiological measures of electrodermal activity (a standard index of stress based on subtle fluctuations in sweat rate) also revealed that, 'deep down', they were far less bothered by being shafted by their tight-fisted playing partners than were the non-psychopaths.

The psychopaths couldn't give a damn whether the offers proposed by their playing partners were fair or unfair.

And they couldn't give a damn how much their partners were making at their expense. All they were focused on was how much *they* were getting.

And it was a heck of a lot more than if they'd decided to take things personally.

THE CHEEK SHALL INHERIT THE MIRTH

'You know I might be wrong,' says Andy, as we turn left on the ring road and head along Newmarket Street (apparently, it didn't escape the notice of the Trivial Pursuit question masters that Hereford is the only city to have a ring road in the centre of town). 'I mean you're the Geek and all that, but what you've just described sounds similar to the experiment you were telling me about with the roulette table – you know, the one where people were given twenty quid but were more focused on what they stood to lose than what they stood to win. Any connection?

'And also that learning task where psychopaths did worse than normal people when mistakes were punished by electric shocks but better when they were given money for getting it right.

'Seems to me the bottom line here is that when there's something on offer psychopaths are just better at cutting through the crap and nailing it. And taking things personally, taking things to heart, is just more of the same. You see this on Selection, for instance, during the R to I [Resistance to Interrogation] phase.

'For Prone to Capture troops like the SAS, this part of the course isn't about getting beaten up to see if anyone caves in and gives out information – though you do get a bit of that of course, because, at the end of the day, you've got to be able to deal with it if the shit *does* hit the fan. It's more about the mental side of things.

'Yes, the training is harsh. Because it has to be. There's no getting away from that. But the funny thing is, some of the candidates do well on the physical side but then fall down when it comes to the verbal stuff. For instance, some guys cracked and lost the plot when a female interrogator told them they had a small cock. I had that—'

'What, a small cock?' I ask.

Andy smiles. 'No,' he continues, 'someone telling me I had one! But when it was my turn with the "bad guy" female I just thought: so what? Fuck it. Just let her crack on and get it out of her system. I mean, they're just words, aren't they? They don't mean anything. Keep your mouth shut and you'll be fine. Besides, when the snow's two foot deep and you're standing naked in an unheated concrete cell, everyone's got a small one!'

Andy's right about psychopaths being better able to nail it when the chips are down. We saw that in Chapter Five. And the connection he makes between the ultimatum game and the roulette table study is valid, too.

Psychopaths tend to overindulge on the positives and starve themselves of the negatives – even when the negatives involve personal affronts and misfortune. Now in some cases, of course, there's no disputing that things can get out of hand. The glass half-full/half-empty diet can be so out of kilter that what we might otherwise consider 'normal' emotional processing goes out the window completely.

In situations like these it's not so much that psychopaths don't feel sorry for themselves but more that they actually don't give a damn about themselves. Their mixing-desk dials have shot through the optimum thresholds and are firmly entrenched in the red.

As a case in point, take George Appel. In New York, in 1928, Appel was sentenced to death for the killing of a policeman.

His last words as he sat in the electric chair?

'Well, gentlemen, you are about to see a baked Appel.'

Admirable under the circumstances, perhaps.

But healthy? I think not.

On the other hand, however, you've got my father.

'As time went on,' I tell Andy, 'things didn't turn out too great for him. His last pitch on the market stall of life turned out to be a bit of a shaky one. Quite literally, as a matter of fact. He ended up with Parkinson's, and went from someone who could pack up a suitcase faster than Usain Bolt can run a hundred metres to someone who, ahem, couldn't even fill out his tax returns without help.

'But he still had his moments. One time, I remember accompanying him down to the local magistrates' court over the nonpayment of a bill. It was for Meals On Wheels. Anyway, my old man rolls up – literally – in a wheelchair, and immediately waives his right to legal representation, insisting, instead, on defending himself.

'"Are you sure that's wise, Mr Dutton," intones one of the magistrates from the bench. "A man in your condition?"

'My father looks straight at him. "Let me tell you something, mate," he says, shaking from head to toe. "I've been in more courts than you've had hot dinners!"

'It brought the house down. Even the bloke from Meals On Wheels – who'd served a few hot dinners in his time – saw the funny side. He got off with paying in instalments.'

Andy laughs.

'Reminds me of this,' he says, pulling out his mobile and swiping through his email as we stand for an age waiting for the lights to change at Widemarsh Street. 'Talk about a brass neck! When we set up Force Select a few years back we interviewed for a couple of jobs. You know, admin, that kind of stuff. Anyway, we turned this guy down and then got this back from him. We couldn't believe it. When we read it we were pissing ourselves.'

Andy hands me the phone and I scroll through the message. After I've read it I can't believe it either!

Dear Sir,

Thank you for your message of May 30. After careful consideration I regret to inform you that I am unable to accept your refusal to offer me employment with your firm.

This year I have been particularly fortunate in receiving an unusually large number of rejection letters. I trust you understand that with such a varied and promising field of candidates it is impossible for me to accept all refusals.

Thus, despite Force Select's outstanding qualifications and previous experience in rejecting applicants, I find that your rejection does not meet with my needs at this time.

Therefore, I will be intending to begin employment with your firm in the second week of June, immediately following my final university exam.

I look forward to seeing you then.

Best of luck in rejecting future applicants.

Sincerely

'I hope you reconsidered,' I say, handing him back the phone.

'We did,' says Andy, reading it again and laughing. 'We offered him a job. Turned out to be a good lad. Ended up joining the army as it happens. He'll be a general one day!'

Moral of the story?

Don't take it personally. Because whatever it is might never even have been meant for you in the first place!

SNITCHCRAFT

We're standing outside Saxty's – a wine bar, restaurant and nightclub not far from the town centre. Andy looks at me.

'What do you reckon?' he says. 'Give it a go?'

I scope the place out. It seems OK but it's not pressing any buttons.

'No, mate,' I say. 'It doesn't really do it for me.'

Andy smiles.

'No, mate, me neither,' he says. 'Too loud. But back in the old days it did. Me and my mates used to spend far too much money and time in there during the weekends. With our pressed shirts, chunky watches and not a hair out of place we'd stand in a group with a bottle of Corona trying to look über cool for the women. By the end of the night, the shirt would have madras stains all over it and at least one of the chunky watches would've disappeared!'

We press on into downtown Hereford. We've lost a lot of the football tribe now but have picked up a new one: shoppers. It's just after five and the streetlights are clocking on – that twilighty Saturday changeover time when the shops are beginning to empty and the pubs are beginning to fill.

'You know,' says Andy as we hang a left on to Broad Street and then do a right on West Street, 'I bet it's going to come as a surprise to a lot of people that psychopaths are good at taking it on the chin. I mean, it didn't surprise me – I'm used to it. But I reckon a lot of people probably think that psychopaths do their nut if people have a go at them.

'And to be honest, I've had my moments. But, it's funny. I'm always in control. I mean, don't get me wrong. I've always been competitive, too – whether it's the army, or business, or even everyday life . . . silly things like auctions, not being late, not being last. *Definitely* not being last. I've always wanted to do the best I can – you know, bring the best out of myself – and to do that you've got to be on the lookout for opportunities.

'But, on the other hand, you've also got to be looking for people who've got their knives out for you; for times when others are trying to cash in at your expense. As the saying goes, a pat on the back can also be a recce for a stabbing.

'Nine times out of ten I get what I want and move on. It's nothing personal, just business. But on the odd occasion when somebody *does* beat me to the punch, I just cut away and move on. Again, I don't take it personally. It's just business. You're on the pitch – you have to expect the tackles to fly in occasionally.'

'I'm not sure how in control you were in that Porsche showroom, mate,' I say. 'I reckon that greaser behind the till knew exactly what he was doing.'

Andy laughs. 'Yeah, fair one!' he says.

But actually, he has a point. When most people think of psychopaths they think of deranged, knife-wielding maniacs who would obliterate a horse as soon as it threw them off. Not indomitable, means-to-an-end pragmatists who would dust themselves down and immediately get back in the saddle.

And yet it's true.

Sure, psychopaths – as we saw in Chapter Five – certainly know how to nail it when it matters. They're certainly not squeamish about putting the boot in when they have to. When they stand to gain something from it. And in that sense they *are* more competitive than the rest of us.

But they are also more resilient.

And when the boot, metaphorically, is on the other foot, they're also more likely – as Andy just explained – to put it down to experience.

'You ever heard of something called the Prisoner's Dilemma?' I ask him.

He shoots me a sideward glance. 'You taking the piss?' he says.

'Ooh,' I say. 'You looked quite mean there for a minute in the light of that teashop window.'

'Yeah, shame it's packed though,' he says, peering through the steamed-up glass. 'I was going to treat you to some scrambled eggs on toast.'

He shakes his head as he takes a step back and looks the place up and down.

'You know,' he says, 'back in the day this was where we all used to meet for breakfast on Saturday and Sunday mornings to compare madras stains from the night before. And hand back whoever's watch we'd nicked! All the sad fuckers who had nowhere else to go would come here too and load up on . . . scrambled eggs and toast.'

'Blimey, I feel honoured, mate,' I say.

As we double back on ourselves on to Broad Street, I explain to Andy what the Prisoner's Dilemma is – a test used by psychologists to see how ruthless and competitive we are. The ins and outs are summarized in the box opposite.

'It works like this,' I say. 'A copper picks up two armed robbers and takes them in for questioning. He interviews each of them separately. It turns out that he doesn't have enough evidence to press charges against them so he decides to see if he can get them to grass each other up.

'He tells each of the blaggers that, if they confess, their confession will be used to send their *partner* down for TEN years. But that they, on the other hand, will be allowed to walk. But – and here's the catch – he also tells them that he'll be offering the same deal *to their partner*.'

Andy stops in his tracks. He's quite interested in this one.

'What if both of them confess?' he asks. 'What happens then?'

'If both of them confess,' I reply, 'they both go down for FIVE years.'

'And if neither of them confesses?'

I smile.

'If neither of them confesses,' I say, 'they both get A YEAR for handling stolen goods.'

	YOUR PARTNER DOES NOT CONFESS	YOUR PARTNER CONFESSES
YOU DO NOT CONFESS	PARTNER GETS 1 YEAR YOU GET 1 YEAR	PARTNER GOES FREE YOU GET 10 YEARS
YOU CONFESS	PARTNER GETS 10 YEARS YOU GO FREE	PARTNER GETS 5 YEARS YOU GET 5 YEARS

THE PRISONER'S DILEMMA

Andy looks at me as if I'm mad.

'Well, that's easy,' he says. 'You confess.'

We start moving again.

'But hang on a minute,' I say. 'If your partner thinks the same way and also confesses you'll each go down for five years. Wouldn't it be best to keep your mouth shut and hope he does the same? Then you both just get a year.'

Andy shakes his head. 'Listen,' he says:

Forget about your partner. If you look at it purely from your own point of view you're always better off coughing.

Let's say your partner decides to keep his mouth shut, right? What are the options? You either go down for a year for doing the same thing or you fuck off by putting your hands up.

Now let's say your partner decides to open *his* mouth. It's the same story. If you decide to hold out you go down for a ten stretch. But if you spill the beans you get off with five.

To me, it's a no-brainer. Take the sentimentality out of it and do the maths and the logical thing to do is to confess. Every time.

As I say, you might even get off completely if the other bloke keeps his mouth shut. But at the same time the *worst* you can get is five years – compared to ten if you keep *your* mouth shut.

No, I'd prefer to be safe rather than sorry. Accept it's nothing at best, a five stretch at worst. And if the other bloke ends up getting ten because he hasn't worked it out, then that's his lookout. Tough shit.

ANYONE FOR GOLF?

Given the GOOD PSYCHOPATH that he is, Andy's appraisal of the situation doesn't surprise me at all.

In fact, when you substitute points for jail terms (getting off = maximum points, 10 years = minimum points etc.) and enact the Prisoner's Dilemma for real in the psychology lab – usually, two people play against each other a number of times and then the points are totted up at the end – his response profile is typical of what you find in psychopaths. Generally speaking, they are less fazed by the need to cooperate and 'play ball' than the rest of us.

But that's not all. Most of us, when we find ourselves on the receiving end of a 'confession', or indeed a string of confessions, tend to start confessing ourselves. We start to get our claws out: partly for reasons of self-preservation but partly out of spite. STRATEGY goes out of the window and PRIDE begins to take over.

In psychopaths this isn't the case.

Psychopaths are more likely than the rest of us to keep their eyes on the prize and *not* to take it personally – shrugging off hostile plays and sticking to a preconceived plan.

'You know, a couple of years ago a Swiss team pitted a bunch of criminal psychopaths – BAD psychopaths – against a bunch of top financial traders on the Prisoner's Dilemma,' I tell Andy. 'What do you reckon happened?'

'The psychopaths came out on top?' he says.

'Exactly,' I say. 'And you know why? Because the traders were way more egotistical and took way more risks. Unlike the psychopaths, they couldn't *control* their responses. Their approach was far more reactive and far less premeditated. And it ended up destroying them. Instead of being clinical and business-like and focusing on the bottom line, which was to maximize their *own* profits, the traders became consumed by the idea of simply getting more than their buddies.'

'Don't tell me,' says Andy. 'And they invested so much time and energy trying to shaft them that their own performance suffered as a result?'

'Got it in one,' I say. 'The traders took it personally while the psychopaths were strictly business.'

He shakes his head.

'You know, I was a board director of a company once where exactly that problem came up for real,' he says. 'The company was about to be sold – which was obviously great news for everyone – but some of the board members started to get sniffy about how much other directors would be getting relative to themselves. Instead of just concentrating on how much *they'd* be walking away with, they took the view that some of the other directors didn't deserve as much of the profit as they hadn't worked hard enough.

'It was crazy. I mean, it wasn't as if there was anything anyone could do about it. The profit allocations were fixed by the number of share holdings that each of us owned. But that didn't stop certain people honking about it and trying to find loopholes in the mandate.

'One thing was for certain, though. When everyone *was* eventually paid off, I know who enjoyed the cash more – the people who were happy with what they got! Money and ego – *not* a good combination!'

Of course, you don't need to be in the finance industry to grasp the moral of the story. The general guiding principle crops up in all walks of life:

- We become so intent on winning the argument, on proving the other person wrong and ourselves right, that we 'lose the plot' and end up saying a whole bunch of stuff we don't mean.
- Political parties get so caught up in dirty tricks campaigns against the opposition that they fail to woo voters with their own policies – and in many cases end up alienating them.
- On the football pitch, individual players get red-carded for senseless reprisals thereby decreasing their team's overall chances of victory.

In short: WE BECOME SO INTENT ON WINNING THAT WE FORGET WHAT IT IS WE WANT!

'I always remember listening to two kids arguing in a shop about which one should have the last bottle of Coke,' I tell Andy as we stop at an ATM so I can get some money out – a precautionary measure just in case he feels like pushing the boat out tonight and doing a side order of onion rings with the inevitable rock and chips. 'They couldn't agree to share it so in the end Mum pulled the plug and neither of them got it. Do you know what? It turned out that one of them wanted it because he was thirsty and the other one wanted it because he was collecting the tokens on the back!'

Andy laughs.

'Love it!' he says. 'And we never grow out of it, do we? If only they'd taken a step back and been less set on winning, both of them would have got what they wanted.'

I grab my cash and we head off towards the cathedral. It's beginning to drizzle and the ghostly golden tower looks like something you'd find on the Silk Road. But a few seconds later I notice that Andy is *still* laughing. Not a good sign, believe me.

'What?' I say, checking my wallet – my watch! – everything.

'Nothing,' he says. 'It's just funny, that's all, that we stopped to get cash back there.'

I nod. 'Well, if it's that bloody funny we can always go back and *you* can get some out.'

That just makes things worse.

'I was with a mate in his VW Golf one evening,' he says, when he's finally got a grip, 'and we saw a lad from D Squadron getting some money out from that ATM. To the right of him, hiding round the corner, were two guys in ski hoods, checking him out.

'We thought something serious might be about to go down as a week or so earlier there had been an attempt to kill another lad as he stood waiting for the school bus with his kids. We didn't want to take action immediately against the ski hoods because we wanted to catch them in the act. So we bided our time and waited at the junction.

'It was quite strange having to get ready to kill people in your home town, but there you go. Anyway, it turned out it was just two teenagers fucking about. They were waiting for some of their mates to come past before jumping them. Funny! They never knew how close they were to being cut in half by a Golf.'

FIRE IN THE MIND

Earlier in the chapter we touched on what we can do in these situations to help ourselves respond calmly, judiciously, and from a position of POWER and CONTROL as opposed to emotionally, irrationally, and from the midst of a psychological matrix that others are twiddling the dials of – how, from a practical point of view, we can be more like the psychopaths and less like the traders in our dealings and interactions with others.

Lesson Number One, if you recall from the fire analogy we used, is to take a step back, feel the build-up of heat, and ask yourself the following questions:

- **What would I do if I didn't take this personally?**
- **What would I do if I *didn't* feel the heat?**

Just the simple act of asking this makes a huge difference to how we handle pressurized and volatile encounters, allowing us a precious few seconds of prefrontal cortex time to RE-EVALUATE a potentially incendiary situation from a safe distance and then to re-enter the fray informed, and enlightened, and with a coherent plan of action.

As Andy points out: 'The advice of "counting to ten" hasn't been around for donkey's years for nothing.'

But asking the question is just the first step.

Once you've asked it, and have cleared the space for re-evaluation, you must then initiate the second step of . . . re-evaluation!

And you must do so quickly because time is extremely limited.

It might take only a split second or two for fire to take hold in the physical world, but that's nothing compared to how fast it can move across our brains. Just like real fire-fighters we have our work well and truly cut out. We have to cram, into a very brief time window, three separate judgement calls.

We have to ascertain:

- **The nature of the initial SPARK that caused the fire (what it was that someone said or did to us).**
- **The nature of the RAW MATERIAL that the fire is feeding off (our particular INTERPRETATION of what they said or did).**
- **The nature of the OXYGEN that is keeping the fire**

going (we don't want to lose face; we don't want to be
disrespected; we don't want the other person to 'get
the better of us' etc.).

Any fire, be it mental or physical, must possess all three of
these components – SPARK, RAW MATERIAL and OXYGEN – in
order to develop.

Snuff out any one of them and you make yourself fire-resistant!

LOSS ADJUSTMENT

As it is with fighting *external* fires, so it is with fighting *internal*
ones: the more practice and experience you get at it the better you
become. This requires building up a good working knowledge not
just of how to put fires out but also of how they start and what keeps
them going.

Prevention is better than cure – and when it comes to the kinds
of blazes that can take hold in our brains, the primary accelerant is
LOSS.

- **Loss of face**
- **Loss of esteem**
- **Loss of status**
- **Loss of respect**

If you recall from earlier in the chapter we learned that the
territorial instinct that we share with much of the rest of the animal
kingdom applies, in humans, just as much to PSYCHOLOGICAL
territory as it does to PHYSICAL territory.

Just as physical territory enhances, say, a wolf's or a seagull's
prestige, so psychological territory can enhance ours, and whenever
we feel that others have encroached upon this territory – upon our
rights, our privileges or upon aspects of 'who we are' – we react
exactly as a wolf or a seagull does when it notices another wolf or

seagull strutting across its 'patch'. We charge right over to it and attempt to shoo it away!

It's impossible for a wolf or a seagull not to take the presence of another wolf or seagull on its patch personally and it is difficult – though not impossible – for us not to do the same. When someone disses us, or insults us, or doesn't take us seriously, we can't help feeling that we're losing something; that they're taking something away from us; that they're invading some of our hard-earned, highly prized identity space.

We do as we do under strict instructions from our evolutionary past, not our cultural present, and our interpersonal behaviour forms as much of a trade mark of our species as does the development of complex language and bipedal locomotion. But the human brain is very different from the brain of a wolf or a seagull. And, as we have seen, the same apparatus that makes us vulnerable to psychological turf wars also enables us to not be drawn into them; to search instead for the diplomatic solution and to commit our troops elsewhere.

So to turn down the heat of territory violation, to exorcize the shadows of psychological loss, let's excavate, in turn, the three incendiary ingredients of fire outlined above . . . beginning with the initial cause, the spark.

THE SPARK

1. It's not you – it's them!

'There are two kinds of people in the world,' says Andy, as we swing right off Broad Street on to King Street. 'Those who are rude and those who aren't. And you know what?'

'What?' I say.

'Those who are rude can be split into two further categories: those who have an issue with you and those who don't.'

He's right (see diagram).

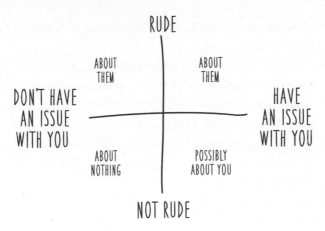

Now this may seem a tad elementary, perhaps. And it is! But when you break things down using this simple binary formula, you arrive at a conclusion that is not, on first inspection, as obvious as it might seem. Which is this:

If, for whatever reason, someone is insulting you, abusing you, or manipulating you, then the problem is not about YOU, it's about THEM.

It's about THEIR issues, not YOURS.

It's about THEIR problems, not YOURS.

It's about THEIR personality, not YOURS.

Of course, the fact that you *think* that it's all about YOU and not about THEM – *that's* about YOU!

As Eleanor Roosevelt once said, 'No one can make you feel inferior without your permission.'

But that's OK because there's something you can do about that. Next time someone says something or does something to you that you perceive as unfair, don't throw caution to the wind and go running into the flames. Instead stop, step back, and then calmly run through the following checklist of questions.

Like any new skill it takes time and discipline to begin with. But the more you get the hang of it, the easier and quicker it becomes, until in the end you'll be doing it automatically.

Ask yourself:

- Was the person acting DELIBERATELY? How do I know? Is there any way I can be sure?
- WHY do I believe that what they did was unfair? Would OTHER PEOPLE also think it was unfair?
- What was the other person's POINT OF VIEW? Is there any way I can find out?
- How would the other person JUSTIFY their actions?
- If I had been in the other person's shoes, how would *I* have handled the situation?
- What EVIDENCE do I have to back up the way that I'm thinking? How can I go about checking it?

The answers to these questions will enable you to assess what psychologists refer to as your ATTRIBUTIONAL STYLE and will allow you to check whether or not you are guilty of committing something called the FUNDAMENTAL ATTRIBUTION ERROR – a common mistake that we all make where we incorrectly attribute INTENT to the things others say or do to us.

Especially if they turn out to be BAD!

Your attributional style describes the way you think about what happens to you in life. Both negative and positive experiences may be evaluated along two psychological dimensions:

- *Locus of control* – whether you believe there to be an *internal* cause for something that happens (i.e. someone is personally responsible) or whether you believe the cause to be *external* (i.e. due to situational factors).*
- *Generality* – whether you view what happened as being just a one-off (*specific*), or the shape of things to come (*general*).

---

*To find out whether you're an 'innie' or an 'outie', why not complete our attributional style questionnaire at the end of the chapter?

Imagine, for example, that you've spent weeks preparing a pitch and have just had it kicked into touch. On the basis of these two dimensions, there are four different ways in which you can make sense of the knockback:

	INTERNAL	EXTERNAL
SPECIFIC	They didn't like my pitch this time	The committee were under instructions from the company board to recruit according to a certain spec this time
GENERAL	They have a problem with ME	From now on the committee are tied to inviting tenders from a particular pool of contractors

ATTRIBUTIONAL STYLE

Now if you're a pessimist, or depressed, or just plain old thin-skinned, then you're more likely to have a GENERAL/INTERNAL attributional style (bottom left box) for negative events like this – and are way more likely to take the rejection PERSONALLY.

On the other hand, however, the more healthy GOOD PSYCHOPATH approach is to go up a floor to the SPECIFIC/INTERNAL box – 'Better luck next time' – and MOVE ON.

Of course, this is not to rule out the possibility that EXTERNAL factors *were* involved in the decision. That, behind the scenes, the hands of the selection committee *were* tied. Without any concrete EVIDENCE you just don't know.

But in the absence of such evidence the best way of shifting your attributional style is to ruthlessly engage in questioning your ASSUMPTIONS – the team we put out when evidence isn't available! – to see if they stand up to scrutiny. And the more you do this, the more fiendish a self-interrogator you become, the more you'll discover that a lot of the players who are running about on the pitch should never have left the dressing room.

But it's not easy.

As Andy points out, this simple act actually requires all three of the core psychological factors necessary to get into the SAS:

It takes discipline.

It takes endurance.

And it takes courage.

And you know why?

Because it's much easier to blame YOUR failure on the failings of OTHER PEOPLE ('They've got it in for me!') than it is to TAKE RESPONSIBILITY for them YOURSELF ('My presentation wasn't good enough.').

Persevere, though, and it'll be worth it.

Walking away and smiling when life gives you the finger – and really *not* giving a damn – is a far better place to be than wasting your time and energy feeling sorry for yourself.

'I mean, your competitors don't feel sorry for you,' comments Andy. 'So why the fuck should YOU?'

2. Get off to a good start

The ever-increasing speed of modern life presents each of us with a simple equation. We either deal with *more* people and put on the airs and graces. Or we deal with *fewer* people and focus on the nuts and bolts.

Many people opt for the latter.

This is especially the case when it comes to email. So starting off your day by firing up your browser may not, if you're inclined to take things personally, be the best idea in the world.

Begin, instead, with something that makes you feel good – something that *affirms* who you are, makes you feel in control and empowers you.

'Work, for instance!' suggests Andy.

Starting each day with a solid foundation sets the tone for the rest of it. You might even become more productive!

THE RAW MATERIAL

3. Take it or leave it

'You know what, Kev?' says Andy as we dive into the Spread Eagle for a swift half. 'It's a basic fact of life that some people are going to love you and some people are going to hate you. But so what? There are some people out there who think even Mother Teresa was a twat. That's the law of averages and you're just going to have to deal with it.

'The quicker you get used to the idea that not everyone thinks the sun shines out of your arse – and that some people think that the stuff that *should* come out of your arse actually comes out of your mouth – the better.'

I agree, I tell him, as I buy the drinks. Again. And, what's more, it's no big deal. I mean, *you* think that way about *others*, don't you?

In fact, while we're on the subject you might also want to get your head around this. Much as you may harbour a secret – or not so secret – desire to control what other people think, you can't. People are free to think and say what they like. And if *you* don't like it – well, tough. That's just the way it is. There's nothing you can do about it.

On the other hand, however, what you *can* do something about is how you react and respond to those people. For a start, you can cut down on the time you spend with them. Or you can choose to put up the 'No vacancies' sign when they come knocking. What is it that they say on twitter? 'Do Not Feed The Trolls!'

Focus on what YOU can do instead of what the other person is doing or saying and you'll find them much easier to deal with.

'Don't give them the finger – that's a waste of a finger!' says Andy. 'Give them NOTHING.'

4. The world doesn't revolve around you

Some people, as we've just established, won't like you. But a lot more people might well like you but simply won't have TIME for you. Not as much as you might want anyway.

These days, everyone is auditioning for everyone else's attention and so the auditions are often kept short. So next time you think that someone has blanked you, cut you off, or not given you the window you reckon you deserve, remember: get your ATTRIBUTIONS in order.

It might not be down to THEM.

It might just be down to CIRCUMSTANCES.

They might, in fact, just be . . . busy!

5. Don't put all your eggs in one basket

'One of the Regiment lads once told me about something that happened to him in India a few years back,' Andy tells me as we fight our way to a quiet corner.

He's been walking in 100-degree heat for a couple of hours or so when he comes across an ice-cream salesman sitting by his cart at the side of a remote dirt track.

He isn't interested in ice cream, just something to drink – he's parched – so he goes up to him and asks for a bottle of water.

But the vendor tells him that he's just closed for lunch and won't be reopening for another hour.

'But I just want a bottle of water,' the lad goes.

The vendor wouldn't budge.

'Come back in an hour,' he says.

Well, anyway, there's nothing for it but to sit there by the side of the road, killing time. They're miles from anywhere. And so that's what he does.

He dosses down in the dust five or so metres away from the vendor and the two of them sit there like idiots, gawping at each other. Fifty-eight minutes later the lad finally gets up and tries his luck again. But the fucker still isn't having any of it and points to his watch indicating that there's still a couple of minutes left.

Anyway, bang on the hour the vendor gets to his feet and stands behind his cart. He's open! Understandably by this time the Regiment lad's doing his nut.

'Water!' he shouts, as the vendor peels open a lolly.

'Sorry,' replies the vendor. 'Sold out.'

When you see it happen on telly, it's funny. But when you spit out your drink for real, it isn't. 'You're joking!' I gasp, coughing and spluttering as if I've just been waterboarded with Guinness. 'That's got to be a wind-up, surely?'

Andy shakes his head.

'Nope,' he says. 'Straight up. He wasn't the kind of bloke to mess about.'

'Yeah,' I say. 'I bet that ice-cream man found that out!'

But actually, hard though it is to believe, Andy's story has more than a ring of truth to it. Sometimes, when our hands are tied, we have no choice but to pin our hopes on one throw of the dice. And that's fair enough.

But more often than not we *don't* . . . but choose to do so anyway.

Think about it. How many times have you said something like this to yourself? And not just to yourself but to anyone who'd listen.

- **If I can't get on to *that* course at *that* university, what's the point?**
- **It's either *that* job or *no* job.**
- **She's the *only one*!**
- **He's the *only one*!**

Reducing complex decisions to dualist, black-and-white choices when there is absolutely no reason to do so is something that we humans particularly excel at – and so it's little wonder that we get especially hot under the collar when our all-or-nothing efforts come to – nothing.

Most of the time, however, unlike Andy's mate and the Indian ice-cream wallah, you do have options.

Instead of applying to just the one university, you can apply to a bunch of them.

Instead of going for just the one job, you can go for several.

Instead of hitting on just the one girl/guy – well, there's plenty more fish in the sea.

By keeping your options open and strategically spreading your bets, you lower the stakes and turn down the emotional gas rings. When it's a zero-sum game and the zero ends up on *your* side of the net, it's hardly surprising you're going to have something to say about it!

6. Get things in perspective

Talking of bets, stakes and zero-sum games, a top international poker player once told me this:

If you're tired, hungry or can't afford to lose what you're bringing to the table, don't sit down in the first place.

Well, what goes for the poker table also goes for the negotiating table.

Sometimes it takes willpower to not take offence and, as we saw in Chapter Five, willpower is a muscle that, just like any other, needs energy to keep it going. If you haven't eaten, haven't slept or simply have to 'win' no matter what, then the risk of you interpreting objective, legitimate challenges as being personally motivated is significantly increased.

It's a rudimentary observation – but one that is backed by a considerable body of evidence within the field of conflict resolution.

The *dual-concern* model of negotiation, for instance, choreographs quite explicitly the dangers of over-commitment to one's own interests when gratuitously conjoined with imperious under-commitment to those of anyone else (see diagram).

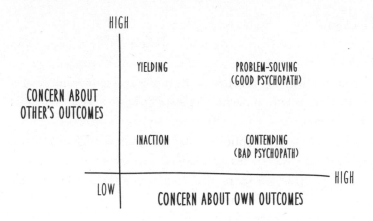

THE DUAL-CONCERN MODEL OF CONFLICT RESOLUTION

Look at the bottom right-hand corner of the quadrant – situations in which one person has a high regard for their *own* outcome but little regard for that of the other – and you'll notice the unchecked flames of naked self-interest devouring all in its path. That's where the BAD PSYCHOPATHS hang out.

Go up a floor, however, to where concern about one's own outcome is mirrored by that for the other, and you get an object lesson in FIRE-FIGHTING: in problem-solving, informed discussion and rational argument. That's where you'll find the GOOD PSYCHOPATHS like Andy.

You can either *lose* your head.

Or *use* your head.

The choice is YOURS.

But if we were sitting round the poker table, we know which one *we'd* go for.

7. Watch what you say

'My turn to tell you a story,' I say to Andy as we knock back our drinks and push our way to the door. We're off to the Orange Tree, a bit further down on King Street, for a steak. Unless hell's frozen over, it's a good job I went to the cashpoint.

I explain:

When I was writing *Flipnosis* a few years ago, I collected examples of what I call 'extreme persuasion'. You know, knife-edge situations where someone says something or does something that completely turns things round. This was one of them.

An 80-year-old woman has been admitted to hospital following a fall and is being looked after on the orthopaedics ward while the wheels of a residential care package are being set in motion.

It's a difficult time for her daughter and her son-in-law, who are there at the bedside with her, and the strain is beginning to tell. As the consultant checks the woman over during the course of his evening rounds, they begin to argue about the various different options available to them. Soon things start to get personal.

'Why do you insist on talking down to me all the time?' yells the son-in-law. 'Most of the time you treat me like a child. It's as if I can't think or do anything by myself any more. It's like I'm a five-year-old or something.'

At that moment, hostilities are interrupted by the sound of a pager alarm going off. It belongs to one of the juniors who regularly accompanies the consultant on his rounds.

Switching it off and perusing the display, the doctor turns to the bloke.

'Hey, mate, it's your mother,' he says, matter-of-factly. 'She wants to know what time you want your hot-water bottle putting in.'

This time it's Andy's turn to piss himself.

But again, outrageous though this story may be on one level, on another it conceals a hard, simple truth. The fact of the matter is this.

If you want to cut down on your chances of taking things personally, one way of doing it is to cut down on your chances of people saying things to you that are ACTUALLY *MEANT* TO BE TAKEN PERSONALLY!

And one way of doing *that* is to watch what *you* say to *them*.

Thankfully, in the example above, the bloke saw the funny side – as he was meant to – and the argument blew over. But if the junior doctor had been a little less socially skilled . . . he might've ended up needing one of the beds himself.

'One of the things I really find amazing out here in the real world,' says Andy, 'is when people start getting all sparked up about something, and point at you with their index finger to ram home their argument. Where I come from, that kind of gesture would immediately be seen as an attack that might very quickly escalate into violence. I mean, why else would somebody be pointing like that?

'Back in my Regiment days, you'd deal with someone like that immediately. I've even seen it happen between best mates. "You were getting lary, so I had to drop you." And the bloke on the receiving end would usually agree. "Fair one."

'That's why in my old world everything is done very calmly and very carefully. Fingers are never pointed at anyone. Unless of course, you really are trying to start a fight. Even if you really need to ram home a point to someone – a good old-fashioned military-style bollocking, for example – you still don't point. You use an open palm with all the fingers pressed together.

'Pencil necks [one of the nicer words the military use for civilians] don't usually "get" this because most of the time they fight with words. Responses are rarely physical. But if you're in a physical world, like the Regiment, what you say and how you say it are very important for your continuing good health.'

'Next round's on you, mate,' I say, jabbing him in the chest.

'Fine,' he says. 'But do that again and you'll be drinking it through a straw.'

THE OXYGEN

8. Get your story straight – with yourself

We all have our personal narratives: stories that we *tell* ourselves *about* ourselves to help us *like* ourselves. An insecure, controlling husband, for instance, might see himself as his wife's 'protector'. A devil-may-care philanderer might view his actions as 'living life to the full'. A basic fear of failure might be psychologically remastered into a 'being sensible' riff.

Whatever our narrative, the chances are that it's not entirely accurate.

And that also, if we're being completely honest with ourselves, we *know* it isn't accurate.

So when someone approaches us with an amendment to our script; when they say something or do something that happens to drill all the way down into the deep subterranean suspicions that we have about ourselves; when they threaten – with a gesture, a remark, or sometimes just a look – to snatch a corner of the doubt duvet away from us . . . we tend to cling on to it for dear life.

At times we take things personally because they're true!

I have a friend I've known since I was five whose parents only ever showed her conditional love as a child. They only ever showed her any real affection when she did something good or when she made them laugh. These days, my friend is married and has kids of her own. But in later life her dysfunctionally provisional upbringing has proved a double-edged sword. It's turned out to be both a blessing and a curse.

On the one hand, through years of dedicated practice, she's the life and soul of every party she goes to. She has a talent that borders on the supernatural for finding out what people want to hear and then giving it to them – and is equally adept at putting strangers at ease and getting them to open up.

On the other hand, however, her genius for instant rapport has a dark side. It disguises a need – a need that began way back in her childhood – to be everyone's 'special' friend; to be the person people can confide in when they can't trust anyone else; to be the person who can 'take the odd liberty or two' because friendship with her is 'like that'. It's 'on a different level'.

Which is fine most of the time because she *is* a very warm person. And fun to be around.

But not on occasions when the other person doesn't buy it. Not when they back off, for instance. Or see things a different way. Or if they *don't* share a confidence. That, unfortunately, is when the laughter turns to tears. That's when the fear, and the pain, and the loneliness of childhood all resurface and she feels abandoned again. The slightest rejection is magnified a thousand times. For reasons, alas, as sad as they are transparent.

It's not my friend as she is *today* that's being rejected but the shut-out little girl who still, even now, many years after their passing, wants Mum and Dad to simply tell her they love her.

If you can see a bit of yourself in my friend then you're not alone. The ghosts of childhood rattle around in all of us, tricking us and spooking us into saying things and doing things that we'd really rather not. We all have our 'buttons' – and people who like to push them. Sometimes deliberately. But often without even knowing.

So here's the deal.

If you want to start moving through life a little bit more smoothly; if you want to stop throwing stones at every dog that barks, as our old friend Churchill memorably put it, Step One is very simple: start doing your homework.

Become your own personal ghostbuster!

Find out what sad, tormented spooks are lurking long-forgotten in the secret childhood stairwells of *your* brain. Get to know what pushes *your* buttons.

On the one hand, like my friend, it may be when someone says something or does something that challenges your personal narrative. On the other it may be something more 'obvious' like your weight. Or your nose. Or being 'stupid'. Something you were bullied for at school . . .

Whatever it is, being aware of these buttons in the first place, knowing that these ghosts exist, makes it much easier to deal with them when they come up in conversation.

Did you know that the light we see from the Pole Star when we look up at the sky on a clear night is 680 years old? When it first set out on its cosmological journey to earth, we still had the Black Death to deal with. It's so far away that it's taken that long to get here.

Well, it's the same with a lot of our feelings.

They belong to a different time.

They are the light from stars that burned out long ago – in the formidably formative firmament of the playground.

9. Communicate

'So, Stevie Wonder is playing his first gig in Tokyo and the place is rammed,' I tell Andy, as we make our way into the Orange Tree.

'To break the ice he asks the audience if anyone would like him to play a request. A little old man jumps out of his seat in the first row and shouts at the top of his voice: "Play a jazz chord! Play a jazz chord!"

'Amazed that this little guy knows about the jazz influences in his long and varied career, Stevie starts to play an E minor scale and then goes into a difficult jazz melody for about 10 minutes.

'When he finishes the whole place erupts. But the little old man jumps up again and shouts: "No, no, play a jazz chord! Play a jazz chord!"

'Stevie's a bit pissed off by this. But being the professional that he is, he dives straight into a jazz improvisation around the B flat minor chord and tears the place apart. As before, the crowd goes wild. But when he's finished, the little old man jumps up again. "No, no. Play a jazz chord! Play a jazz chord!"

Well and truly hacked off that this little guy doesn't seem to appreciate his technical virtuosity, Stevie grabs the mike. "OK, smart arse," he shouts. "You get up here and do it!"

'The little old man climbs up on to the stage, takes hold of the mike and starts to sing . . . "A jazz chord to say I loved you . . ."'

Andy asks for the menus.

'The T-Bones are good,' he says.

I laugh.

Perfect timing.

One of the most common reasons why we take things to heart – and the main point of the joke! – is down to MISCOMMUNICA-TION. We misunderstand what another person is trying to say or do and we become frustrated and jump to conclusions.

So next time something sounds odd, uncalled for or just plain stupid, don't sit there ruminating over all the possible connotations and letting things stew in your head. Instead, seek clarification. Ask the other person, calmly and non-defensively, what they mean. Because the chances are they probably don't mean anything.

10. Don't become a victim of victimhood

How do you get a bunch of people who have never met each other before to dislike each other?

Simple.

Divide them into two arbitrary groups (the red group versus the blue group; the warriors versus the hawks . . . it doesn't matter what you call them) and give each group time to gel.

In no time at all, individuals will start to show favouritism towards members of their own group and antagonism towards those of the other group. So deeply hardwired is our need for affiliation that even these so-called MINIMAL GROUPS have the power to make us loyal.

These days, it goes without saying, with the rise of social networking sites, minimal groups have a habit of springing up all over the place – and our highly responsive group loyalty buttons are being pressed constantly. Often, the psychological glue holding such groups together is a grudge against, a disliking of or an antipathy towards a certain cause, individual or collective.

Sometimes, of course, these groups offer an invaluable support network for their members.

But sometimes they don't, and constitute little more than a professional bitching forum for those for whom victimhood is a convenient and lifelong vocation. (Indeed, it's a moot point whether the increased tendency in modern society to take things personally might in fact be related to the unprecedented recourse now offered to us by the internet to fashion an 'identity' out of our grievances.)

Bottom line?

If you want to *keep* taking things personally, join a *group* that takes them personally.

11. Give yourself a pat on the back

Take five minutes each day to remember that some people *do* like you, *do* have time for you and *are* on your side.

'Don't turn into a raging narcissist doing this, though,' as Andy points out.

We said five minutes not five hours.

12. Put yourself in the other person's position

A doctor and a lawyer are attending a cocktail party together when the doctor is approached by a man seeking advice about his ulcer. The doctor mumbles some general words of standard medical counsel, and then, when the man has gone, turns to the lawyer and says: 'You know what? I'm never quite sure how to handle situations like that where I'm asked for advice in public. Do you think it's OK to issue an invoice for one's services under such circumstances?'

The lawyer nods enthusiastically.

'Absolutely!' he says. 'I think it's perfectly OK.'

The next day, the doctor duly obliges and sends the man with the ulcer a bill.

And the lawyer sends one to the doctor.

'Yeah, yeah, I know,' says Andy, attempting to become the only man in the history of human achievement to pour water out of a bottle without first removing the cap, 'typical dodgy lawyer! What do you expect, right? But at least this one's better than your dodgy Stevie Wonder joke. That really *was* shit.'

Fair enough. I put my hands up to that. Not only that, but this little gag contains a fundamental truth about the way we deal with others – a truth that we discover as kids and never really ever stop learning.

Next time someone says something or does something to you that you regard as unfair, don't fly off the handle immediately. Instead, take a step back and ask yourself this:

- **Actually, are the actions of this other person justified?**
- **Would I not do exactly the same if I were in their position?**

Chances are you might!

Just because we don't happen to like something doesn't automatically mean that it's unfair. All it means is that we don't happen to like it.

SO WHAT?

'You know,' says Andy – cap now off, water safely poured – 'in diplomatic circles there's a technique called the "fatal hug". It's basically a way of taking out your enemies by being nice to them. I'll give you an example. Imagine if the Yanks went up to Kim Jong-Un in North Korea and said: "Let's forget all these sanctions. We can see the problem you have with us and we want to do something about it. So let's start again. Let's talk. Let's open an embassy in Pyongyang. Let's start importing some of your stuff and let's start selling you some of ours: Apple Macs, Big Macs . . ."

'He wouldn't know what the fuck had hit him! All these people queuing up round the block to get green cards stuffing their faces with McFlurries?'

Fiendish. Brutal. Brilliant.

You see, putting yourself in the other person's position has hidden advantages. Not only does it make it easier to see where they're coming from. It also allows you to set up diversions and roadblocks.

But in order to do either you need to see things through THEIR eyes, not your OWN.

You need to stand in their shoes – and *then* take it personally!

QUESTIONNAIRE
HOW THICK-SKINNED ARE YOU?

Assign a rating to each of the following statements, then add up your total and check it with the scores on the next page.

		strongly agree 0	agree 1	disagree 2	strongly disagree 3
1.	I bear grudges.	○	○	○	○
2.	I have a tendency to take things the wrong way.	○	○	○	○
3.	It matters a lot to me how others see me.	○	○	○	○
4.	If someone says something bad about me, I find it hard to get it out of my head.	○	○	○	○
5.	I have trouble seeing things from another person's point of view.	○	○	○	○
6.	I worry that other people are talking about me behind my back.	○	○	○	○
7.	I 'read into things' a lot.	○	○	○	○
8.	I get irritable if I don't get what I want.	○	○	○	○
9.	My friendships and relationships are often rocky or stormy.	○	○	○	○
10.	I often interpret accidental mishaps as deliberate.	○	○	○	○
11.	If my boss doesn't like a pitch or presentation that I have prepared he's making a judgement about me personally.	○	○	○	○

0–11 You're so thin-skinned you make Miley Cyrus look like she's made of kryptonite. We're guessing you probably didn't like that . . . ?

12–17 You're definitely a bit on the touchy side. Sometimes you don't just get the wrong end of the stick. You get the wrong stick.

18–22 You generally give people the benefit of the doubt but occasionally have your 'moments'. After all, enough is enough, right?

23–28 It takes a lot to push your buttons. You are pretty happy in your own skin and if other people have a problem with you, so what? It's *their* problem.

29–33 We could take a sledgehammer to your ego and it still wouldn't break. You are unoffendable!

QUESTIONNAIRE
ATTRIBUTIONAL STYLE TEST

The following ten statements refer to different ways of looking at life events. Indicate on the scales provided the extent to which you agree or disagree with each statement.

	strongly disagree 1	disagree 2	agree 3	strongly agree 4
1. When I perform well on a task at work or sail through an exam, it's mainly because it was easy.	○	○	○	○
2. If I fail an exam I can do better next time by studying harder.	○	○	○	○
3. 'Right place, right time' is the recipe for success.	○	○	○	○
4. Attending political rallies is usually ineffective: nobody takes much notice.	○	○	○	○
5. Intelligence is determined at birth – there's not much you can do about it.	○	○	○	○
6. I attribute my successes to my abilities rather than to chance.	○	○	○	○
7. The impression people form of you is down to them – you can't really change it.	○	○	○	○
8. If you're going to get sick, you're going to get sick – there's nothing much you can do about it.	○	○	○	○
9. You can't cheat destiny.	○	○	○	○
10. If your true love is out there they'll find you – it's written in the stars.	○	○	○	○

Scoring For items 2 and 6, reverse your score so that 1 = 4 and 2 = 3 etc. Then total your score for all ten items.

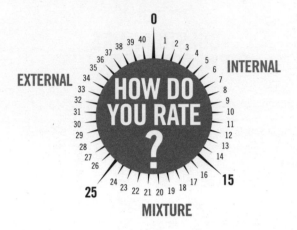

Scores of 15 or below generally indicate an INTERNAL attributional style – you take personal responsibility for your actions and believe that 'life is what you make it'.

Scores above 25 indicate an EXTERNAL attributional style – you believe in fate, chance and loaded dice.

Scores in the 15 to 25 range indicate a MIXTURE of both.

 CHAPTER NINE

LIVE IN THE MOMENT

Regret is unprofessional.

M

HANG ON A MINUTE

A convicted murderer is sentenced to death and the judge informs him that he will be sent to the gallows at noon one weekday of the following week.

There is, however, a catch.

The judge explains to the man that since his victim could not possibly have foreseen the fatal attack that killed him, his own punishment should mirror the fate of the deceased. It should, in other words, come as a total surprise to him. In fact, the judge concludes, he will not know the date of his execution until the hangman knocks on his cell door at noon of the appointed day.

The prisoner is taken down and, on returning to his cell, is told that he is allowed one visitor. Being rather despondent, he decides to summon his oldest friend, who is, as it happens, a philosopher. The philosopher listens to what his friend has to say and then, when he has finished, suddenly jumps to his feet.

'But you've got nothing to worry about!' he shouts, punching the air. 'You're in the clear! If what the judge has said is true then they cannot possibly execute you!'

The prisoner is confused to say the least.

'What do you mean?' he asks.

'Well,' explains the philosopher, 'it's simple. Let's take it in stages. They can't hang you on Friday, because if they haven't hung you by Thursday then it *has* to be Friday and that won't come as a surprise, will it?'

'Er, I guess not,' mumbles the prisoner.

'Which means,' continues the philosopher, 'that by the same logic they can't hang you on Thursday either. Think about it. If

Friday is already out of the question then if they haven't done you in by Wednesday night the execution *must* occur on Thursday. So once again, it won't come as a surprise.'

Enlightenment begins to dawn.

'Wait a minute,' ponders the prisoner. 'That means that they can't hang me on Wednesday either because—'

'That's right,' interjects the philosopher. 'If Thursday is already accounted for then if you're still alive and kicking on Tuesday night it won't be a surprise.'

The prisoner is ecstatic. He hugs the philosopher and the philosopher is escorted away.

'Drinks on me Friday night then!' the prisoner shouts after him.

'You got it!' replies the philosopher.

But the prisoner never makes it to the bar.

This paradox, the so-called 'hangman paradox', is an A-lister in philosophical circles. Its fiendish background reasoning ties logic up in knots. In psychological circles, in contrast, it's a virtual unknown – a curious omission since its devious prognostications conceal a profound and surprising truth about the world in which we live.

Stay in the present and just 'let life happen' – as opposed to ruminating over the past or sweating over the future – and you'll leave yourself much less open to the nasty little surprises that it is sometimes in the habit of throwing at us. In the case of the prisoner – death!

Check out these recent figures for depression and anxiety:

- In the UK, 1 in 4 people have been diagnosed with depression.
- In the UK, 15 per cent of people have taken time off work due to depression.
- The estimated cost of depression-related problems to UK businesses is around £1,000 per employee – approximately £26 billion per annum. The total cost to the UK economy is estimated at £105 billion a year.

- In the US, anxiety disorders affect 40 million adults aged 18 and over (18 per cent of the US population).
- According to a study commissioned by the Anxiety and Depression Association of America ('The Economic Burden of Anxiety Disorders'), anxiety disorders cost the US more than $42 billion a year, almost one-third of the country's $148 billion total mental health bill.

The bottom line is simple. Regret over the past or anxiety over the future doesn't do any of us any favours.* You can have all the plans, dreams and good intentions in the world. But if, for whatever reason, you don't have the confidence or the motivation to carry them out, then you may as well forget it.

You might, for example, have the drive to lead your company to greatness.

You might have the desire to ask your boss about that annual pay increase.

You might have a yearning to commit to a new relationship.

And if you do – all well and good!

BUT . . .

If you dread the idea of Steve Jobs-style public launches . . .

If the thought of entering your boss's office puts you in a cold sweat . . .

If you still have trust issues over a failed relationship . . .

. . . then, let's face it, you're going to have your work cut out for you.

When Dickens visited upon Scrooge the ghosts of the past, present and future in *A Christmas Carol*, he didn't do so by accident. The master storyteller and equally masterful psychologist chose,

---

*This is in no way to deny that in many cases depression and anxiety are illnesses that require professional intervention. What we are referring to here are sub-clinical levels of these illnesses. For more information on treatment for anxiety, depression and other mental health and behavioural conditions, visit the National Institute for Clinical Excellence (NICE) website: http://www.nice.org.uk/guidance/index.jsp?action=bytopic&o=7281.

entirely deliberately, a trio of spectres that scare the hell out of all of us.

Except that the middle of the three needn't scare us at all.

The 'ghost' of the present can actually be our friend.

THE CLOSING OF A LIFE

'What did you think of that email I sent you?' asks Andy, as we load up the boot of his car. 'Good, wasn't it?'

It's the crack of dawn and our precious cargo is body-boards. I've come down to Cornwall to get lessons from the 'world's leading expert'. But it's not who I was expecting. Or rather, it *is* who I was expecting . . . a barrow boy from Peckham with a Madness 'One Step Beyond' T-shirt, an 'I Love Minehead' pork-pie hat, and a pair of Hawaii Five-O shorts, who's firing up the 'Capri gear' as I speak.

Nag's Head later then, I think.

The email that Del – sorry, Andy – is referring to was indeed good.

In fact, it was *very* good.

It was an account by a New York taxi driver of a fare he picked up early one morning. There's not much more I can say about it really apart from just to show it to you. The sparse, beautiful, hauntingly workaday narrative simply speaks for itself.

> I arrived at the address and honked the horn. After waiting a few minutes I walked to the door and knocked.
>
> 'Just a minute,' answered a frail, elderly voice.
>
> I could hear something being dragged across the floor. After a long pause, the door opened. A small woman in her nineties stood before me. She was wearing a print dress and a pillbox hat with a veil pinned on it, like somebody out of a 1940s movie. By her side was a small nylon suitcase.
>
> The apartment looked as if no one had lived in it for years. All the furniture was covered with sheets. There were no clocks

on the walls, no knickknacks or utensils on the counters. In the corner was a cardboard box filled with photos and glassware.

'Would you carry my bag out to the car?' she said.

I took the suitcase to the cab, then returned to assist the woman. She took my arm and we walked slowly toward the curb. She kept thanking me for my kindness.

'It's nothing,' I told her. 'I just try to treat my passengers the way I would want my mother treated.'

'Oh, you're such a good boy,' she said.

When we got in the cab, she gave me an address and then asked: 'Could you drive through downtown?'

'It's not the shortest way,' I answered quickly.

'Oh, I don't mind,' she said. 'I'm in no hurry. I'm on my way to a hospice.'

I looked in the rear-view mirror. Her eyes were glistening.

'I don't have any family left,' she continued in a soft voice. 'The doctor says I don't have very long.'

I quietly reached over and shut off the meter.

'What route would you like me to take?' I asked.

For the next two hours, we drove through the city.

She showed me the building where she had once worked as an elevator operator.

We drove through the neighborhood where she and her husband had lived when they were newlyweds.

She had me pull up in front of a furniture warehouse that had once been a ballroom where she had gone dancing as a girl.

Sometimes she'd ask me to slow in front of a particular building or corner and would sit staring into the darkness, saying nothing.

As the first hint of sun was creasing the horizon, she suddenly said: 'I'm tired. Let's go now.'

We drove in silence to the address she had given me. It was a low building, like a small convalescent home, with a driveway that passed under a portico.

Two orderlies came out to the cab as soon as we pulled up. They were solicitous and intent, watching her every move. They must have been expecting her.

I opened the trunk and took the small suitcase to the door. The woman was already seated in a wheelchair.

'How much do I owe you?' she asked, reaching into her purse.

'Nothing,' I said.

'You have to make a living,' she answered.

'There are other passengers,' I responded.

Almost without thinking, I bent and gave her a hug. She held on to me tightly.

'You gave an old woman a little moment of joy,' she said. 'Thank you.'

I squeezed her hand, and then walked into the dim morning light.

Behind me, a door shut.

It was the sound of the closing of a life.

I didn't pick up any more passengers that shift. I drove aimlessly lost in thought. For the rest of that day, I could hardly talk. What if that woman had gotten an angry driver, or one who was impatient to end his shift? What if I had refused to take the run, or had honked once, then driven away?

On a quick review, I don't think that I have done anything more important in my life.

We're conditioned to think that our lives revolve around great moments.

But great moments often catch us unaware – beautifully wrapped in what others may consider a small one.

If ever there was an advert for why we should live in the present it is this – a moral, spiritual, psychological truth reduced to a quantum quintessence in a single, simple encounter.

As the taxi driver rightly points out, if he'd been in any way preoccupied that morning – angry about something that had happened to him the day before or anxious to end his shift and be doing something else – then the old woman's ride to the hospice would most certainly have turned out differently.

How lucky for her – and indeed for him – that his powers of social awareness rose to the occasion.

'But don't forget the old woman,' Andy says, as we jump in the car and rumble off into the sunrise. 'She played her part, too. She was the one who closed the door on the past. Nobody else. She might not have had much time left. But what she *did* have left she was ready to face down the barrel. Right here right now. That takes a lot of courage.'

It does, indeed.

To begin with.

But reading between the lines I got the impression that that old woman was a past master at it. Or should I say, a *present* master. And I think that as well as teaching that taxi driver a thing or two, there's a lot she could teach the rest of us.

PRESENT AND CORRECT

You hear quite a bit about the benefits of living in the moment these days. And with good reason. They *exist*!

I blame my old mate Mark Williams.

Several years ago now Mark, a professor of clinical psychology at Oxford University, brought out a book called *Mindfulness – A Practical Guide to Finding Peace in a Frantic World*, in which he advocated the practice of immersion in the present moment as a life-changing alternative to letting our thoughts run wild, to submerging ourselves in painful, stressful memories from the past or fretful, nerve-jangling anxiety over the future.

Starting with a fruity Buddhist bass line and then overlaying it with some classic riffs from the cognitive psychology archives, mindfulness teaches you to observe your thoughts and feelings as if they were monkeys in a forest swinging from tree to tree. Or traffic on a busy road. To notice them, yes. But not to get caught up in them, over-identify with them, or think that they are 'you'.

Mindfulness daubs a big yellow box junction in the heaving gridlocked downtown area of our brains into which only thoughts from the immediately streaming present are permitted. But there are some of us whose brains possess this box junction naturally – whose cognitive traffic-calming system was part of the original blueprint.

Psychopaths!

Coincidence that these guys, on the one hand, are renowned for their carpe diem attitude – their impermeability to regret and their imperviousness to consequence – yet on the other are conspicuously free from the depression and anxiety that haunt so many of the rest of us?

Mark Williams didn't seem to think so when I put it to him – but suggested that the difference between the psychopathic brain state and the mindful one might lie in what we 'do' with the present once we have it. Mindfulness teaches you to *savour* it, he pointed out. Whereas psychopaths tend to *devour* it.

'Yep,' says Andy, as we swoop into a deserted clifftop car park, 'fair one, that. I've always been more of a devourer than a savourer. But do you think it really matters? I mean, whether you devour it or savour it – it's got to be better than missing it altogether.'

THERE'S SOMETHING I WANT TO GET OFF MY CHEST

As we head out of the car park down a heather-flanked path to the beach, Andy tells me about how he used mindfulness – the naturally occurring variety! – to get through SAS selection.

'Every morning I woke up as if that day was the first day of Selection. If I had fucked up the day before, or even had a brilliant day, so what? There was no point worrying about yesterday's fuck-ups or crowing over its highpoints. That was history.

'During Selection, "today" was the most important day of my life. That was the only day I had any control over – and in the world

I was trying to become part of, you were only as good as your worst day anyway. So why even bother worrying about tomorrow?

'I never cared about what kind of task they were going to give us that day because I was going to get on and do it anyway. I could be running about on the Black Mountains with the world's heaviest Bergen on my back; in the jungle getting eaten alive by God knows what insect; or stuck in a classroom trying to get my head around some complicated maths formula or other which would tell me the exact amount of explosives I'd need to blow up a bridge.

'I treated every single day, for seven months, as if each one was the first day of Selection: a selection I believed I had the ability to pass, otherwise I wouldn't have volunteered for it in the first place. So . . . no need to think about *that* again!

'Even then, I knew that Selection was nothing compared to what it would be like once I was finally in a Sabre Squadron. But I'd worry about that once I'd made it. For now, all that mattered was passing. One day at a time.

'There were some excellent soldiers on that course. Some got through but there were others who just couldn't focus on what mattered. They spent so much time thinking about what had happened to them, and what might be about to happen to them, that they couldn't focus on what was actually happening to them right now.

'The secret is to think of every single day as just one revolution of a wheel, and to repeat that revolution day after day as if today's revolution is the only time that wheel is ever going to turn. In my book, that's the only way you ever get anywhere. Even now, I only think in three-hour blocks. It drives the missus mad! I might have a lunchtime presentation to do the next day and that evening she'll say: "Now, do you know what you're going to say tomorrow?" and I'll go: "No, I'll think about that in the morning. I'll get what I need to get done today and crack on with tomorrow, tomorrow."'

I got my own little taste of what Andy's talking about several years ago when we did a TV pilot together for a show on interrogation.

'Fucking hell, do you remember that?' he roars, as the path begins to narrow and I get a first glimpse of the sea – a long way down, I can't help noticing. 'I was pissing myself when that forklift jammed!'

'Yes,' I reply sarcastically. 'A barrel of laughs, wasn't it?'

The forklift to which Andy is referring just so happened to be carrying a pallet of reinforced concrete which it proceeded to lower, with meticulous and excruciating precision, to within a millimetre of my chest while I lay chained to the floor of a freezing, minging warehouse.

Of course, what I didn't know at the time was that the concrete wasn't concrete at all but fiendishly disguised polystyrene. And that the forklift hadn't jammed either: it was all part of an elaborate – and highly successful – ruse to get me to reveal the details of my 'mission'.

But when I ran this jolly little jape past a couple of BAD psychopaths whom I chatted to on a visit to Broadmoor, they, oddly enough, had a distinctly different take on it to mine. They couldn't, for the life of them, see what all the fuss was about.*

'But even if the mechanism had jammed,' one of them pointed out, 'that doesn't mean to say the rig's going to come crashing down on top of you, does it? It just means you're stuck there for a while. So what?'

The other one agreed.

'While you were lying under that lump of concrete, or rather, what you thought was concrete,' he said, 'nothing bad was really happening to you, was it? OK, a four-poster might've been more relaxing. But actually, if you'd been asleep, you'd really have been none the wiser, would you? Instead, what freaked you out was your imagination. Your brain was on fast-forward mode, whizzing and whirring through all the possible disasters that might unfold. But *didn't*.

'So the trick, whenever possible, is to stop your brain from running on ahead of you. The thing about fear, or the way I understand fear, I suppose – because, to be honest, I don't think I've ever really felt it – is that most of the time it's completely unwarranted anyway.

---

*Because of the restrictions regarding recording equipment, some degree of narrative licence has inevitably been employed in reporting this dialogue. However, the interaction has been reproduced as accurately as possible.

What is it they say? Ninety-nine per cent of the things people worry about never happen. So what's the point?

'I think the problem is that people spend so much time worrying about what might happen, what might go wrong, that they lose sight of the present. They completely overlook the fact that, actually, right now, everything's perfectly fine. You can see that quite clearly in your interrogation exercise . . . so why not just stay in the moment?'

THANK YOU PRESENT

We've been walking for a good quarter of an hour now and the path has gone rapidly downhill.

Not just in elevation but in condition.

If we were talking about a human being here it would've been put on a life-support machine five minutes ago. That was the point when the rough stony track went into a coma and entered a fugue state of narrow ledges and rocky leaps of faith. It's not for the faint-hearted.

Luckily, I'm not carrying anything. But Andy, with towels under his arm and body-boards and breakfast on his back, has pranced on ahead, jumping nonchalantly from ledge to ledge as if he was at Centre Parcs.

It's dawn. Cold, brand-new sunlight spills across the sea and fifty or so feet below us the soupy peppermint depths simmer and seethe in giant Jurassic saucepans of interleaving basalt.

I can't help thinking how beautiful it is – this raw, primeval, elemental sunrise.

And how nice it would be to live to see another one!

'You OK, mate?' I hear Andy shout from somewhere down below. 'Nearly there. One step at a time. Live in the moment!'

'Right,' I squeak, grappling my way around a sharp, jagged corner on my arse. 'I thought we were going surfing, not bloody rock-climbing.'

I hear Andy laugh and then the sound of footsteps continuing on down. But he's got a point. A lot of the positives you hear about living in the present concern general, more overarching benefits to health and wellbeing. Not concrete improvements in performance or decision-making.

Sure: lower stress levels, better immune functioning, lower blood pressure, higher self-esteem and a more 'laid-back' attitude to problems and negative feedback – all of which mindfulness can give you – undoubtedly, by their very nature, contribute to enhanced productivity (as we've seen in previous chapters).

But is there a more direct link between this 'living in the moment' mindset and success? Can it actually help you get what you want in the short term?

A couple of recent studies suggest that, perhaps, it can. And not just when it comes to the short term, but also when it comes to longer-term goals as well.

The studies in question looked at the dynamics of temptation. Or, more specifically, at how we handle it: how, when we're working towards a goal or making a resolution we keep ourselves focused and cope with the inevitable 'distractions'. Oscar Wilde might've pondered, as he reclined in the meadows at Magdalen, that the best way to resist temptation was to give in to it. But could science go one better?

The first study involved healthy eating. Students were split into two groups, each of which was given a subtly different mantra to keep them on the straight and narrow.

One group was instructed that every time they were faced with something they shouldn't eat they should repeat to themselves the phrase: 'I CAN'T eat X': a negative, self-limiting strategy that casts the present in a 'bad' light as the enemy.

The other group was given a slight variation: 'I DON'T eat X': a positive, self-affirming strategy that casts the present in a 'good' light as an ally.

Once they'd been given their mantras, the students were asked to repeat them in the lab in order for them to stick. Then, when they had done so, they were handed a questionnaire – unrelated to the study – to fill out. Once they'd completed it, they were free to leave the room.

But there was a catch.

As each student handed in their answer sheet and filed out of the lab, they were offered a choice of complimentary treats.

Yes, you guessed it.

Either a big fat chocolate bar.

Or a nice healthy granola bar.

Who said anything about the experiment being over? It was just about to begin! Here's what happened.

Those students who were given the 'I CAN'T eat X' mantra went for the chocolate bar 61 per cent of the time.

In contrast, however, the students who repeated 'I DON'T eat X' to themselves did so only 36 per cent of the time.

Just that simple change in wording made all the difference. And that's not all. If 'I don't' beats 'I can't' when it comes to one-shot choices, the researchers wondered, might it also make a difference in the long run? Could *embracing* the present and harnessing its empowering mojo – as opposed to wrestling with it and treating it as a gaoler – help us persevere over time?

To find out they set up a similar study to the first. But this time, instead of recruiting students, the experiment involved thirty professional women who signed up for a specially designed 'health and wellness seminar'. To get the ball rolling, each of the women was first told to think of a long-term health and wellness goal that was important to them – and then the group was divided into three subsets of ten.

The idea was the same as before.

Group 1 was told that whenever they felt the urge to give up on their goals, they should tell themselves:
'I CAN'T miss my workout today.'
Group 2 was told that any time they felt tempted to throw in the towel they should tell themselves:
'I DON'T miss workouts.'

Group 3 were given no specific strategy and were told simply that they should 'just say no'.

At regular intervals during the next ten days, each of the women received email reminders of their temptation-busting strategy and were asked to report back instances where it did or did not work.

Then, when the ten days were up, the researchers looked at how many women from each group remained 'undefeated': how many had persisted with their goals for the entire ten days.

The results were even more extraordinary this time around than they had been for the students.

For **Group 1** – the 'I CAN'T' group –
the figure was 1 out of 10.
For **Group 2** – the 'I DON'T' group –
the figure was 8 out of 10.
For **Group 3** – the 'JUST SAY NO' group –
the figure was 3 out of 10.

The message seems pretty clear.

Identifying with the here and now, as opposed to merely *tolerating* it, not only strengthens our resolve to make good decisions. It strengthens our *resolve* to resolve to make good decisions.

JUMPING TO CONCLUSIONS

'Looks like the tide's in!' I hear a voice boom up at me from behind a huge overhanging boulder. 'Fuck! Should've checked that before we set off. We'll just have to leave the towels and breakfast stuff here and jump in. Then we can climb back up to the path again when we're finished.'

It takes me a minute or so to catch up.

But when I do – when I've finally managed to negotiate the insanely narrow ledge around the overhang, with Andy steadying me from the other side – I finally get all the proof I need that he's stark raving mad.

The beach is ten metres away to our left – a secluded, turquoise bay of pristine, powdery sand. But to get there we have to go through hell: a twenty-foot jump into an icy, inky, raging, fomenting cauldron.

I stand rooted to the spot.

No way.

'How did you get round that overhang, you fat bastard?' is all I can think of to say.

Andy laughs. 'Now do you want to jump?' he says. 'Or do you want me to push you?'

He yanks off the Madness T-shirt and hangs it on an upturned spindle of rock out of reach of the spray. Next to go is the Minehead hat.

'Do you mind?' he grins, pointing back to the boulder. 'This is my dressing room. Yours is next door.'

'We're sharing,' I snarl.

Down below in the foam, I notice a couple of body-boards bobbing about in the entrance to what looks like a cave.

They're ours. He's already chucked them in.

Maybe some freak current will wash them into the looming, booming darkness, I think. Or some hideous form of prehistoric marine life will creep out and drag them under. Then that will be that. We'll have our bacon butties and clamber back up to the car.

But on second thoughts, I muse, maybe that's not such a good idea. He'll probably produce an 'I Love Skegness' oxygen rig from somewhere and insist we go in after them.

Too late! There's a splash, and he's in.

'Fucking brilliant!' he shouts, clearing his head and rounding up the boards. 'Your turn, mate – jump!'

I teeter on the edge. I go to jump but my brain's not having it.

'Come on!' shouts Andy. 'What's the matter with you? It's water, mate. Not quick-drying cement!'

Again, I go to jump. But again, something holds me back. The desire to stay alive, quite possibly.

'Look,' yells Andy, 'just imagine blokes with guns are creeping along the ledge and they're after you.'

I peer down at him swirling around in the giant, relentless washing machine of the North Atlantic.

No, hasn't worked.

'I think I'd prefer to take my chances with the men with guns,' I shout back. 'It's not called tombstoning for nothing, mate!'

Twenty foot below in the spin cycle, Andy's having a ball.

'OK,' he shouts. 'This is what's going to happen. I'm going to tell you a joke and then you're going to jump. Got it?'

'Better to die laughing than crying I suppose,' I holler, trying to psych myself up. 'So you might as well go for it.'

'OK,' yells Andy. 'So, it's like this:

There's a passenger in a taxi and he leans forward and taps the driver on the shoulder to ask him a question. The driver screams, loses control of the cab, swerves into the path of an oncoming bus, mounts the kerb, and pulls up just a few inches from a shop window. For a few moments no one says anything. Then the driver, still shaking, says: 'Sorry, mate – but you scared the shit out of me.'

The passenger can't understand it. 'You're a bit jumpy,' he says. 'All I did was tap you on the shoulder.'

'Yeah, yeah, I know,' says the driver. 'I should've said. You see, today's my first day driving a cab.'

'Right . . . So what were you doing before?'

'Driving a hearse,' says the driver . . .

TIME AND A PLACE

There's no feeling quite like it when you catch a wave just right!

And there's no feeling quite like it when you catch a wave just wrong – when you're 'dumped', go under, and for a few terrifying seconds can't figure out which way is up or down.

I managed to do both that morning. And loved every minute of it. I was glad I took the plunge. Even if I *was* coughing up seaweed for the next half hour.

Moral of the story? If you're going off the deep end, keep a straight face!

'You know, that little trick you used about imagining there were men with guns behind me,' I tell Andy, as – back in his 'dressing room' – we root out our stash of butties, 'reminds me of a study that was done on psychopaths a couple of years ago. Funnily enough, a study not unrelated to me jumping off that ledge because it showed that, in the heat of the moment when the chips are really down, psychopaths are much better at just "getting it done" than normal people.'

'Go on,' says Andy, munching away.

'Well,' I say, 'basically what happened was this. A bunch of psychopaths and a group of normal people were given some moral dilemmas to solve. In some of them the stakes were high and in some they were low.'

'You've lost me already,' says Andy.

'OK,' I say, 'let me give you a couple of examples. Enemy soldiers have taken over your village, right? They're under strict instructions to kill anyone they find. You and some others are hiding in a basement when you hear the soldiers enter the house above you. Your baby begins to cry loudly. You cover his mouth to block out the sound but you know that if you remove your hand he'll keep on blubbing. Obviously, that will alert the soldiers to the fact that you're there and they'll come and kill you, your baby and everyone else.

'Now, here's the deal. In order to save yourself and the others, you have to smother your baby to death. 'Is it morally acceptable for you to do that to keep everyone else alive?'

'Yes,' says Andy without hesitation. 'We've been down that road already. The shepherd boy in the desert?'

'OK,' I say. 'That's an example of a high-stakes dilemma. Now let me give you an example of a low-stakes one. You're visiting your grandmother for the weekend. Usually she slips you a few quid when she sees you. But this time, she doesn't. You ask her why and she moans about you not keeping in touch or something. You're pissed off so you decide to teach her a lesson. You find some pills in her bathroom cabinet and slip them into her tea, thinking that this will lay her up for a few days.

'Is it morally acceptable to screw your granny over like that?'

'No,' says Andy, again without hesitation.

I laugh.

'Well, mate,' I say, 'you've pretty much proved the point right there because that's exactly the pattern of results that the people who ran the study found. It turned out that the psychopaths were way better at smothering babies – and staying alive! – than normal people. But when it came to doing Granny in with the pills it was a draw. Not only that, but the psychopaths also made up their minds a lot quicker about what they thought was the right thing to do.

'They weren't put off by guilt, or doubt, or anger, or anything like that. They were responding, purely and simply, to the demands of the moment. And the greater those demands were, the greater the difference between the way they reacted and between . . . well, between you and me. The psychopaths were "there" in a way that the normal people weren't.'

FIGHTING TALK

The climb back up to the car passes without incident. And that's going some for Andy. In fact, he's uncharacteristically quiet – reflecting, perhaps, on the results of the study.

I didn't even tell him the full story.

Actually, when they were contemplating smothering babies and keeping everyone alive, the researchers found a remarkable neural signature in the brains of the psychopaths that they didn't find in normal people: a pattern of activity similar to that found in elite sportspeople when they enter a state of automatic effortlessness or 'flow' – and in superstar Buddhist monk meditators when they're deep in a trance.

What the rest of us have to work years for, psychopaths appear to be born with.

'Again, it reminds me of that roulette table study,' says Andy as, back at the car, he unscrews a thermos of coffee and does the honours. 'And also that other study you were talking about – you know, the one where you carve up the money either fairly or unfairly. It's all about concentrating on what you're getting out of something as opposed to what you're losing – and finding the right balance. Fair enough, smothering your baby isn't exactly going to make you parent of the year. But if it's going to save lots of lives . . .'

He hands me a cup and we perch on the bonnet staring out to sea across the car park.

The coffee looks like crude oil – and tastes like it, too.

'You know,' he says, 'back in the summer of 1998, me and the missus threw a Eurovision Song Contest party. Don't ask me why! It was fancy dress and we ended up with about 200 friends and family at our home, including a big contingent of SAS guys. A couple of blokes from my old troop, Nish and Frank, turned up as 1970s porn stars, complete with stick-on droopy moustaches, sideburns, plat- forms, velvet jackets, the lot. Anyway, we got chatting about another ex-member of the troop, Tommy, who'd recently been handed a life sentence for killing his girlfriend. Apparently, they'd had a row in a pub car park which clearly hadn't gone well because out from the boot of his car came an AK47 and he gave her a couple of bursts with it.

'Tommy had left the Regiment by then and had put himself through medical school to become an anaesthetist of all things. Can't say his bedside manner was up to much. Frank had also left the Regiment – trading in his M4 assault rifle for a dog collar. Tommy put them away and Frank buried them! As always, being Frank – and especially now he was Reverend Frank – he was over-thinking things.

'"What makes a man do such a thing?" he kept repeating to me and Nish.

'"Because he's even madder than I am," said Nish.

'Actually, that would've been going some because Nish had

been diagnosed as a paranoid schizophrenic. Four years earlier he'd stabbed his girlfriend with a pair of scissors thinking she was the Devil. He'd been in and out of a couple of loony bins but with the help of his meds appeared to have got through the worst of it. To be honest, he still seemed the same old Nish I'd known fifteen years ago when he'd been admitted to the biggest loony bin of all: the Regiment. In fact, on balance he'd probably improved.

'Now these three men, Kev – apart from the fact that each of them had once served in Seven Troop – all had something in common. Know what it was? They all had PTSD. Of course, none of us called it that at the time. But looking back on it there's no question in my mind that's what it was.

'Within a couple of months of our party, Nish had jumped out of a plane without a parachute and Frank had got shot of himself by having a night in with his car exhaust.

'Maybe it was the vol-au-vents, who knows?

'But actually, Kev, I *do* know. And the thing is, it's all down to exactly what we've been talking about. You see, Frank and Nish just couldn't move on. Both of them were stuck in the past – on an operation in Northern Ireland a few years earlier that had resulted in a good mate, Al Slater, getting shot.

'All three of us were on the border that night, mate. A PIRA [Provisional Irish Republican Army] active service unit was about to plant 1000 pounds and it was our job to find them. I'll never forget it. It was a frozen, pitch-black, fog-covered night – perfect for hide and seek.

'Anyway, eventually, when we did catch up with them, a contact ensued and Al took a burst while he was returning fire. Two lads from the troop tried to save him while the others went after the players. But it was never going to happen. The only way Al would've made it that night was by helicopter. And that was a non-starter because of the fog. So he slipped away in one of our guys' arms.'

'That really *is* tragic,' I say.

'Yeah,' says Andy. 'It was. No question. Of course, PIRA also shipped a bit of lead during the contact. But that didn't stop Nish and Frank taking Al's death very badly. The three of them were big time free-fall nuts and thick as thieves. They used to go on and on about the different things they could've done that night that might've meant Al was in a different place at a different time. But it was all crazy shit. In fact, they were beginning to do *my* head in by constantly banging on about it!

'I was with Frank the whole time we were on that job. And Nish had more radio time than Tony Blackburn. There was absolutely nothing that could've been done differently that would have put Al anywhere else. He was doing his job! But Frank and Nish weren't satisfied by that. For years they just kept raking over what happened, what didn't happen, what could've happened that night. Again and again. I mean, don't get me wrong. Of course it's a fucker when mates are killed. But that wasn't the first time. And sadly, it wasn't the last.

'The fact is: Al died on that job. And there's nothing any of us can say or do that will change that. In the end, you've just got to crack on and not over-think things. You have to do what that old woman did: pull the dust sheets over the furniture and close the door on the past.'

'And what the taxi driver did, too,' I add, taking a sip of coffee. 'Treat every day, every encounter, on its own merits. No emotional hangovers.'

'Exactly,' says Andy. 'But you know, Kev, it's all very well talking about the dangers of looking back. But as a soldier there's also the other side of things. You've also got to be careful not to let your mind get *ahead* of you.

'When I was captured and tortured by the Iraqis during the 1991 Gulf War, for instance, they did all sorts. One little trick they used to get up to was to shove the muzzles of their weapons into my mouth and take the safety catch off. Great laugh!

'Another time, some guards came into my cell and one of them had a Makharov pistol. He cocked it, aimed it at my head and pulled the trigger. The hammer came down on an empty chamber. The other guards were pissing themselves. So fuck it, I thought. I may as well join them.

'I mean, why not? It wasn't as if I had a full diary! I was hand-cuffed, lying on the floor, beaten black and blue, and stark bollock naked. I had no control over what was happening. So I thought: "Mate, you might as well enjoy it while it lasts."

'And you know what? The more I just focused on each event in isolation the more it just washed off. You focus on the feeling of the cold steel inside your mouth – OK, that's kind of interesting! How does it taste? Shit – how do you think guns taste?'

'Better than this fucking stuff, I reckon,' I say, chucking the remainder of my cup on to the grass.

Andy laughs.

'You focus on the loud bang, the looks on the guards' faces, the smell of cheap aftershave, your breathing, the fact that – yep – you're still alive! When all you've got is the present, it's amazing how fascinating it can become.

'Anyway, it turned out that the grand finale was still to come because after the war was over the Red Cross did a deal with the Iraqis to get all of us POWs back home. Just hours before we were due to fly out of Baghdad, they blindfolded and handcuffed a group of us and drove us to the airstrip – or what we hoped was the airstrip – where we knew the Red Cross had a plane waiting.

'After a couple of hours or so – something like that – the wagon stopped and they started dragging us out. I felt two sets of hands grab my arms and pull me out of my seat. That was OK. As far as I was concerned it was more good news. We were still moving. There was still forward motion. Again, take each moment as it comes. Stay in the present.

'There were echoes outside the wagon so that was promising. At least it sounded like an aircraft hangar. Great! Soon we'd be drinking hot chocolate and eating sticky buns all the way to Saudi. But don't get ahead of yourself. Don't take anything for granted. Focus on your sensations. Concentrate on your immediate surroundings.

'We were pushed and shoved into a long line, still handcuffed and blindfolded. There was a loud hiss and the smell of oil-filled Tilly lamps. There was the noise of soldiers moving around behind us. There was the sound of people breathing heavily either side of me. No, hang on a minute. All of a sudden something was telling me something wasn't right. Didn't know what . . . just something.

'We stood there for ages with no idea what was happening. To put the tin lid on it my stomach was playing up again and was about to put something in the post. First class. I'd been made to eat my own shit a few days earlier and it wasn't exactly Michelin-starred.'

'Don't tell me,' I say. 'It tasted like . . .'

'Shit!' Andy grins. 'But again, that was OK. When I got fed up of focusing on the pain of my smashed-up teeth, broken fingers, dislocated shoulder and the world's best collection of cuts, bruises and cigarette burns, diarrhoea was another sensation I could hand the baton over to.

'Anyway, I leaned forward trying to relieve the pain of the handcuffs around my wrists as my stomach approached the letter box. My nose brushed against a brick wall and I rested my forehead against it. Dehydration was now coming into the equation and I was starting to get very weak. Again, I focused on the texture of the bricks, the roughness of them against my skin. That's what bricks feel like, I told myself.

'But soon I was telling myself something very different. A sudden flurry of Arabic commands was followed by the ominous, heavy metallic echo of AK-47 assault rifles being cocked.

'Well, there you go, I thought. This one has to be for real. So much for getting released. I kept my head against the bricks calmly focusing on every lump, bump and indentation. What else could I do? Fuck it, if death was about to happen I still had no control over it, did I? And let's face it, when it comes to a choice between bricks, bullets, diarrhoea and a mouth full of smashed-up crockery, it's going to be bricks every time, isn't it?

'Besides, I'd never really looked that far ahead in life anyway. Like I said, three hours is about it. And that's on a good day!

'And it wasn't as if I'd rolled the dice with my eyes closed. I'd signed a non-liability contract to play the fighting game and, just like Al Slater, I was very aware that getting zapped was one of the downsides.

'But anyway, that was me, and, as you can imagine, some of the other POWs didn't quite see it like that. Bizarrely, they weren't exactly ecstatic at the prospect of having a couple of AK-47 rounds drilled into their backs.

'A lot started to pray. Some started to sob. And others begged. Me? I started to concentrate on not shitting myself. I thought, "If I shit myself now, before we all get dropped, the Iraqis might think I lost control because I was flapping and get an even bigger laugh out of the situation."'

'Christ,' I say. 'You really are as cold as ice, aren't you?'

Andy smiles, nudging my arm.

'But you haven't heard the best bit yet,' he continues. 'To the right of me there was this American – a US Marine Corps pilot as it turned out – who I noticed was taking very short, sharp breaths. To begin with, I thought he was just trying to control himself, fighting back the tears, trying to die with some dignity, that sort of thing.

'How wrong I was! He was just mightily pissed off at all the blubbing and couldn't hold back any longer. "Shut the fuck up!" he shouted, his words bouncing off the walls. "The last thing I want to hear right now is all this fucking God bollocks, you pathetic fucking wimps!"

'Well, how do you top that? You can't! So I chimed in with the first thing that came into my head: "And I need a shit!"

'Well, what do you know but the Iraqis started pissing themselves. A right old barrel of fucking laughs, wasn't it? Turned out the plane to take us home was just outside the hangar on the tarmac. Hot chocolate was on its way!'

THE PRESENT OF THE PRESENT

'Everyone agrees it's important to live in the moment, but the problem is how,' says the Harvard psychologist Ellen Langer. 'When people are not in the moment, they're not there to know that they're not there.'

She's right – unless of course, like Andy, you've been afforded the luxury of staring death in the face. What was it Samuel Johnson said? There's nothing like the prospect of being hanged to concentrate a man's mind.

So how do we go about it?

How, in the absence of the prospect of a sudden, violent end, do we overcome our powerful distraction reflexes and gain control of our thoughts – as opposed to letting those thoughts control us?

How do we step out of the deafening narrative waterfall coursing through our heads, the eternal rapids of anxiety and regret, into the calmer, stiller waters of the here and now: untroubled by expectation, unclouded by guilt and grief?

Predictably, perhaps, it's not easy. To truly commit – and we know from Chapter Five the difference between committing and truly committing – takes practice, dedication and willpower. But the benefits are huge.

The ability to focus on the task at hand with ruthlessly streamlined intention, with thoughts as drilled and as tightly knit as any Special Forces unit, confers a supreme advantage in a world becoming ever faster and ever more complex by the minute.

So with that in mind – or rather, with that *not* in mind – here are a few tricks to get the ball rolling. You might never get to *quite* the level that GOOD PSYCHOPATHS like Andy are at. You might never be *that* free and easy.

But then again . . . maybe you don't aspire to be.

Wake up and smell the coffee

'A few years ago I was in Edinburgh for the festival,' Andy tells me as we jump in the car and head back to base. 'One morning, because the hotel was so shit, I went into a café to kill a bit of time. "Do you mind if I get the computer out and do a bit of work?" I ask the owner. Sure, he says, no problem. So long as you're out by lunchtime.

'As the morning wears on, I order a couple of coffees and the owner and I get talking. He's ex Para Regiment and had been in the Falklands – a really good bloke. Sure enough, as lunchtime approaches and the phone begins to ring, he starts placing reservation signs on the various tables that are dotted about. To begin with, he puts a sign on the table to my left: table reserved for 1.00 p.m. Then he puts another sign on the table to my right: table reserved for 12.45 p.m.

'Finally, he comes up to my table and puts a sign behind my laptop screen. I peer over it and read: FUCK OFF!

'Both of us were falling about laughing. Even now it makes me giggle. Hilarious!'

It's hard not to see the funny side of this story. But there's a serious side to it, too. Things happen, events unfold, in their own time – and getting ahead of yourself and worrying about what the future might hold doesn't change that one bit.

Mark Twain once said: 'I have known a great many troubles, but most of them never happened.'

That's not just true for Mark Twain. It's true for all of us. But what *does* happen – what *is* happening – is happening NOW. Right this moment. In the present. So practise being there when it does. Start showing up for a change!

When you wake up – really *do* smell the coffee! And don't just smell it, *savour* it. Savouring, as psychologists call it, is the act of immersing yourself in something so that you notice all the minute details about it – and you can't do that by being anywhere else but the present.

It's a simple way to start but one that has proven benefits. Research shows that people who begin taking a few minutes each day – that's all – to actively savour something that they would usually rush, like eating a meal or going for the train, for instance, experience, on average, a higher percentage of positive emotions and fewer depressive ones.

Here's an example.

In one study, volunteers were told that other participants were forming a group and were going to hold a vote on whether or not they could join. It was nonsense, of course. There was no group. And there was no vote – the researchers were just interested in pissing some of them off!

Five minutes later, when the 'vote' had taken place, half the volunteers were informed that it had turned out favourably and that they could join, while the other half – the half the researchers wanted to wind up – were told that they'd been given the thumbs down.

But there was a catch.

Prior to the announcement, half of each group – both those who'd been 'accepted' and those who'd been 'rejected' – took part in a mindfulness induction exercise in which they slowly and deliberatively ate a raisin, savouring how it tasted and focusing on every sensation.

Then the fun really started!

Some time later, in a separate task that the volunteers had no idea was still part of the study, they were given the opportunity of inflicting a painful burst of noise on another person. Would the mindfulness intervention make any difference to who pushed the button and who didn't, wondered the researchers?

The answer couldn't have been clearer.

Of the volunteers who'd supposedly been given the heave-ho, those who *hadn't* eaten the raisin were significantly more aggressive, dispensing prolonged and painful acoustic bursts without provocation. Rejected by their peers, they were more than happy to take out their anger on complete strangers.

But for those volunteers who *had* eaten the raisin, neither rejection nor acceptance made a blind bit of difference. Either way, they remained chilled and laid-back, showing not the slightest flicker of interest in 'getting their own back'.

Savouring that previous experience had inoculated them against infection from their own toxic emotions, allowing them, rather than lashing out, to ask themselves the question: 'So this is how I'm feeling. How should I respond?'

'You know,' says Andy, shoving an Undertones CD into the player and whacking up the volume, 'I've come across that raisin trick before. When we were barely more than kids in the Infantry,

I had a mate who went through some pretty hairy experiences in Northern Ireland. Years later he got PTSD. But only after he'd left the army and become a well-known club singer in the East End of London. Things got so bad that his work and marriage were starting to suffer big time. The guy was really spiralling down. It was only when his wife poked him in the chest and told him he needed to sort himself out – otherwise she was history! – that he went to seek help.

'Anyway, it was mindfulness that got him over it. And you know what? One of the practices they taught him was exactly what you just said.

'They got him to put a raisin in the palm of his hand; to look at it really, really carefully, noticing every detail about it; to touch it and feel its texture; and then to put it in his mouth and do the same thing again before chewing it very slowly, savouring the taste, and then taking in the moment before swallowing it . . . all the time being mindful of every little detail of every little act. It saved him.

'The only trouble now is, half the East End have got PTSD listening to his bloody singing!'

The power of friendship, eh? Never ceases to amaze.

But anyway . . . next time you get the chance, *do* make the most of that coffee! Focus on how it tastes. Its colour. How it pours. The aroma. The way the steam rises from the surface.

Because you never know what might be round the corner.

Unless, of course, Andy's made it.

Then you're better off just chucking it in the bushes.

Press Reset

Here's a little puzzle for you.

> Jack is looking at Anne.
> But Anne is looking at George.
> Jack is married.
> But George is not.

Is a married person looking at an unmarried person?
1. Yes   2. No   3. Cannot be determined.

If you're like 80 per cent of people you'll go for Option 3. And get it wrong!

But if you're like Andy you'll go for Option 1. And get it right. Let's go through it.

The only person whose marital status is not known here is Anne. So let's start off by imagining that she is married. If Anne is married, then we know that a married person is looking at an unmarried person because we know that she's looking at George. But the same thing also applies if Anne is unmarried. Because this time we know that Jack, who is married, is looking at her. So . . . it's Option 1.

Now, the reason that this puzzle is so powerful is very simple. (If you got it right by the way, well done!) It's because, on a superficial examination, it really does seem as if we don't have enough information to answer it. It's only by looking at it more closely and systematically breaking the information down into its working parts that we realize that autopilot has a heck of a lot to answer for. It makes us miss stuff – quite literally in this case – that's staring us in the face.

Of course, we do this so often in life that we're simply not aware of it. Over evolutionary time, flicking on the autopilot has become so endemic a response to the speed and complexity of an increasingly informational society that it's virtually impossible, somewhat ironically, to catch ourselves in the act.

Until, that is, a simple puzzle like this one happens to trip us up!

But that's in everyday life. In the workplace, needless to say, it's a different story. Many professions – such as surgery, for instance – rely on their exponents *not* being on cruise control for successful outcomes. Miss something obvious in the operating theatre and often that's that. It's lights out.

Here's what one neurosurgeon – a GOOD PSYCHOPATH like Andy – told me when I asked him about the mindset he enters into before an operation:

Yes, when you're scrubbing up before a difficult operation, it's true: a chill does go through the veins. The only way I can describe it is to compare it to intoxication. Only, it's an intoxication that sharpens, rather than dulls, the senses; an altered state of consciousness that feeds on precision and clarity, rather than fuzziness and incoherence . . . Perhaps 'supersane' would be a better way of describing it. Less sinister. More, I don't know, spiritual . . .

And here's Andy – on a different kind of 'head shot'.

'For me everything becomes more sharply focused and the pace slows, like you're in slow motion. I don't seem to get that heavy pumping pulse that I know some mates get when shit happens. It's as if the man in front of me, who's trying to kill me, has deliberately slowed himself down so I can get a clear picture of what the fuck is happening. It's almost as if he's giving me loads of time to draw down a weapon from my holster, bring it up into the aim and take a head shot rather than going for the centre mass of the chaos that's in front of me. Not always, but most of the time it's been very easy.'

When conditions are tricky, you take full control of the cockpit.

Now, the mindset that Andy and the surgeon are describing here is not something that is attainable only by Zen masters or psychopaths. It's a state of mind that we can all aspire to. And we can get there surprisingly easily . . . by setting ourselves a very simple challenge. In whatever situation you might find yourself in: NOTICE SOMETHING NEW.

In the higher echelons of the martial arts they have a term for doing precisely this. It's called *shoshin*, or 'beginner's mind'.

'In the beginner's mind there are many possibilities,' explains Shunryu Suzuki, a well-known Buddhist teacher. 'In the expert's mind there are few.'

But this isn't just the case in the martial arts. It's the same everywhere.

Noticing new things anchors you firmly in the here and now

because it's only once we think we know something that we stop paying attention to it and our minds begin to wander.

We run through the contract in a haze because we've done it a thousand times.

We go with the same supplier because it's 'better the devil you know'.

We don't bother looking at *that* particular junction because there's never anything coming!

Pressing the reset button on our expectations makes life more interesting for all the right reasons.

'Like keeping it going for a start!' observes Andy.

CAN YOU FIND THE THE **MISTAKE?** 123456789

OK, that was easy!

But how about in the following pictures?
Anything strike you as . . . odd?
Answers at the end of the chapter!

Don't think about it

Last summer, in a small gym close to where I live, Andy pulled off an amazing stunt that really has to be seen to be believed.

The stunt involves one man kneeling down – arms by his side, blindfolded – while another man stands behind him with a weapon raised above his head. Whenever he likes, the man with the weapon can bring it down on to the man kneeling in front of him, killing or badly injuring him, unless the blow is somehow anticipated and the assailant subsequently disarmed. It seems impossible, I know. But it isn't. I saw it with my own eyes once, in a martial arts dojo in Japan, and ever since then I've been fascinated by it.

'Let's give it a go,' said Andy, when I told him about it. So we did: with me brandishing a rolled-up copy of the *Sun* – Samurai swords are a bit hard to come by at short notice in rural Oxfordshire – and him kneeling down between a couple of kettle bells.

I was on my back in no time!

'One must empty one's mind totally,' an old sensei told me when I'd first seen it done. 'One must focus purely on the now. When one enters a state like that, one is able to smell time. To feel its waves washing over one's senses. The tiniest ripple may be detected over great distances. And the signal intercepted. Often it appears that the two combatants move simultaneously. But this is not so. It is not difficult. With practice it can be mastered.'

'You've just got to stop thinking,' was Andy's more prosaic take on it. 'In my case, not difficult!'

'Not thinking about it' is something that we could all do with a little bit more of. Seems a bit odd to say that in a book about success, doesn't it? You'd expect the opposite. But it's true.

Think about it – or rather, don't!

Let's say you're in a situation that makes you feel anxious. You're about to stand up in front of a crowd of people and give a speech, for example. Or you're about to do a bungee jump. Does thinking about it make it any better?

Most people would say that it doesn't. In fact, it makes it worse.

A colleague of mine, Peter Lovatt, is a cognitive psychologist at the University of Hertfordshire. Peter uses dance to help people resolve their emotional, psychological and interpersonal difficulties.

That's why they call him . . . Dr Dance!

Peter and I were at a Christmas bash together once and Peter was strutting his stuff.

'Come on, Kev!' he shouted. 'What are you waiting for?'

'I'm waiting for a time when I can actually dance,' I replied.

He pulled me on to the floor.

'Everyone can dance,' he said. 'The problem is that most people just *think* they can't. Just forget about what you're doing. Forget about what other people are doing. Just move your body about, let it do its own thing, and enjoy being part of the party. Step *outside* your head and *on to* the dance floor.'

I did – and was still crap.

But I get where Peter is coming from. It's the same place that Andy and the sensei are coming from.

Clear your mind and focus on your immediate experience without attaching it to all the background chatter, the incessant loop of 'breaking news' constantly going around inside your head – the doubts about your self-esteem; the fear of looking silly; the self-comparison and self-evaluation updates; or any other unpleasant or intrusive thoughts that contaminate the purity of raw experience – and everything suddenly seems much 'cleaner' and less threatening.

That's how I felt for half an hour after I got my own taste of what it's like to be a psychopath – my 'psychopath makeover' – with Andy in the lab. For the briefest of periods, with the help of some Harry Potteresque electromagnetic brain magic, I 'got over myself'.*

Sadly, though, it wore off.

As Andy wrote at the time: 'Dutton is a wimp. He could only stand being me for fifteen minutes!'

---

*To find out more about my psychopath makeover, go to:
http://www.thegoodpsychopath.com/my-psychopath-makeover/

Don't get the world inside your head confused with the one outside

'When I was an undergraduate I had a rather inventive tutor who was always coming up with new ways to teach us stuff,' I tell Andy as, back at the ranch, we unload the car.

One morning, as we filed into his office for a seminar on paranoia, he handed each of us an envelope.

'Don't sit down,' he said. 'In each of these envelopes is a customized delusion that I've prepared for you in advance. Take it away, open it up and then, for the rest of the day, I want you to actively seek out evidence that it's true!'

We all looked at each other, grabbed our envelopes and filed back out.

'Great!' we all thought. 'Morning off!'

I took my envelope into a café on campus and opened it up. Inside was a piece of A4 paper. I unfolded it and read the following statement: 'PEOPLE ARE LAUGHING AT YOUR SHOES.'

I looked around.

No they weren't.

But wait, I thought. That's not what this is about, is it? What this is about is *believing* that they are and then finding the evidence to *prove* it.

I went and bought a coffee and sat back down.

On the table next to me were a group of girls having a chat. One of them said something funny and the others laughed. But just before she laughed the girl sitting nearest me happened to glance away from the table and down at my shoes.

Coincidence?

Then there was the guy on the payphone in the sports hall. He turned round, saw that I was waiting, looked me up and down . . . and started laughing.

And the chap on the bus who laughed 'apologetically' as he 'accidentally' trod on my foot.

You know what, mate? By the end of the day I really *was* genuinely starting to believe it – even though, deep down, I 'knew' it was just an exercise and had a piece of paper to prove it!

'I bet that was the last time you wore those pink Doc Martens,' Andy says, chucking the boards into the garage and shaking the sand out of the towels. 'But I get where you're coming from. It's easy to put two and two together and come up with five, to let what's going on *inside* your head dictate how you see what's outside.

'Which is why, when we were talking about the interrogation phase of SAS Selection, I told you that some of the candidates end up binning it. They lose track of the fact that they're on Selection – that it's just an exercise – and start thinking it's real.

'You have to keep yourself firmly grounded in the present at all times. That's why, when you're captured for real, switched-on interrogators will never wear a watch. And why they'll keep you in an enclosed space well away from any natural light. Deprive someone of a sense of time for long enough and the present ceases to exist. That's the brain's gravitational field gone – and without it you float away into oblivion.'

Andy's absolutely right.

Wrong conclusions, incorrect assumptions, muddled attributions (if you recall from the previous chapter) are all the products of an ungrounded mind – a mind whose thoughts and feelings drift off at random into cognitive outer space, into the psychological ether of past or future, into either a time that is gone or a time that is yet to come.

But stay in the moment – adopt the 'beginner's' mindset – and you'll gradually find that your thought processes start becoming a little bit more 'nailed down'.

Maybe it *was* a genuine oversight that you didn't receive the invitation.

Maybe the other candidate for the job *was* just that little bit more experienced.

Maybe people *aren't* laughing at your shoes after all.

Andy gets out his phone.

'Here,' he says, 'if you need any convincing that the brain sometimes brings more to the party than it needs to, have a look at this and tell me very quickly what you see.'

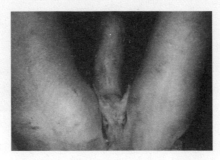

'I see three pigs,' I say.

'Funny,' he says. 'That's exactly what I saw!'

Take it one step at a time

How do you make a million quid?

Easy.

First you make ten quid, then twenty, then fifty . . .

Yes, we know. Sounds like a cop-out doesn't it?

But not so fast!

Research shows that people who think like this – people who have a clear, long-range goal that can be broken down into a series of specific, attainable, smaller goals to track their efforts along the way – are far more likely to get what they want than those who simply 'think big' all the time.

If your goal is too abstract or too intimidating at the outset then it's much more difficult to stay motivated and focused. But chopping your one, all-encompassing 'championship' goal into a series of smaller, interim 'early round' successes enables you to do a number of important things.

It allows you to:

- Make positive, evidence-based progress.
- Gain concrete, in-the-moment feedback on your performance.
- Get some confidence-boosting 'small wins' under your belt on your way to the 'Big One'.

Even something as small and insignificant as doing the breakfast dishes before you leave the house for work in the morning has been shown to deliver a 'reward high' that sustains performance throughout the rest of the day – another good reason, to go with those already mentioned, why a morning routine works wonders. The importance of getting off to a good start should not be under-estimated.

Such one-step-at-a-time thinking is, you might say, the more 'commercial' arm of the coffee-smelling, raisin-eating present that we've been looking at so far.

In the workplace in general, for instance, research has shown that little rewards such as solving a problem or getting a pat on the back from a supervisor or colleague have a significant impact on both personal motivation and job satisfaction.

And when 'small wins' strategies of short-term goal setting are pitted more scientifically against 'big bang' strategies of long-term evaluation in corporate settings, it's the former that come out on top in the productivity stakes – something that app designers and video-game producers have known for quite some time. Mere coin-cidence, do you think, that millions of people become addicted to games like Grand Theft Auto with their carefully calibrated progress levels . . . but very few to their work?

Quests, tasks, challenges and adversaries that can be readily met and deftly overcome deliver regular pellets of minor accom-plishment to the reward centres of our brains – and give us a feel-good hit just like any other drug.

But there's good news for all of us.

By:

- splitting the day into individual elements, sections or tasks,
- keeping a daily 'to do' list, and
- recording our 'small wins' in a diary (in the same way that video games automatically 'save' where you are up to),

we can all increase our engagement, motivation and productivity levels at work.

Another way is not to multi-task!

Not only is multi-tasking the complete opposite of staying in the moment – switching on numerous little spotlights across a variety of different fronts that the brain must then frantically shuttle back and forth between – research also shows that it actually *impairs* performance, sometimes resulting in up to four times as many mistakes!

The appeal of multi-tasking is predicated upon an illusion. It lies in the fact that when we're engaged in it we *feel* like we're getting things done because we make a little bit of progress in lots of different areas. We get that cheap ding-ding-ding reward thrill across the board.

But you know how it is . . . as soon as you encounter difficulties on one of the tasks you neglect it in favour of the easier ones. Until they, too, start to cut up rough. In the end you struggle to complete any of them. And your mind, rather than being clean, fresh and focused, is all over the place.

'I heard a nice little story once,' Andy shouts from the kitchen as he powers up the go-faster Gaggia for a drinkable version of the stuff that came out of the flask earlier, 'which proves the point in a different way.'

He plonks some Ginger Nuts down on the table.

'A bloke is driving down a country lane one dark, foggy night when his car breaks down. He gets out and shines his torch straight ahead of him into the fog but the light just bounces back and blinds him. He can't see a thing. He's cursing his luck and resigning himself to the fact that it's going to be an overnighter on the backseat, when a wise man suddenly appears from nowhere.'

'Convenient,' I say.

'Yeah,' says Andy. 'Anyway, the bloke explains his predicament to the wise man and the wise man asks him for the torch. When he gives it to him he points it at the ground and shines it just a few inches in front of his feet.

'"To get where you want to go," says the wise man, "the most important thing is to concentrate on what's immediately in front of you. Nothing else."'

'So what happened then?' I ask. 'The wise man gave him a lift?'

'Shut up,' says Andy.

Meet life head on

When I was writing *Flipnosis* I dropped in on a friend of mine at the University of Western Australia, in Perth. Colin MacLeod is a professor of clinical psychology and an expert in anxiety disorders – and is only too well aware from years of clinical practice how the brain can wind itself up and get itself in a tizzy over absolutely nothing.

'A lot of the time we worry about the worry,' Colin explained to me. 'We conflate the thing we're worrying about with the worry that the thing we're worrying about gives rise to! This "second order" worry then takes over and things get confused. The second-order worry gradually becomes the focal point of the problem – the first-order worry, in other words . . .'

I think we all know what Colin is getting at. The brain's natural response when faced with anxiety, depression, or any unpleasant thought for that matter, is to turn a blind eye.

We go into denial over our financial problems.

We experience a 'mid-life crisis' when trying to recapture our youth.

We do things we shouldn't 'on the rebound'.

And yet at the same time we all know, if we're being totally honest with ourselves, that we're fighting a losing battle. That, in a squalid little bolt hole deep inside our brains, fear and sadness are sitting up late for us and waiting for us to return 'home'.

So what do we do? We use every trick in the book to stay out just that little bit longer – and encounter, in dimly lit neural dive bars, the second-order emotions, the emotions about other emotions, that Colin is talking about.

The original, PRIMARY emotion might be stress over an upcoming deadline.

The spin-off, SECONDARY emotion is: 'I'm stressed about being stressed.'

The irony, of course, is that it doesn't have to be like this. And that if we 'stay in' the moment instead of 'going out'; if we just accept the emotion as it is – as a fully paid-up tenant who has every right to be there – without trying to evict it, tidy up after it, or have strong words with it, then things get a whole lot easier.

As a case in point, Colin introduced me to Tania – a patient of his whose seatbelt phobia eventually got so bad that she was forced into selling her car.

'So, ironically, what we're going to be doing with Tania is getting her to focus her anxiety on the *seatbelt*,' Colin told me, 'because in doing so what we're actually doing, unbeknownst to her, is taking her mind off the *real* source of her anxiety – the worry about the worry – and transplanting it on to a "ghost" anxiety: the original hub that now lies emotionally dormant. Basically it's distraction in disguise. What Tania will be unconsciously "concentrating away" will not, in fact, be the actual phobia *itself* – but a satellite anxiety associated with the phobia's onset.'

The technical term for this technique, Colin enumerated, was *paradoxical intention* – the eradication of a problem by embracing, and explicitly focusing one's attention on it, in the present moment.

When you experience it first hand it's really quite something.

'What I need to do to begin with,' Colin explained to Tania when she arrived, 'is to observe your symptoms for myself so I can get a handle on them. Is that OK?'

'Fine,' said Tania.

'Good,' said Colin. 'So we'll take it in stages. First, tell me how you feel right now, as we approach the car park. Concentrate hard on your anxiety and try to convey to me what it's like.'

Tania went quiet for a moment as she rummaged around inside her head trying to put into words how she felt.

After a few seconds she said, 'Actually, I seem to be all right at the moment.'

'No problem,' said Colin. 'That's OK. We'll come back to it in a minute.'

Once we'd walked across the car park and got to her car, Colin had another go. Focus on your anxiety, he encouraged her, and tell me how it feels.

Once again, Tania was at a loss to put it into words. Mysteriously, she felt OK.

Amazingly, when Colin asked her the same question a few seconds later as she was getting into the car she drew another blank.

And another, even more amazingly, as she did up her seatbelt!

Pootling around the car park didn't seem to bother her. And neither did going on the freeway.

A miracle?

No – just a bit of ingenious mind-whispering!

You see, up until then Tania – without being aware of it – had been worried about being worried. Her fear, behind the scenes, had metastasized – and had started to turn on itself.

But as soon as she was anchored into the moment, as soon as she was made to *savour* her anxiety, it vanished into thin air.

Several years ago, I chatted to a BAD PSYCHOPATH who was behind bars in a secure unit. When you're in the sea and standing in a position where the waves are crashing down on top of you, he told me, you've got two choices. Either you can retreat and come out – and miss all the fun. Or you can go further in and be buoyed up by the waves instead of being flattened by them.

There's a lot in what he says.

'Or,' says the GOOD PSYCHOPATH, a mug of fresh, steaming coffee in each hand, 'you can ride them like we did earlier!'

There's a lot in what *he* says, too!

QUESTIONNAIRE
HOW 'IN THE MOMENT' ARE YOU?

Assign a rating to each of the following statements and then add up your total and check it with the scores on the next page:

	strongly disagree **0**	disagree **1**	agree **2**	strongly agree **3**
1. In difficult situations I am able to pause before reacting.	○	○	○	○
2. I am good at breaking big tasks and projects down into smaller ones.	○	○	○	○
3. I find it easy to put things that are worrying me out of my head until later.	○	○	○	○
4. I am able to make an itch go away by concentrating on it.	○	○	○	○
5. I am good at taking just one thing at a time and not getting ahead of myself.	○	○	○	○
6. Every so often I slow myself down and savour every aspect of what I'm doing.	○	○	○	○
7. I take regular time outs to relax and clear my mind.	○	○	○	○
8. I find it easy to just focus purely on my breathing for one minute and not have any intrusive thoughts.	○	○	○	○
9. I recover from setbacks well.	○	○	○	○
10 When I'm engaged on a task I'm not easily distracted.	○	○	○	○
11. I rarely beat myself up for feeling or thinking the way I do.	○	○	○	○

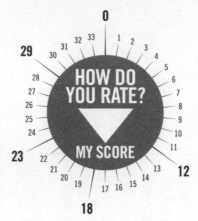

0-11 It's amazing you managed to get through the questionnaire! Your mind is everywhere but here.

12-17 Your thoughts are about as grounded as a helium balloon – constantly floating off into your brain's emotional atmosphere. Time to invest in some string.

18-22 Sometimes you are top dog inside your own head but at others your thoughts can get round you very easily and take over the place. You need to crack down more regularly.

23-28 Eight out of Zen. For you, it's more the pleasure of the moment than momentary pleasure.

29-33 You are at one with everything!

NOTICE ANYTHING UNUSUAL?

MISTAKE The word 'the' is repeated.

HORSE Is that a Bond girl silhouetted in white on his face?

FOOTBALL TEAM Where's that coach's left hand going?

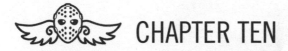 CHAPTER TEN

UNCOUPLE BEHAVIOUR FROM EMOTION

Emotional qualities are antagonistic to clear reasoning.

Sherlock Holmes, *The Sign of Four*

TAXI FOR MR DUTTON?

They say that going to India is an assault on the senses. But they're wrong. It is an assault on the soul.

Senses are collateral damage.

The road from New Delhi to Dharamsala takes 16 hours by taxi and swoops, swooshes, teeters and judders through three provinces – Uttar Pradesh, Haryana and the Punjab – before rollercoastering through the clouds into Himachal Pradesh.

I have no choice but to take it.

At this time of year, October, the baby monsoons make air travel unreliable and I need to be in McLeod Ganj, the Narnian headquarters of the Dalai Lama's Central Tibetan Administration, by eight o'clock tomorrow morning. There I will meet a monk who, for the next couple of weeks, shall be my guide in a land where magicians are reputed to prowl: reclusive *tsanbalas* who meditate high in the mountains and who have psychological powers the rest of us can only dream of.

I have come to test them – to see whether their renowned capacity for emotional detachment is greater than that of psychopaths.

I reckon it'll go to penalties.

I'm off to a funny old start. At the airport in Delhi the taxi driver holding the 'Kevin Dutton' sign isn't who I'm expecting.

'Morning, mate, welcome to India!' crows a familiar voice as soon as I come through arrivals.

I stop dead.

'What the . . . ?'

Andy laughs.

'It was all sorted weeks ago,' he says. 'That missus of yours can certainly keep a secret!'

Over in the car park is a gleaming Toyota Hilux with a full tank of petrol and a route map on the dashboard. I sling my rucksack on to the backseat and Andy steers us out into the vehicular bear pit of New Delhi. Cars, rickshaws, lorries, buses and motorbikes come at us from all angles.

But he couldn't give a damn.

'I hope you took out insurance on this thing,' he smiles, one arm out the window, the other fiddling around with the CD player.

'Yeah, that's a point,' I say. 'How did you . . . ?'

'There's some beers under your seat,' he says. 'Why don't you have one and just chill out, for fuck's sake?'

The sun rises and we zoom north.

I snap open the top of an ice-cold Kingfisher and take a swig.

For once, I could've kissed the old bastard.

SQUEALS ON WHEELS

It's just after eight as we enter the town of Panipat on the National Highway – part of the Grand Trunk Road, which, for over two millennia, has linked the easternmost and westernmost regions of the Indian subcontinent, from Chittagong in Bangladesh in the east to Kabul in the west.

Just like anywhere else at that time of the morning, it's rush hour. Roadside shanties selling everything from silks to car tyres to electrical goods are pushing up the shutters and traffic is at a standstill.

Andy has a slug of Diet Coke and rips open a Mars bar.

'Nice to see the Peckham diet of the mid-Seventies is still going strong then,' I say.

He smiles.

'Yours is in the glove compartment,' he mumbles.

I open it up and find a small jar of Jelly Brains. But they've all coagulated into one *big* Albert Einstein Jelly Brain in the heat and it's stuck fast. I'd need a Black and Decker to get it out.

'When I was in the Regiment I had a mate called Clive,' Andy says, as a cow mopes past the window and peers in at us. 'Clive had just moved into a new flat in town and everything was perfect except for one thing: his neighbour, a taxi driver, who got up at the crack of dawn and sang very loudly in the shower. Normally this wouldn't have been a problem. But the walls in the flat were like paper. And the neighbour – well, he wasn't exactly going to get a record deal any time soon.

'To make matters worse, the taxi driver seemed like a bit of a drama queen. Already, in the fortnight or so since Clive had been living there, he'd twice heard him lose his temper in the flat – and on both occasions it'd been over something trivial. So if it was a quiet life you were after – and Clive was like that: he came from Woking and was into Sibelius – knocking on someone's door and telling him to shut up probably wasn't a good idea. But on the other hand, things clearly couldn't go on the way they were. So, what to do? Well, what happened was this:

> Very cleverly, Clive made use of the fact that by this stage he hadn't actually met his neighbour face-to-face. Yep, he certainly knew what he looked like – had seen him through the window a couple of times – but his neighbour had never seen *him*.
>
> So one evening, what Clive does is this. He notes down the guy's number plate in the car park outside and then, a couple of days later, gets me to flag him down outside Hereford train station.
>
> We get talking.
>
> 'My mate's just moved into a new apartment,' I say.
>
> 'Oh yeah?' says the driver. 'How is it?'
>
> 'Well,' I say, 'it's great except for one thing. His next-door neighbour has got the worst voice he's ever heard in his life. Can't sing for shit, apparently. But you know what? At half five every morning, at the top of his voice, he sings – or rather squeals – in the shower!
>
> 'Can you believe that? To be honest, it doesn't really bother him all that much. He quite likes Queen and George

Michael as it happens. Plus, my mate reckons this neighbour's actually quite a nice bloke.

'But hey, maybe he should say something anyway. You know, for the neighbour's benefit. Just in case someone else puts in an *official* complaint. What do you think?'

There's a pause.

'Hmmh,' says the driver, a bit uneasy. 'Yeah . . . maybe he should.'

He checks his rear-view mirror.

'By the way, where did you say you were going again?'

'I'm actually going round my mate's now,' I say. 'Asquith Court. Number 7.'

'You know what, Kev? The rest of the journey passed in silence, mate. As did the mornings round at Clive's from then on!'

THE EVOLUTION OF TACT

Throughout this book we've touched at various points on the origins and function of two very important parts of the brain. On the one hand, the amygdala, the ancient emotional control tower which splits the world into 'good' and 'bad' experiences based on primeval survival values. And on the other, the prefrontal cortex: the newer, more diplomatic, more metrosexual voice of reason.

During the course of our evolutionary history, natural selection, as we've seen, began to install phone lines between these two neural ministries. And channels of communication were opened.

Slowly, as the millennia rolled by and language, consciousness and society began showing up to the party, the Department of Emotion started talking to the Department of Rational Thought and a political sea change began to take place in our brains. Our problem-solving and decision-making strategies became markedly less 'autocratic' and decidedly more 'democratic'.

Back in the day, many was the occasion when we simply had

to fight; when *thinking* about fighting would have entailed that we thought no more. But, over time, our priorities changed. And after millions of years of ruling the brain by itself, *precedence*, all of a sudden, was forced to share power with *preference*.

'Good and bad' and 'better and worse' formed a coalition.

If you need any convincing that natural selection nailed it and that this was the right move, then the story that Andy just told about his mate Clive and the taxi driver is all the evidence you need.

Understandably, Clive was getting a bit pissed off with the early morning Bohemian Crapsodies scaramouching through his bedroom wall. But if the bottom line was a quiet, hassle-free life in his new apartment, then venting his anger in what would undoubtedly have been a volatile confrontation wasn't, perhaps, the best way of going about it.

OK, on the one hand the singing might've stopped. But, on the other, who knows what might have come crashing through the bedroom wall in its place. Instead what he did – decoupling the emotion from his behaviour – *was* the most effective strategy.

The singing did stop.

The taxi driver saved face.

And no harm was done.

Emotions are great. They save our lives; make us fall in love; forge lifelong friendships; and help us appreciate great works of art.

But they can also be a pain in the arse.

Especially the big hairy ones like anger.

ANGRY McNAB

'You know, Kev, I've been angry for at least half of my life,' Andy tells me as we grind to a halt in a sea of cows and cars.

'For years, I hated everyone and everything, mostly because I didn't have what they had. As you know, I spent the first fifteen years of my life on a housing estate in South London. But, as I'm sure you're aware, despite what *Only Fools and Horses* would have you believe, Peckham was never full of Del Boy cheeky chappies having a laugh on the market and then going off to drink cocktails in the pub. It was full of unemployment, drugs, guns, and mindless vandalism just to fill in the time.

'I didn't do the drugs or the guns. That was a mug's game. But I did do my fair share of vandalism. I felt angry with people who had shiny new cars or spotless motorbikes so I used to kick them in just because I could. I'd vandalize people's shops and mess up their goods – simply because they had stuff, and I didn't.

'I can also remember being very angry with my teachers. I went to nine different schools between the ages of five and fifteen, so there were a lot of them to be angry with. I was angry that they kept putting me in remedial classes. But then again, I wasn't exactly doing anything to get out of them.

'In fact, I used to like being bottom of the class. It gave me yet another reason to feel angry. I liked the feeling of being a minority, the feeling that everyone was against me. It was like being part of my own select club. It made me feel that my anger was justified and that I was entitled to do things that others couldn't, or shouldn't, do.

'There was only one problem. Not everyone saw things the same way and by the age of fifteen I ended up in juvenile detention for destroying a flat full of nice shiny things that someone else had worked really hard for. Sadly, my time in borstal didn't teach me anything. In fact, it just made me even more angry. As I saw it, the reason I was in there was no fault of my own. It was everyone else's. Borstal's short, sharp shock treatment just reinforced the fact that no one cared about me.'

'And if *they* didn't care, then why should you, right?' I say, turning up the air conditioning.

'Exactly,' says Andy. 'But there was one good thing about borstal, Kev. It was there, as you know, mate, that I was recruited into the army. OK, I didn't get to be a helicopter pilot like the sergeant said I would. I was packed off to join the infantry. But, on the other hand, things pretty soon turned out to be even better than I'd imagined.'

'Go on,' I say.

'Well,' Andy continues, 'I soon found out that the army *liked* its young men to be angry. And when I found *that* out, mate, *I* got to like the army. Big time!

'I especially liked milling. Milling is where you're thrown into the middle of a human boxing ring and told to fight the other 16-year-old lad thrown in there with you. Each fight lasts for two minutes – or until one of you drops. Milling was designed to get the blood up. To make you angry. There's no technique. No style. You just get in there and try to drop your opponent before he does the same to you. I couldn't believe my luck. I was actually somewhere where they *wanted* me to be angry.'

'And, what's more, they were paying you for it!' I say.

'A perfect storm!' says Andy. 'And that's not all they were paying me for. They also paid me to stick a steel bayonet on to the end of my rifle, think about all the people who had ever made me angry, and then charge towards a sandbag with it, screaming at the top of my voice. Again and again, I would ram home that lump of steel into all my teachers, all the borstal staff . . . into anyone I could think of who'd ever had more in their lives than me.

'It was great. Here was a talent I had plenty of! For once in my life, I could do something right.'

'Must've felt very liberating,' I say, as the cows tinkle off into a siding and we get on the move again. 'Finally, you were on your way. And all the previous shit had been worth it.'

Andy nods. 'That's exactly how it felt,' he says. 'And it got better! After my year as a boy soldier, I was sent to my infantry battalion. The guys there were all pretty similar to me and we got on like a house on fire.

'They were angry, too. But, unlike me, their anger seemed to be directed more towards the system than individuals. They were pissed off with bigger things. Like the government, for instance. And the army itself, for that matter. And you know what, Kev? I could see why. Because at the time, as a hard-as-nails baby infantryman, I just couldn't get my head around the army's attitude towards the aggression that they instilled in us soldiers.

'They trained us to be aggressive. To get really angry and fight. But then, when that anger spilled out into civilian life – as it inevitably would in garrison towns up and down the country on a Saturday night – they seemed surprised and we'd get severely punished for it. I mean, what was all that about? They *paid* us to fight, didn't they?

'One Saturday night I was in the thick of it myself. The pubs had shut and a fight broke out between the squaddies and the townies.'

'No!' I say. 'Really?'

Andy chuckles. 'Yeah, funny that,' he says. 'Anyway, someone called the military police and they came down in their vans to arrest us. But somehow – can't remember how – I managed to escape. So all of a sudden there I am running down this cobblestone road in the middle of the night being chased by a big fat military copper who I know doesn't stand a chance in hell of catching me, with him screaming orders at me to stop.'

Andy pauses, a bemused smile etched across his face.

'And you know what I did, Kev?'

'Yeah,' I say. 'You stopped.'

He looks at me in amazement.

'Yeah,' he says. 'I did. But you know why? Not because he was ordering me to. Or because I knew I'd done something wrong. It was nothing like that.

'The reason I stopped was because my anger towards him and the system that he represented got the better of me and I decided that right there and then might be a good moment to have a go back. You know, hurl a few insults at him, allow him to get up close, then fuck off into the distance leaving him playing catch-up again.'

'And?' I say. 'What happened?'

Andy shrugs.

'Well, it was a good plan in *theory*,' he says. 'But in practice, I never got the chance.'

'Why?' I ask.

'Because, out of frustration, the fucker goes and lobs his truncheon at me, and as I turn round, it cracks me right across the side of the head and knocks me spark out!'

We both laugh.

'Mind you,' Andy continues, 'then the boot really was on the other foot and it was the Royal Military Police's turn to take their anger out on me. I got a good kicking and they carted me off.'

'So what was the turning point, then?' I ask, as the road opens up again and the kaleidoscopic shanties give way to hot green fields. 'When did you change – assuming you *have*, that is?'

Andy smiles.

'Actually, Kev,' he says, 'the turning point came when I joined the Regiment. By the time I'd reached my mid-twenties and had been promoted to sergeant, I began to wonder if my anger might be put to better use elsewhere. And, I mean, the SAS fought all the time, didn't they? But how wrong I was! Once I'd passed Selection I very quickly discovered that there was no place at all for anger in the Regiment. None whatsoever. The vibe was completely different to that in the regular army.

'All of a sudden I found myself in a much calmer, much less aggressive environment. Nobody seemed to need to shout or chest-poke any more to get things done. People treated each other more respectfully. Even called each other by their first names.

'A lot of the army's rules and regulations had disappeared, too. For a start, there was no marching. And no uniform either. Most of the men were in jeans. This was a whole new world for me. And one that I had to learn to adapt to fast.'

'So what was the main difference?' I ask. 'You were talking about a different "vibe" just now. But can you put your finger on what that vibe was, exactly?'

'Easy!' says Andy. 'In a nutshell, the focus was less about anger, and more about self-control. There was enough violence going on in the Regiment as part of the job anyway. They didn't need you to work yourself up until you were red in the face and had steam coming out your ears in order to get yourself ready for it. They needed you to be able to control your aggression, so that you could take your time to think, assess a situation, and be ready to take whatever action was necessary. Regiment guys never got into fights downtown on a Saturday night, for instance. If you were caught fighting or drink-driving you were RTU'd – Returned to Unit. Kicked out of the SAS.

'Besides, Regiment guys were more interested in trying to pull in bars than fight in them! But there were other, more subtle differences. "The enemy", for example, were no longer called, or even *viewed*, as the enemy. Like I've said before, they were simply called "players". As *we* were, too.

'And our "tasks" weren't called tasks any more, either. They were called "jobs". Or "the business". You see, in the Regiment, Kev, the concept of "right" and "wrong" is a little more vague. In short, my new world couldn't have been more different to my old one. It was hard to believe both were part of the same army. In my new world, I discovered, being "kinetic" – a wonderful military understatement that means blowing things up and killing people – didn't require anger. It required something else entirely. It required being cool, calm and collected.

'It didn't take long for the penny to drop. And when it did, it was quite a shock. The message was crystal clear: I didn't need anger any more. It certainly wasn't going to make me an efficient Special Forces soldier. It was just going to get in the way. So, bit by bit, I learned to bin the old habits I'd learned in the regular army – the ones that had served me well up to then – and take a different approach on jobs. Tone it down a notch. Quite a few notches, in fact.

'I mean, anger wasn't going to help you blend in as an undercover operator in Derry, was it? Long hair and cheap trainers might. But getting sparked up definitely wouldn't. In order to carry out the business and stay alive as an undercover operator, Kev, you have to become the grey man. And the thing about grey men is: they don't get angry.'

FROM CROSSWORDS TO CROSS WORDS

Andy's account of life in the SAS and how it differed from life in the regular army is a good example of how sometimes, when you focus on the bottom line – when you weigh up what you really want out of a situation – you can get there much more efficiently by surgically removing emotion from the equation.

That's what his mate Clive did with the taxi driver – an SAS sting operation if ever there was one! – and the devilish wheeze went off without a hitch. But if Clive had got 'sparked up' on that 'job', if his blood had started to boil when the 'business' became 'kinetic', chances are things might've turned out rather differently.

Yes, there's a time and a place for anger. There's no denying that. And in the 'old world' Andy came from, as he said, it served him well. But in the world of Special Forces it's a dangerous and unnecessary impediment to cool and clinical judgement – whether you're dealing with hijackers, insurgents . . . or karaoke cabbies.

'You know, legend has it that there's a little office on the top floor of Harrods in which a man sits – feet up all day – doing crosswords, making pot-noodles and watching television,' I say, as the road gets hotter and dustier and we pass people sleeping in the middle of it – sprawled out in rags in the grime and the dirt and the rubble. 'He sits there all day every day in jeans and a T-shirt and gets paid to do absolutely nothing.

'Well, almost nothing. On a desk in the corner sits a telephone. The telephone doesn't ring all that often. Once or twice a month, at most. But when it does the man puts down his crossword, changes out of his jeans and T-shirt, slips on the Harrods uniform that he keeps in a little suit-cover behind the door, and descends to the shop floor of whichever department has summoned him. There, the following ritual ensues:

> MANAGER: Smithers, it was you that was responsible for ordering Professor Blatherwick's exorbitantly over-priced Greco-Roman figurine, was it not?
>
> SMITHERS: Yes, sir.
>
> MANAGER: Then could you possibly explain to Professor Blatherwick here how it has come to acquire this hairline crack along the base?

SMITHERS: No, sir. I'm afraid I couldn't.

MANAGER: Thank you, Smithers. You're fired. Gather up your things right away and get out!

SMITHERS: Very good, sir.

At which point Smithers, suitably admonished in front of the irate customer the manager has been unable to appease, slopes off dejectedly to the elevator, heads back upstairs to his little office on the top floor, changes back into his jeans and T-shirt, and resumes his crossword until the next time the telephone rings . . .

MANAGER: Smithers, it was you that was responsible for delivering Lord Farqhuar Pilkington-Bland's ludicrously expensive white truffles, was it not . . . ?

'Such is the nature of the cushiest job in the world. The man who gets paid to get fired!'

ALL CHANGE

It's noon, and we've stopped off at a roadside café a few miles north of the city of Karnal. It's a pleasant enough spot with toilets out back you can smell in the forecourt out front and a zoo's supply of lizards on the walls.

Much to the surprise of the waiters, Andy endeavours to catch one – to demonstrate to me that this particular variety has an evolutionary trick up its sleeve: when captured, it jettisons its tail.

Either it doesn't feel especially threatened or David Attenborough is having a bad one because a minute or so later he releases it, tail intact.

We sit in the shade and order dhal, chapathis and water. When it comes, it's bloody good.

'You know, we were talking back there about anger being a barrier to clear thinking,' says Andy tucking in, 'but it's not the only emotion that gets in the way. You can become paralysed by fear, too. In the Regiment, to be honest, I never really saw it – there's more than just the one psychopath in there, you know. But in the regular army it's actually pretty common: young lads so shit-scared they can't even pick up a weapon.'

'Isn't that natural, though?' I ask. 'You go from Basildon to Basra in pretty much the blink of an eye and the next thing you know you've got bullets whistling past your ear?'

Andy nods. 'Absolutely,' he says. 'And I'm not saying it isn't. All I'm saying is that just as there's no place for anger in Special Forces, there's no place for fear either. Fear is just another obstacle that gets in the way of the job. And that doesn't just go for Special Forces, of course. It goes for everyone. I heard a great story once – you couldn't get a better example. Can't remember where it was: Australia maybe? But anyway, a bus pulls over to pick up a couple of pedestrians:

> No sooner do the doors open than one of them – a big old boy with tattoos, you know, the works – begins effing and blinding at the driver. The reason? He and his girlfriend won't cough up the fare and the driver isn't having it.
>
> The clock starts ticking.
> The traffic starts building.
> And the standoff begins to escalate.
> Then up steps one of the passengers.
> 'Look, mate,' he says in a calm, reasoned voice. 'It's not the driver's fault you don't have the money. So why don't you just back off, yeah?'
> The dickhead stops in his tracks. He looks at the passenger. Then at his girlfriend. And then back at the passenger. You could hear a pin drop.
> 'You wanna fucking 'ave some, you cunt?' he snarls.
> The passenger stands his ground.
> 'Er, actually, yes I do,' he replies coolly. 'But not here, eh? If we're going to have a fight, let's do it properly. Outside, on the street.'
> The bus holds its breath as he gestures towards the door.

The Terminator and his girlfriend can't believe it. They look at each other – and then, ready to rumble, step out on to the sidewalk.

The passenger turns to the driver.

'I'd shut the doors now if I were you, mate,' he says. 'Let's hit the road!'

RISK ASSESSMENT

In the finance industry they have something called the Sharpe Ratio. Put simply, the Sharpe Ratio is an equation which tells you whether the return on the end of a particular investment is worth the amount of risk associated with it.

Imagine if we had something similar for the dilemmas of everyday life!

Certainly, if we did, then for the passenger in Andy's story the numbers would've stacked up. Here was a situation that entailed high risk (he could've got the shit kicked out of him) for large gain (a peaceful resolution to what was increasingly becoming a rather nasty situation). And, in true GOOD PSYCHOPATH style, he decided to play the odds.

Luckily, he came out on top. But there's no denying that his ice-cool intervention took balls.

Do the opposite, in contrast – take a high risk for a small gain – and you're in different territory altogether. That *doesn't* take balls, it takes something else entirely: recklessness.

Which is what BAD PSYCHOPATHS do.

Their fearlessness dials are permanently set on max – which means that they lack the cognitive flexibility necessary for intelligent shot selection. They can't differentiate when to go for the backhand down the line and when to play safe. The result, as we know, is that they *always* go for the backhand down the line. And most of the time they end up hitting it out.

Of course, *not* going for your shots when you *should* go for them is equally self-defeating – and that's where the rest of us come in.

Having the bottle of the GOOD PSYCHOPATH to hit the outright winner when necessary, to take the emotion out of the decision-making *in the right context*, is a personality characteristic that many aspire to but relatively few possess.

The key, as always, is CONTEXT.

THE SHARPE RATIO

Several years ago – talking of Sharpe Ratios – an American study looked at the way we make financial decisions. It illustrates this point perfectly. The study took the form of a gambling game consisting of twenty rounds. At the beginning of the game each participant was handed a roll of $20 bills and, at the start of each new round, was asked whether they were prepared to risk the princely sum of $1 on the toss of a coin.

A loss incurred the penalty of that $1 invested, but a win swelled the coffers by a cool $2.50.

Now, it doesn't take a genius to work out the winning formula.

Logically, as one of the authors pointed out, the right thing to do is to invest in every round. But logic, as someone else once rather sagely pointed out, is often in the eye of the logician.

Prior to the experiment participants were divided up into two groups. Those with lesions – damage – to the emotion areas of their brains. And those with lesions in other areas.

Now if, as neuroeconomic theory suggests, it's an overdose of emotion that is responsible for the unnecessary risk aversion, then, according to the dynamics of the game, those participants with the 'right' kind of lesions (in other words, those in the first group) should clean up. They should outperform those with the 'wrong' kind – the kind unrelated to emotion (those in the second group).

Surprise surprise, that was exactly how the study shook down. As the game unfolded, 'normal' participants began declining the opportunity to gamble, preferring instead to conserve their winnings.

But participants with problems in their brains' *emotion* neighbourhoods – participants whose brains were not equipped with the bobby-on-the-beat, everyday emotional police force that the rest of us take for granted – kept right on going. And ended the game doing quite a bit better than their thriftier, more cautious competitors.

'This may be the first study,' claims one of the authors, 'that documents a situation in which people with brain damage make better financial decisions than normal people.'

His colleague goes one better:

'Research needs to determine the circumstances in which emotions can be useful or disruptive, [in which they] can be a guide for human behaviour . . . The most successful stockbrokers might plausibly be termed "functional psychopaths" – individuals who are either more adept at controlling their emotions or who do not experience them to the same degree of intensity as others.'

'Many CEOs,' adds another author, 'and many top lawyers might also share this trait.'

YOUR MONEY OR YOUR LIFE

It's late afternoon, and at Jalandhar we branch north off the Grand Trunk Road and head for the Himalayas. The sky fries in a pale blue oil and entire families perch on the back of dodgy-looking mopeds as they weave in and out of traffic like clapped-out human toast racks.

This is the Punjab where the roads are smooth and tarmacked (relatively speaking, at least); where the mountains start getting their act together; and where everybody wears the brightest colours imaginable.

Even the elephants are painted.

'You know,' says Andy, swerving suddenly to avoid a crateful of chickens that's fallen off the wagon in front, 'it's funny you should mention that because I was going to tell you about something very similar that also happened in America a few years back – an experiment that compared financial decision-making with military decision-making.

'You've heard of the United States Marine Corps, right? Well, the US Marine Corps is twice the size of the British Army. In fact it's bigger than the army, navy and RAF put together . . . but is commanded by way fewer generals than we have. Which means that not only do these generals need to have big brains, they also need to have big shoulders. Because when the shit hits the fan, there are only so many uniforms it can land on. 'Anyway, in the late Nineties, to try to cut down on their dry- cleaning bills, the Marine Corps head shed decided to make a little trip to Wall Street to see what they could learn from stockbrokers about making decisions. You see, it'd suddenly dawned on some bright spark that the City and the battlefield have more in common than you might think. For a start, stockbrokers work in a continuous state of confusion, rumour and conflicting information, accompanied, all the time, by the constant risk of things going tits-up big style – exactly the same conditions that any general experiences when they're commanding their forces in battle.

'Then there's the question of battle plans. Stockbrokers always have a plan of action for the day's trades. They plan to win – obviously – and to make a shedload of money in the process, so they can shell out even more of the green stuff on hair gel and Rolexes.

'But the problem for these slicked-backed stockbrokers is that all the other slicked-back stockbrokers are trying to do the same –

just as the problem for our crew-cut generals is that whoever they're up against in Iraq, Afghanistan or wherever is trying to mess up *their* plans. So, could these cigar-chomping Gordon Gekkos offer them any tips? Turned out the answer was yes! The main thing the generals were interested in was how the stockbrokers made decisions so quickly.

'You've got your double-decker-high digital displays; you've got computer screens by the hundred displaying rolling share prices; you've got all the shouting and hand signals coming at you from across the floor . . . how the fuck were they able to download into their heads the shitload of data bombarding them from every corner and then, within just a matter of seconds, make instant decisions, instant trades, and risk hundreds of millions of dollars? If the generals could work *that* out, they reckoned, they really would have it made – because it was exactly how they fought *their* battles.

'We've all seen the war films with the "situation room" – windowless spaces with dozens of bodies hunched over computer screens showing everything from aircraft bombings to naval positions, everyone punching keyboards and rabbiting away on radios as they communicate with the guys in the battle space. In the middle of it all is the general. The one big body in the one big chair – taking no notice of any of the surrounding mayhem but instead just absorbing the data.

'The parallels were certainly there, all right. But what if the two of them actually went head to head? What if the stockbrokers could somehow compete with the generals? Play them at their own game? Who'd come out on top?

'To find out, two separate situation rooms were set up into which were fed identical descriptions of battle information. The information came from a simulated military exercise in which the battle space changed interactively according to strategy – you know, in line with the decisions that were made by the occupants of each room.

'In one room were the generals. In the other, yep, were the stockbrokers. Would the Gekkos beat the Eisenhowers on their home turf? Or would military savvy and combat zone experience win the day?

'The answer blew everyone out of the water, mate!

'Both groups won their battle. But guess what: it was the stockbrokers, not the generals, who ended up with way more of their troops still alive and their ships and aircraft intact.

'Why? Well, when they looked into it, it turned out that there was one humongous difference between the way the generals were making decisions and the way the stockbrokers were making them. The generals were "fighting". But the stockbrokers weren't.

'Far from taking things personally, the stockbrokers were just solving equations. They were reading the data, crunching the numbers, getting information dumps, then making up their minds, quickly and coolly, purely on the basis of that. There was no emotion behind their decisions. Just cold, hard maths.

'The generals, on the other hand, were also reading the data. But they were seeing it through compassion-tinted glasses: their feelings were coming into play. With their wealth of conflict experience, they knew first hand the implications that any wrong decision might have for a young man or woman in the battle space. Yes, there will always be lives lost in combat. Unfortunately, that's the nature of war.

'But because the generals belonged to the same tribe as the men and women who were fighting, at the back of their minds all the time was damage limitation. They were constantly doing their best to keep casualties to a minimum. Which was honourable and commendable and all that. But also a bit of a problem. Because by doing so, by that slight hesitation in trying to work out an alternative, possibly safer way of getting the job done, they were actually costing more lives, more ships and more aircraft than if they'd gone with the emotionless option.

'It was a bit like I was telling you about rugby that time. Go into a tackle not fully committed and you put yourself at greater risk of injury. But if you go into it a hundred per cent then you're more likely to come out of it OK.

'Which is not to say that empathy isn't good. Of course it is.

But it does have a downside – you start feeling it when you can least afford it. And those warm, buzzy feelings can *cost* lives rather than save them.

'Emotion doesn't cut it if it's "on" all the time. But if you've got a switch to turn it on and off – that's when it *can* really work for you.'

THE EMPATHY SWITCH

Andy's observations couldn't come at a more opportune time in psychopathy research. For years it had been thought that psychopaths just didn't experience empathy, just didn't have the necessary operating systems installed in their brains to support it.

But a recent study has changed all that and suggests – exactly in line with Andy's recommendations – that, rather than being incapable of experiencing empathy, psychopaths in fact have an empathy 'switch' that they can turn on and off at will . . . and the default setting just happens to be programmed to 'off'.

The study in question, I tell him, as the air gets clearer, the roads get higher and narrower, and twilight settles like a dust blanket over the foothills of the Himalayas, stuck a bunch of criminal psychopaths in a brain scanner while showing them a series of video clips featuring a pair of hands touching.

The hands touched in four different kinds of ways:

- **One hand stroked the other hand affectionately.**
- **One hand inflicted pain on the other hand.**
- **One hand 'rejected' or pushed the other hand away.**
- **The two hands made contact in a neutral way.**

The study was divided into two parts.

In the first part, the psychopaths were simply shown the clips without any prior instructions and their brain activity was recorded.

But in the second part things got more interesting.

This time, the psychopaths were shown the clips again but

were specifically asked beforehand to try to put themselves in the position of the other person and to feel what they might be feeling. To empathize with them, in other words.

The results were extraordinary.

When the researchers examined the psychopaths' brain scans from the first part of the study they drew a blank. Compared with the brain activity in an equivalent group of non-psychopaths who watched one hand inflicting pain on the other, the psychopaths' brains just shrugged.

Activity in their mirror neuron system – a network of brain cells specifically equipped to mimic or 'mirror' the actions and feelings of others – was way down on the level observed in normal people. But when it came to the scans from the second part of the study, where the psychopaths were explicitly requested to put themselves in the other person's shoes, it was a completely different story. This time around there was no significant difference in levels of mirror neuron activity between their brains and anyone else's.

'So when we want to, then, we can feel.' Andy smiles. 'The question is: do we want to?'

A couple of years ago, Andy introduced me to a Japanese Special Forces sergeant by the name of Yoshiji Hayashi (Japanese for Andy McNab!). Hayashi had been one of the first off the helicopter in the city of Nihonmatsu, evacuating men, women and children who'd been exposed to radiation from the Fukushima nuclear plant. Like Andy, and certain other Special Forces soldiers I know, he had a certain 'something' about him.

A vibe.

A confidence.

A psychological force field of limitless possibility: as if his brain was some kind of neural tax haven, eerily exempt from the standard rate of everyday emotional duty.

'I was just going through the motions,' Hayashi told me. 'Don't misunderstand. It wasn't that I didn't care. It was that, at the time, I couldn't *afford* to care. My training didn't let me. If I had thought: "These are my people. These are my brothers and sisters. Look what has happened to them . . ." then maybe I couldn't have done it.

'Yes, people are scared. People are screaming. People are in pain. But you just deal with it. You have to. You kind of switch yourself off inside. And go on to autopilot. You think about it later.'

I was reminded of Hayashi's comments when, some time later, I interviewed a leading neurosurgeon. He told me:

> I have no compassion for those whom I operate on. That is a luxury I simply cannot afford. In the theatre I am reborn: as a cold, heartless machine, totally at one with scalpel, drill and saw.
>
> When you're cutting loose and cheating death high above the snowline of the brain, feelings aren't fit for purpose. Emotion is entropy and seriously bad for business. I've hunted it down to extinction over the years.

Sounds chilling, doesn't it? Something that you might expect from a Special Forces soldier, maybe, but not from someone who's going to saw open your skull and rummage around in your brain.

But think again!

Henry Marsh, a consultant neurosurgeon at St George's Hospital in London, has a new book out entitled: *Do No Harm: Stories of Life, Death and Brain Surgery*. Here is a passage from it:

> It's one of the painful truths about neurosurgery that you only get good at doing the really difficult cases if you get lots of practice, but that means making lots of mistakes at first and leaving a trail of injured patients behind you.
>
> I suspect that you've got to be a bit of a psychopath to carry on, or at least have a pretty thick skin. If you're a nice doctor, you'll probably give up, let Nature take its course and stick to the simpler cases . . .
>
> It is an experience unique to neurosurgeons, and one with which all neurosurgeons are familiar. With other surgical specialties, on the whole, the patients either die or recover, and do not linger on the ward for months.

It is not something we discuss among ourselves, other than perhaps to sigh and nod your head when you hear of such a case, but at least you know that somebody understands what you feel. A few seem to be able to shrug it off, but they are a minority. Perhaps they are the ones who will become great neurosurgeons.

Or perhaps they're the ones who happen to know where the switch is!

'Hey,' I say to Andy, as we meander through the Kangra valley on our final approach to Dharamsala, 'I've got a conundrum for *you*.'*

You are a commander in a war zone. You are about to send thousands of troops into a major battle.

You feel you have a good chance of winning the upcoming battle, but victory will come marginally more quickly and with lower casualties if the enemy is fooled by misinformation regarding your intentions.

At the same time you have a spy who has proved his loyalty to your cause many times, and been extremely effective at great personal risk. What if you feed him false information and send him into a location where you know he'll be captured?

He will be horrendously tortured, mutilated and ultimately killed. But in the process he will divulge the false information in a convincing way that will strengthen your hand in the battle.

Do you send him?

We pull into a passing place to let a busload of tourists from McLeod Ganj – Upper Dharamsala or 'Little Lhasa' as they call it – come through.

Andy looks at me nonplussed.

'Of course I would,' he says. 'Why *wouldn't* I?'

'Because he's loyal and brilliant?' I hazard.

---

*Thanks go to Crispin Rovere for this dilemma.

Andy laughs.

'Then all the more reason to use him!' he says, swinging back out. 'I mean, you're not going to send someone who's fucking dodgy, are you?'

EMOTHERAPY

OK. It's highly unlikely that you're ever going to be first off the helicopter in a nuclear disaster. Or operating way behind enemy lines deep inside the brain. Or sending a brilliant secret service agent to his death. And anyway, even if you do happen to find yourself in any of those positions, it's highly likely that you're already pretty adept at keeping your house of emotions in order.

But if you're not a fan of heights, even the most insignificant of molehills really can seem like a mountain – and none of us go through life entirely on the flat. So next time you encounter a longer, steeper gradient than you might, perhaps, feel comfortable with, here are some tips to keep you moving forward and stop you looking down.

Ask yourself: what if . . . ?

Kerry Packer, the Australian billionaire, was a familiar face in Las Vegas from the 1970s through the 1990s. The amount of money both won and lost by the media tycoon is legendary – and, when he was in town, casino bosses would regularly fall over themselves to offer him their hospitality. Meals, girls, suites, cars – you name it – were all laid on for him compliments of the house. And every whim, no matter how small, was catered for.

But there were occasions, unsurprisingly, when Packer's star billing didn't exactly endear him to his fellow guests. On one such occasion – at the Stratosphere Casino – a wealthy Texan oil-investor, irate at yet another show-stopping performance by the Australian high-roller, decided to have it out with him.

'What makes you so special?' he growled. 'I've got $100 million in the bank.'

Packer smiled. 'That's great,' he replied. 'Tell you what – I'll toss you for it.'

A hundred million dollars is a heck of a lot of money. And rolled up tightly in that mountain of dollar bills is a heck of a lot of emotion. People tend to get quite attached to what they've got in their bank accounts! So when the oil baron asked Packer what made him so special, he got his answer right there and then in no uncertain terms.

It wasn't the fact that he was able to part with a hundred million dollars just like that. Actually, that was the easy part. No. It was the fact that he could part with a hundred million dollars' worth of *emotion* just like that.

That's a bit more difficult!

Now we're not suggesting here that you go throwing away your life's savings or anything like that.

'Unless you want to throw it in our direction,' Andy chimes in.

But what we *are* recommending is a very basic technique that's as simple as it is powerful. Next time you find yourself stressing out over a difficult task, take a step back from it and ask yourself this:

- **What would I do if I *didn't* feel this way?**
- **What would I do if I *didn't* give a damn what other people thought?**
- **What would I do if it just didn't matter?**

And then, when you've got the answers to those questions . . . just go ahead and do it. Simple! It's not rocket science. Just do it.

When Steve Davis, the six-time world snooker champion, was asked the secret to being a great player, he replied: 'Playing like it means nothing when it means everything.'

'I mean, I've told you before, since when did you need to *feel* like doing something in order to actually *do* it?' says Andy, nursing us steadily upwards into the sandalwood-scented night through the candlelit bazaars of Lower Dharamsala. 'If that was the case most people wouldn't even get out of bed in the morning. Did I ever *feel* like shooting anyone? No. To be honest, I would've been worried if I had. It's just part and parcel of the job. Did I ever feel *bad* about shooting someone? No. Again, it's just part of the job.

'I heard a great little story once. Well, more a parable actually. A Muslim warrior goes to war against infidels. On the battlefield, an enemy soldier spits in his face. About to slay the soldier, the Muslim warrior stops and lets him go. Dumbfounded, the soldier asks him why.

'Before you spat on me I was going to kill you in the name of Allah,' replies the warrior. 'But after you did I was going to kill you to preserve my ego.

'That is a sin.'

Remember: 'it's all in your head'

'You know, the way you feel isn't real, is it?' says Andy, coining, without realizing it, a half decent mantra. 'I mean, it is but it isn't . . . if you get where I'm coming from. It's just different tribes of cells migrating about in different directions in your brain. It doesn't actually mean anything. If you watch a film without the soundtrack it's still the same film. The soundtrack doesn't change what happens. That's how I think about feelings.'

If Andy's take on the relationship between emotion and experience – between the world within and the world without – seems familiar, then you're not mistaken. It would, on the face of it, make a great mission statement for mindfulness – the living-in-the-moment mindset that we looked at in the previous chapter.

Lots of stuff goes on between our ears which bears absolutely no relation to reality whatsoever – and in many cases this can include the way we feel about things.

So keeping that in mind – remembering that it's often 'all in your head' – is a great first step towards asking yourself the $100-million question 'What if . . . ?' And then cracking on regardless.

When I was writing *The Wisdom of Psychopaths*, mindfulness expert Mark Williams gave me perhaps the best example of the power of this way of thinking that I've ever heard, when explaining how you might use it to help someone get over a fear of flying.

'One approach,' Mark elucidated, 'might be to take the person on a plane and seat them next to a flying buff. You know, someone who absolutely loves being up in the air. Then, mid-flight, you hand them a pair of brain scans. One of them depicts a happy brain. The other one depicts an anxious brain. A brain in a state of terror:

> 'This pair of pictures,' you say, 'represent exactly what's going on in each of your heads right now, at this precise moment in time. So, obviously, because they're so different, neither of them really means anything, do they? Neither of them predicts the physical state of the plane. That truth is in the engines. So, what *do* they signify? Well, what, in fact, they do represent is . . . precisely what you're holding in your hands. A brain state. Nothing more. Nothing less.
>
> 'What you're feeling,' you say to the anxious passenger, 'is simply that. A feeling. A neural network, an electrical ensemble, a chemical configuration, caused by thoughts in your head that drift in and out, that come and go, like clouds.
>
> 'Now, if you can bring yourself round to somehow accepting that fact; to dispassionately observe your inner virtual reality; to let the clouds float by, to let their shadows fall and linger where they please, and focus, instead, on what's going on around you – each pixelated second of each ambient sound and sensation – then eventually, over time, your condition should begin to improve.'

Take your mind off it

The South African golfer Louis Oosthuizen won the 2010 British Open Championship against all the odds. He hadn't had the best of build-ups to the tournament and most of the pundits fully expected him to surrender the four-shot lead that he was carrying into the final round.

But they were wrong. The Oosthuizen of the previous year might've choked. But not this one. And the reason was very simple. A small red spot, just below the base of his thumb. On his glove.

The spot was the brainchild of sports psychologist and performance coach Karl Morris. A short time earlier, Oosthuizen had paid Morris a visit to help him deal with intrusive thoughts of failure that had begun to creep into his mind at exactly the wrong moment – such as whenever he was about to play a crucial shot. And Morris came up with a very simple solution.

Whenever Oosthuizen was about to play a shot, he was to deliberately distract himself. He was to zone in exclusively on the dot on the base of his thumb and concentrate on that. At the critical moment, it was the dot, not the shot, that mattered. The golfing part of his brain knew all too well how to play the shot, thank you very much – without the rest of 'him' being there and screwing things up.

He won by seven strokes.

Morris's 'dot con' solution to Oosthuizen's psychological woes has a name in sports psychology. It's called a *process goal*. A process goal is when a performer is made to focus on *something* else in order to take their mind off *everything* else.

The idea, as Oosthuizen proved, is that much of the time we know what we've got to do. But the anxiety of not being able to do it gets in the way of us doing exactly that.

Doing it!

Anyone who's ever had trouble getting to sleep will understand this only too well. The harder you try, the harder it gets – because, as Andy points out, 'If performance anxiety is going to get in the way of *anything* it's going to be getting to sleep.'

Instead, the thing to do is to set up the best possible conditions for 'optimal performance' to occur – a dark, quiet room with a nice, comfortable bed – and let things take their course.

The power of distraction to deal with emotional distress is well documented in the scientific literature. Distraction reorients our attention away from the main issue at hand – and the agonizing uncertainty often inherent to its outcome – and diverts it on to something less 'meaningful'.

Now, this distinction between the event itself and the intrinsically probabilistic nature of its occurrence is actually extremely important. Because, although it may not seem like it, it is, ironically, the *uncertainty* over bad things happening that's the killer. Not the bad things themselves!

One study, for instance, found that people whose jobs are chronically insecure report significantly higher rates of depression and poorer health than those who've actually lost their jobs. Another found that when people were asked to predict whether some unresolved issue in their life would turn out badly, they got it WRONG 85 per cent of the time.

'It was the same during SAS Selection,' Andy says. 'The tabs over the Black Mountains are specifically designed not just to test candidates' physical fitness but also their mental fitness. Most of the lads are fit enough to cover the ground with the weight on their backs and are able to map-read. But the problem is that no one knows the cut-off times – how long you actually have to go each distance. That constantly nagging uncertainty really fucks people over. It makes everyone insecure.

'But the remedy is simple. You read the map and put one boot in front of the other as quickly as possible. Nothing else matters.'

The message is crystal clear. We find uncertainty so hard to deal with that we're prepared to assume the worst just to get shot of it. So next time you're faced with a 'crucial shot' of your own, reflect, before you play it, on the following:

- Uncertainty, by its very nature, is uncertain.
- Things *could* go badly. But they could just as easily turn out OK.
- Even if things do turn out for the worse, IMAGINING them turning out for the worst is worse!

On the other hand, however, distraction can be just as powerful a tool for emotionally disarming others as it is for disarming ourselves.

In Chapter Seven, if you recall, we saw how the Incongruity Principle of persuasion utilizes distraction by lobbing a psychological stun grenade through the expectancy window of the brain. And then, in the ensuing pandemonium, slipping in whatever it is that's required sub-radar.

It's an extremely effective technique – especially in conflict situations where the assassination of negative emotions is particularly important for successful resolutions. As we finally pull up outside our hotel in McLeod Ganj, Andy comes up with a brilliant example.

'Back in my Regiment days I had a mate who was a copper in Hereford called Dave. Dave was a football nut and his team, Brentford, had been drawn against Liverpool in the FA Cup at Anfield. Anyway, he goes up there to cheer them on and they get hammered 38–0 or something. On the train home Dave also gets hammered and, arriving back in Hereford, hits the bars big time.

'When he gets back to his house, he's not a happy camper. He kicks over the living-room table, puts his fist through a door, then turns on his missus, pushing her about and that. So she's shitting herself and runs out of the house into the street. She doesn't want to call the Old Bill in case she gets one of his mates, so she gets on the blower to me. I tell her to stay where she is until I get there.

'So I jump in the car, nip round to Scouse Billy's – another Regiment lad's – house to borrow a Liverpool shirt and then five minutes later I'm marching up Dave's drive in the pissing rain and knocking on his door. His wife can't believe it!

'"Hello, mate," I say, when it opens. "Just passing and wondered if you happened to know how Brentford got on?"

'There's a moment of silence as he takes it all in. The rain. The cold. The missus. The LIVERPOOL TOP! Then he laughs.

'"You stupid bastard," he says. "You'd better come in."

TOUGHEN UP

You hear about the benefits of regular exercise everywhere. But there's evidence to suggest – and you won't thank us for saying this – that regular exercise accompanied by a freezing cold shower at the end of it is even better.

On its own, exercise helps combat anxiety, stress and depression by placing the body under manageable, controllable, adjustable physical strain, which, in the same way that a flu jab protects your immune system against the lurgy, inoculates the mind against more virulent emotional stressors.

But so too, it would seem, can regular exposure to cold water.

At least, that is, in rats!

Scientists have discovered that getting rats to swim regularly in cold water makes them less prone to the malaise of learned helplessness – the inability, if you recall from Chapter Three, to 'take the initiative' and 'fight back'.

Whether such benefits in resilience and emotion-hardening extend to us humans is a moot point. But some researchers claim that they do, suggesting that regular exposure to intermittent periods of stress and recovery of the kind that a regular exercise regime may give you – accompanied by the acute thermal rigours that a cold dunk at the end may provide – constitutes an incremental affective toughening process that renders those who go through it more emotionally stable when confronted by prolonged stress.

Such evidence is, as I say, speculative. But there may well be something in it.

Beginning with the premises, as some evolutionary biologists argue, that back in the days of our prehistoric ancestors the neurobiological hardware underpinning mammalian thermoregulation might also have paved the way for subsequent mechanisms of emotional arousal, the American psychologist Richard Dienstbier proposes that cold tolerance and emotional stability may well be correlated. And that by building up the former you may well be increasing the latter.

Coincidence that road rage was pretty much unheard of in the days before sophisticated climate-control systems became fitted as standard in cars, homes and offices? Perhaps. But then again, perhaps not.

Recent evidence implicates the widespread proliferation of such systems in the equally pervasive increase in obesity levels.

Studies conducted in enclosed chambers, for instance, have shown that reducing the temperature by a mere five degrees Celsius – from 27 to 22 – results in an extra 239 calories being burned per day.

When you consider that temperatures in the average British home have gone up from 13 degrees in 1970 to 18 degrees in the year 2000, it doesn't take a rocket scientist to figure out how such a hike might well, over time, translate into significant rates of weight gain, a general reduction in fitness levels . . . and increased emotional lability.

Thermal stress is something we learned to handle – over millions of years of our evolutionary history. If, as some suggest, and as the experiment with the rats seems to indicate, the neurophysiological mechanisms of thermoregulation and emotional regulation might at some point have converged during the course of that history, then it's entirely possible that micromanaging the temperature of our indoor environment might well have an impact on our ability to deal with stress.

'There might be more to the phrase "letting off steam" than we think!' I say to Andy, as we stand on the balcony of our appropriately monastic room and gaze across town at the twinkling golden lights of the Dalai Lama's palace.

'Anyone for a run, a sauna and an ice-cold plunge?'

He grins, shakes his head and cranes his neck up and down the street.

'What do you reckon the chances are of grabbing a bacon sandwich round here at this time of night?' he says.

QUESTIONNAIRE
HOW GOOD ARE YOU AT UNCOUPLING BEHAVIOUR FROM EMOTION?

Assign a rating to each of the following statements and then add up your total and check it with the scores on the next page:

		strongly agree **0**	agree **1**	disagree **2**	strongly disagree **3**
1.	I get easily frustrated if things don't go my way.	○	○	○	○
2.	I find it difficult to concentrate if things are 'hanging over me'.	○	○	○	○
3.	I find it hard to give people bad news or tell them the hard truth.	○	○	○	○
4.	I often don't get what I really want because I don't like upsetting or inconveniencing others.	○	○	○	○
5.	Even if every second counted towards a tight deadline I would find it difficult to resist opening a crucial email.	○	○	○	○
6.	I often later regret decisions that I've made or things I've done in the heat of the moment.	○	○	○	○
7.	I find it difficult to watch my team if they're involved in a critical shoot-out or decider.	○	○	○	○
8.	I am not good in an emergency because I find it hard to keep a clear head.	○	○	○	○
9.	I don't like taking risks, however well justified.	○	○	○	○
10.	If I were facing the final question on *Who Wants to be a Millionaire* I would not be able to think clearly.	○	○	○	○
11.	I would have trouble giving a young child an insulin injection in an emergency.	○	○	○	○

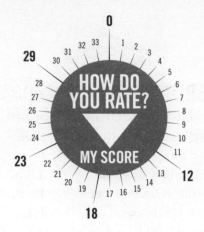

0–11 Your brain is a dictatorship governed by emotion. Time for a coup, perhaps?

12–17 Your brain may not be an emotional dictatorship but emotion is certainly the ruling party. Vote of confidence in order?

18–22 50 per cent Jo Brand, 50 per cent Russell Brand.

23–28 Your head definitely rules your heart. You weigh things up before you act and are good at getting things in perspective.

29–33 You'd give Spock a run for his money!

THE GREAT BRITISH GOOD PSYCHOPATH SURVEY

We hope that our little questionnaires at the end of each chapter have told you something useful about yourself. If it's something you didn't know, then so much the better. If you did already know, tough. But all is not lost! To find out your final GOOD PSYCHOPATH score, and where you sit on the overall spectrum, why not go on to our website and enter your scores individually for the Seven Deadly Wins? By doing so, you will be helping us conduct a unique GOOD PSYCHOPATH survey of the nation, which will analyse the precise links between GOOD PSYCHOPATH personality traits and various other aspects of life in general.

Here's where you click: www.thegoodpsychopath.com

Over 1.5 MILLION people have already filled out our general psychopath questionnaire.

So, go on – you know you want to! And it won't take long.

JUST DO IT!

# ABOUT THE AUTHORS

Dr Kevin Dutton is a research fellow at the Department of Experimental Psychology, University of Oxford. He is an affiliated member of the Royal Society of Medicine and of the Society for the Scientific Study of Psychopathy. He is the author of the acclaimed *Flipnosis: The Art of Split-Second Persuasion* and *The Wisdom of Psychopaths: Lessons in Life from Saints, Spies and Serial Killers*. He lives in the Cotswolds.

From the day he was found in a carrier bag on the steps of Guy's Hospital in London, **Andy McNab** has led an extraordinary life.

As a teenage delinquent, Andy McNab kicked against society. As a young soldier he waged war against the IRA in the streets and fields of South Armagh. As a member of 22 SAS he was at the centre of covert operations for nine years – on five continents. During the Gulf War he commanded Bravo Two Zero, a patrol that, in the words of his commanding officer, 'will remain in regimental history for ever'. Awarded the Distinguished Conduct Medal (DCM) and Military Medal (MM) during his military career, McNab was the British Army's most highly decorated serving soldier when he finally left the SAS. Since then Andy McNab has become one of the world's bestselling writers, drawing on his insider knowledge and experience. As well as three nonfiction bestsellers including *Bravo Two Zero*, the bestselling British work of military history, he is the author of the bestselling Nick Stone thrillers. He has also written a number of books for children. Besides his writing work, he lectures to security and intelligence agencies in both the USA and UK, works in the film industry advising

Hollywood on everything from covert procedure to training civilian actors to act like soldiers, and he continues to be a spokesperson and fundraiser for both military and literacy charities.